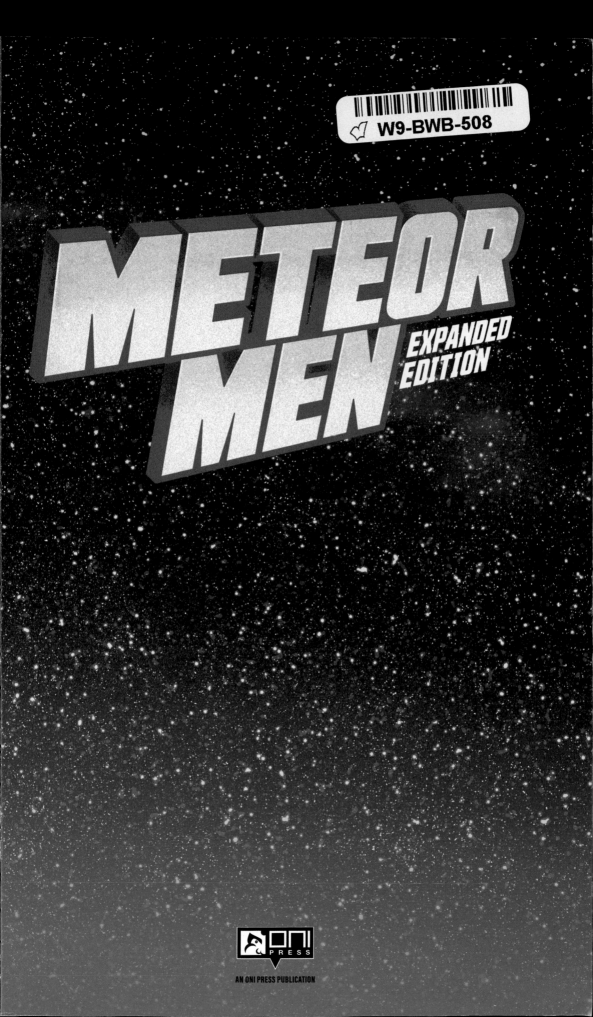

W9-BWB-508

METEOR MEN

EXPANDED EDITION

ONI PRESS

AN ONI PRESS PUBLICATION

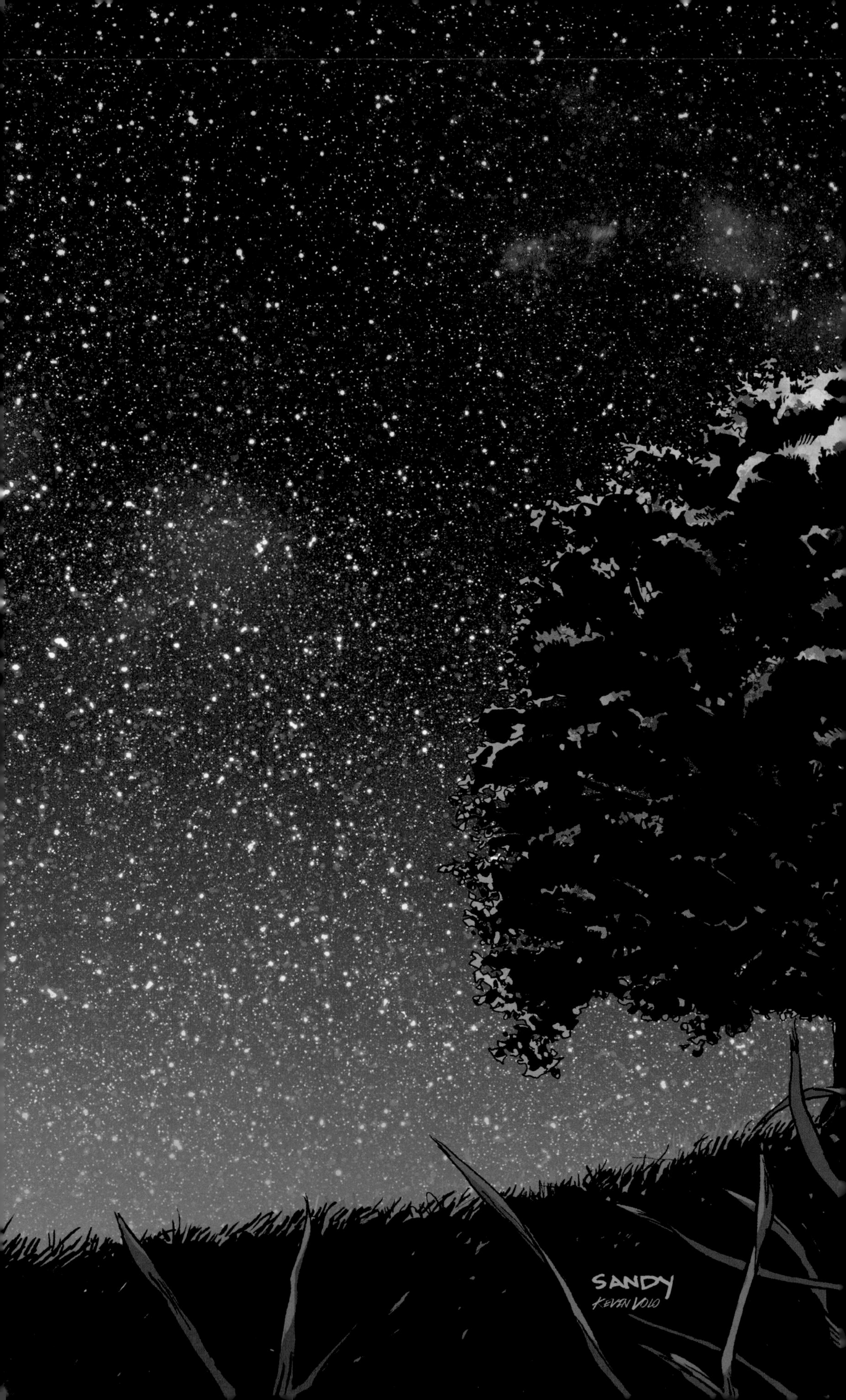

SANDY
KEVIN VOLO

WRITTEN BY
JEFF PARKER

ILLUSTRATED BY
SANDY JARRELL

COLORED BY
**KEVIN VOLO &
SANDY JARRELL**

LETTERED BY
CRANK!

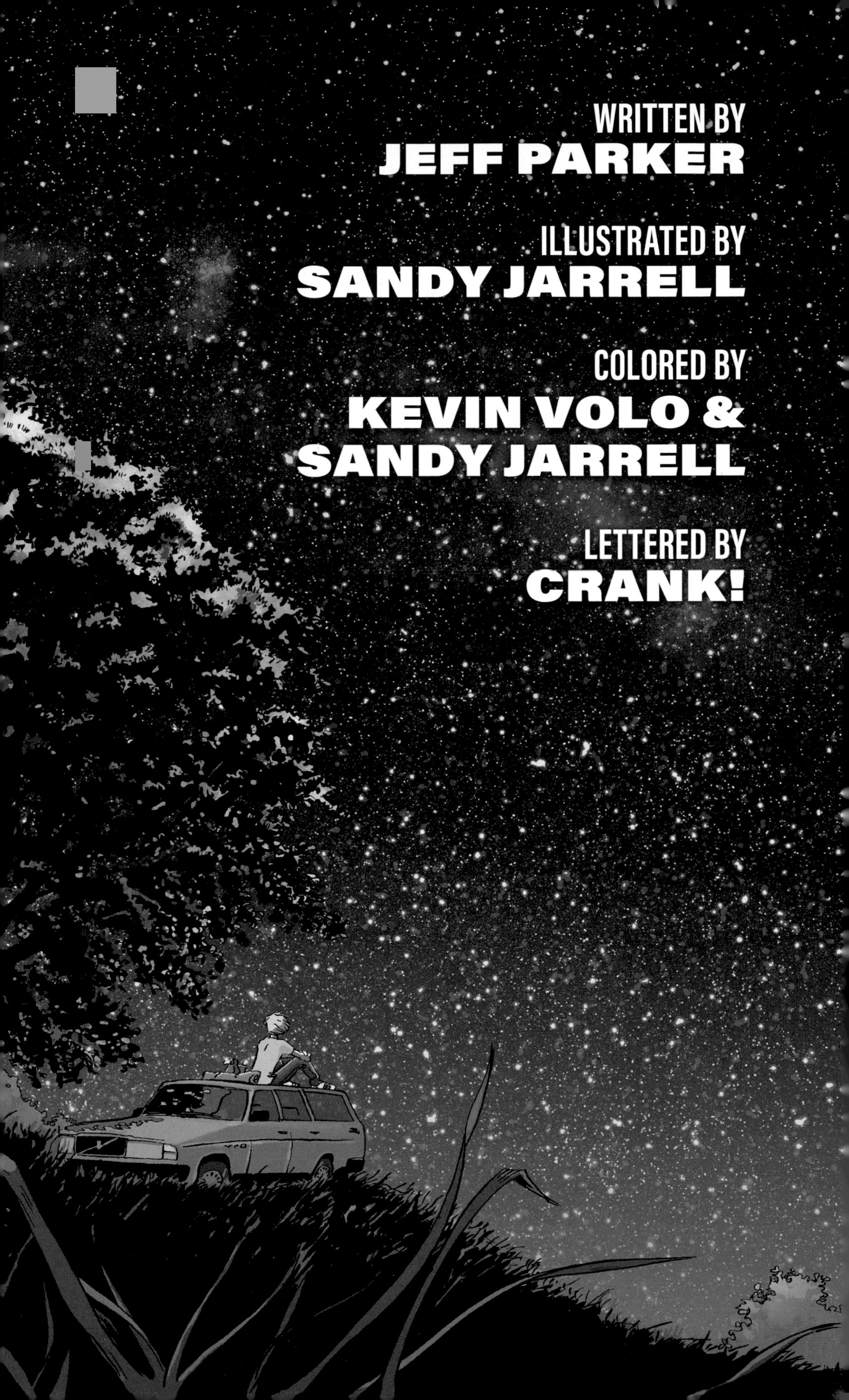

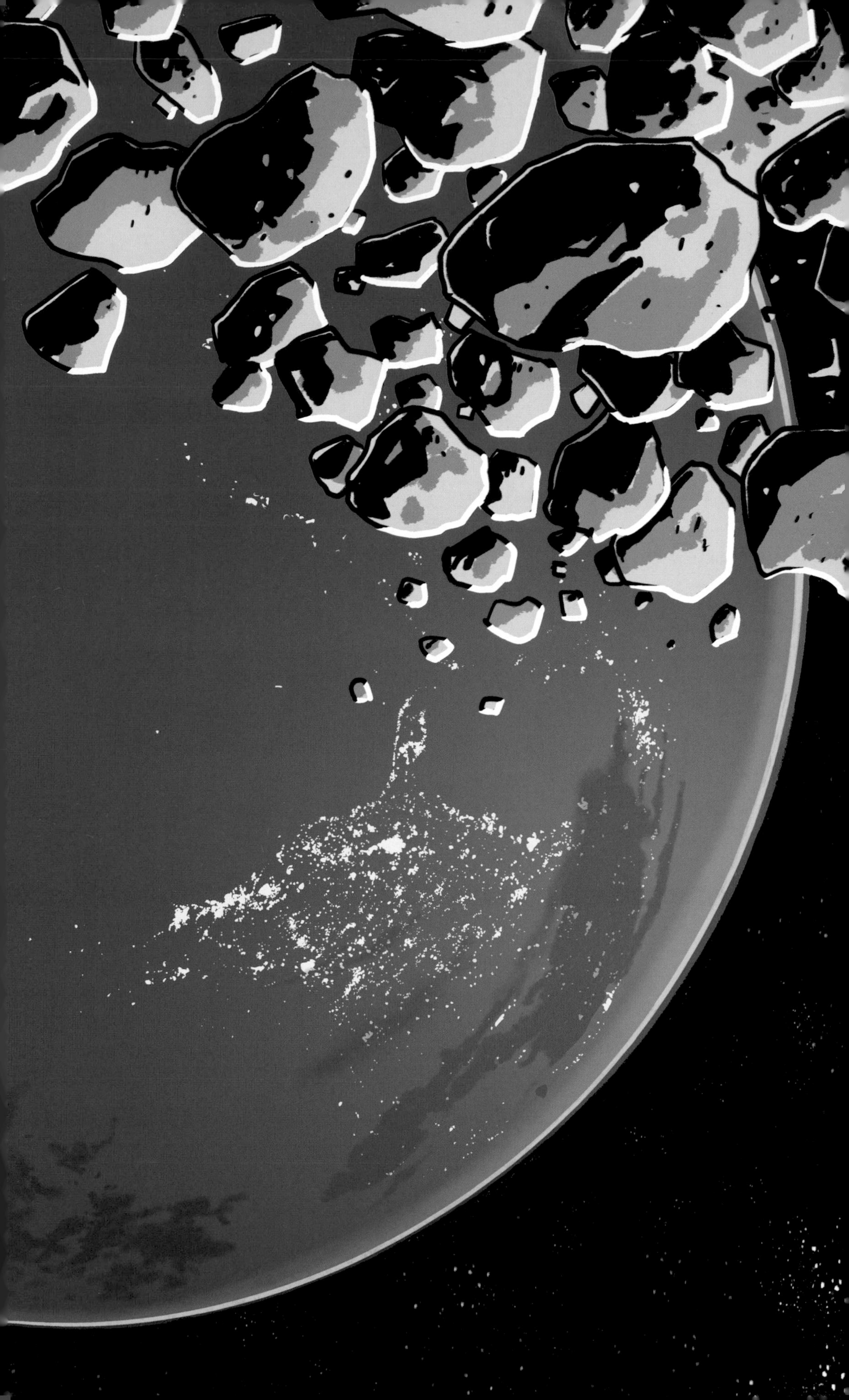

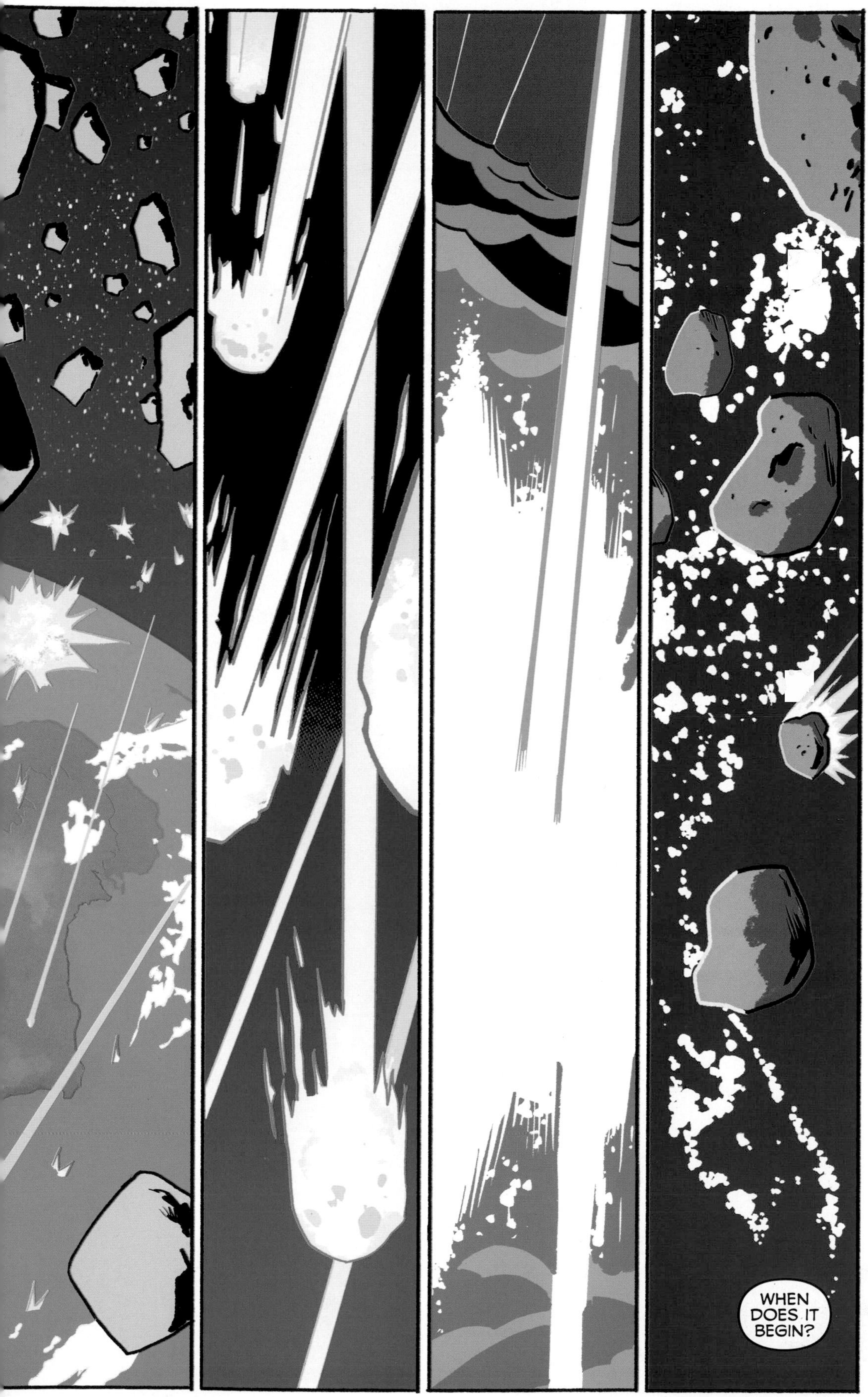
WHEN DOES IT BEGIN?

COLOR FLATS BY
ROXY POLK, MATT RAINWATER & CHARO SOLIS

DESIGNED BY
JASON STOREY & CAREY HALL

ORIGINAL EDITED BY
CHARLIE CHU & ARI YARWOOD

EXPANDED EDITION EDITED BY
ZACK SOTO

METEOR MEN

PUBLISHED BY ONI-LION FORGE PUBLISHING GROUP, LLC.

JAMES LUCAS JONES PRESIDENT & PUBLISHER

CHARLIE CHU E.V.P. OF CREATIVE & BUSINESS DEVELOPMENT

STEVE ELLIS S.V.P. OF GAMES & OPERATIONS

ALEX SEGURA S.V.P OF MARKETING & SALES

MICHELLE NGUYEN ASSOCIATE PUBLISHER

BRAD ROOKS DIRECTOR OF OPERATIONS

AMBER O'NEILL SPECIAL PROJECTS MANAGER

MARGOT WOOD DIRECTOR OF MARKETING & SALES

KATIE SAINZ MARKETING MANAGER

TARA LEHMANN PUBLICIST

HOLLY AITCHISON CONSUMER MARKETING MANAGER

HENRY BARAJAS SALES MANAGER

TROY LOOK DIRECTOR OF DESIGN & PRODUCTION

ANGIE KNOWLES PRODUCTION MANAGER

KATE Z. STONE SENIOR GRAPHIC DESIGNER

CAREY HALL GRAPHIC DESIGNER

SARAH ROCKWELL GRAPHIC DESIGNER

HILARY THOMPSON GRAPHIC DESIGNER

VINCENT KUKUA DIGITAL PREPRESS TECHNICIAN

CHRIS CERASI MANAGING EDITOR

JASMINE AMIRI SENIOR EDITOR

SHAWNA GORE SENIOR EDITOR

AMANDA MEADOWS SENIOR EDITOR

ROBERT MEYERS SENIOR EDITOR, LICENSING

DESIREE RODRIGUEZ EDITOR

GRACE SCHEIPETER EDITOR

ZACK SOTO EDITOR

BEN EISNER GAME DEVELOPER

JUNG LEE LOGISTICS COORDINATOR

KUIAN KELLUM WAREHOUSE ASSISTANT

JOE NOZEMACK PUBLISHER EMERITUS

METEOR MEN: EXPANDED EDITION, April 2022. Published by Oni-Lion Forge Publishing Group, LLC., 1319 SE Martin Luther King Jr. Blvd., Suite 240, Portland, OR 97214. Meteor Men: Expanded Edition is ™ & © 2022 Jeff Parker & Sandy Jarrell. All rights reserved. Oni Press logo and icon ™ & © 2022 Oni-Lion Forge Publishing Group, LLC. All rights reserved. Oni Press logo and icon artwork created by Keith A. Wood. The events, institutions, and characters presented in this book are fictional. Any resemblance to actual persons, living or dead, is purely coincidental. No portion of this publication may be reproduced, by any means, without the express written permission of the copyright holders.

FIRST EDITION: APRIL 2022

ISBN 978-1-62010-846-8

EISBN 978-1-63715-013-9

PRINTED IN CHINA

LIBRARY OF CONGRESS CONTROL NUMBER: 2021940868

1 2 3 4 5 6 7 8 9 10

ONIPRESS.COM

FACEBOOK.COM/ONIPRESS   TWITTER.COM/ONIPRESS | TWITTER.COM/LIONFORGE   INSTAGRAM.COM/ONIPRESS | INSTAGRAM.COM/LIONFORGE

To my own stellar event, Jill, who would never bring about the end of mankind.
—JEFF PARKER

To Karen, for her endless encouragement and support.
—SANDY JARRELL

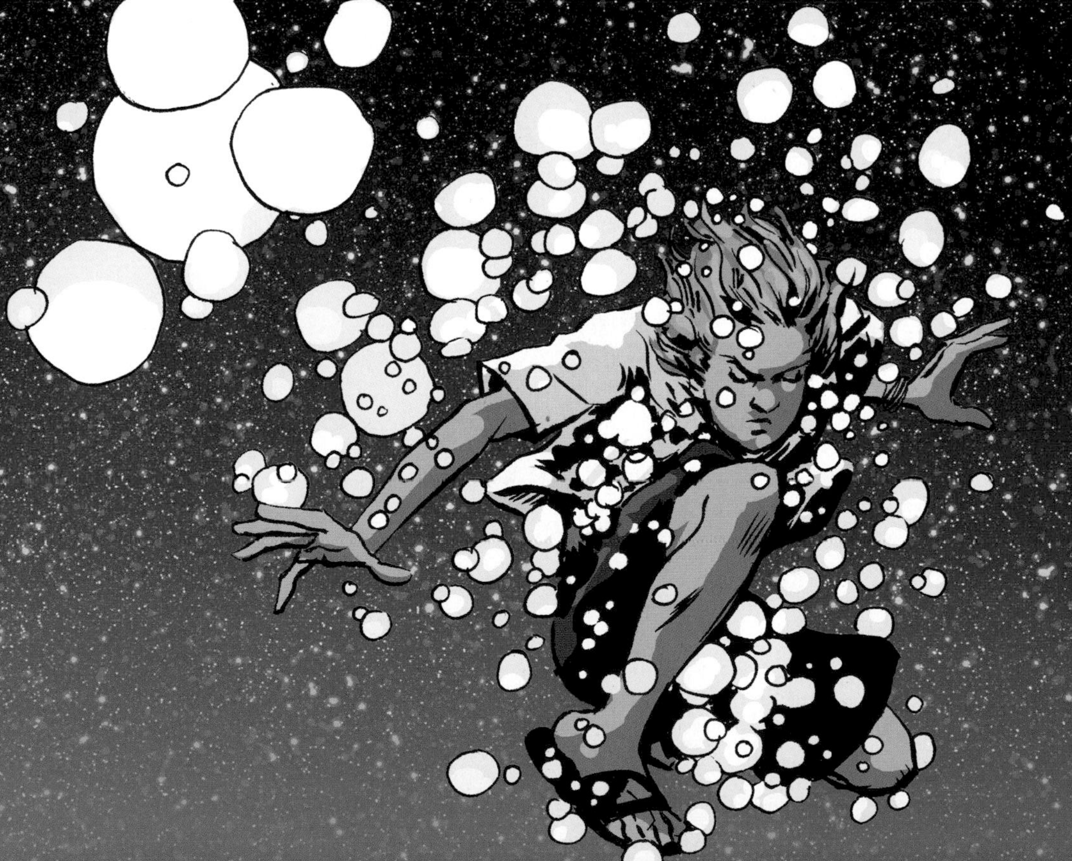

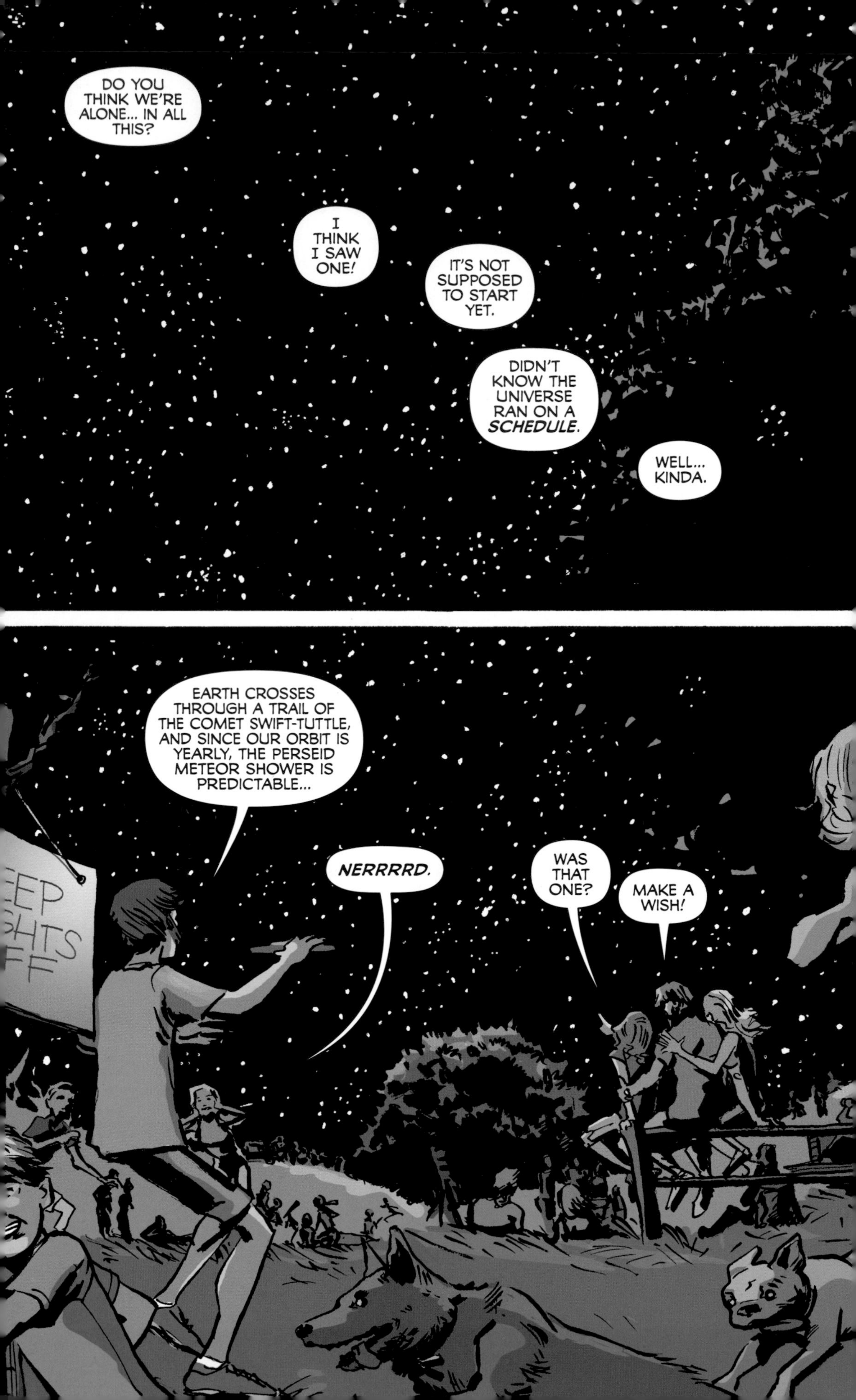
DO YOU THINK WE'RE ALONE... IN ALL THIS?
I THINK I SAW ONE!
IT'S NOT SUPPOSED TO START YET.
DIDN'T KNOW THE UNIVERSE RAN ON A *SCHEDULE*.
WELL... KINDA.
EARTH CROSSES THROUGH A TRAIL OF THE COMET SWIFT-TUTTLE, AND SINCE OUR ORBIT IS YEARLY, THE PERSEID METEOR SHOWER IS PREDICTABLE...
NERRRRD.
WAS THAT ONE?
MAKE A WISH!

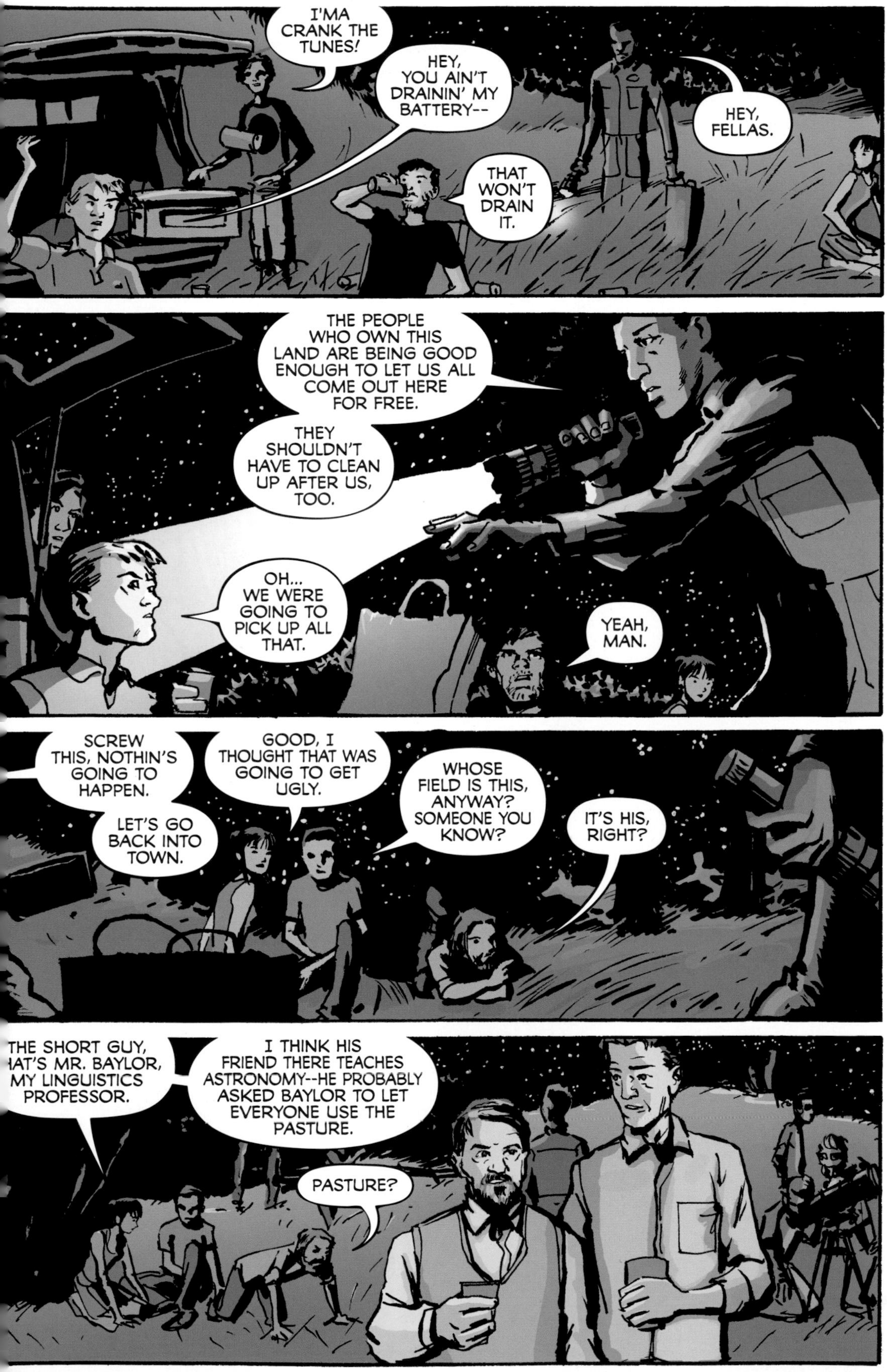
I'MA CRANK THE TUNES!
HEY, YOU AIN'T DRAININ' MY BATTERY--
THAT WON'T DRAIN IT.
HEY, FELLAS.
THE PEOPLE WHO OWN THIS LAND ARE BEING GOOD ENOUGH TO LET US ALL COME OUT HERE FOR FREE.
THEY SHOULDN'T HAVE TO CLEAN UP AFTER US, TOO.
OH... WE WERE GOING TO PICK UP ALL THAT.
YEAH, MAN.
SCREW THIS, NOTHIN'S GOING TO HAPPEN.
LET'S GO BACK INTO TOWN.
GOOD, I THOUGHT THAT WAS GOING TO GET UGLY.
WHOSE FIELD IS THIS, ANYWAY? SOMEONE YOU KNOW?
IT'S HIS, RIGHT?
THE SHORT GUY, HAT'S MR. BAYLOR, MY LINGUISTICS PROFESSOR.
I THINK HIS FRIEND THERE TEACHES ASTRONOMY--HE PROBABLY ASKED BAYLOR TO LET EVERYONE USE THE PASTURE.
PASTURE?

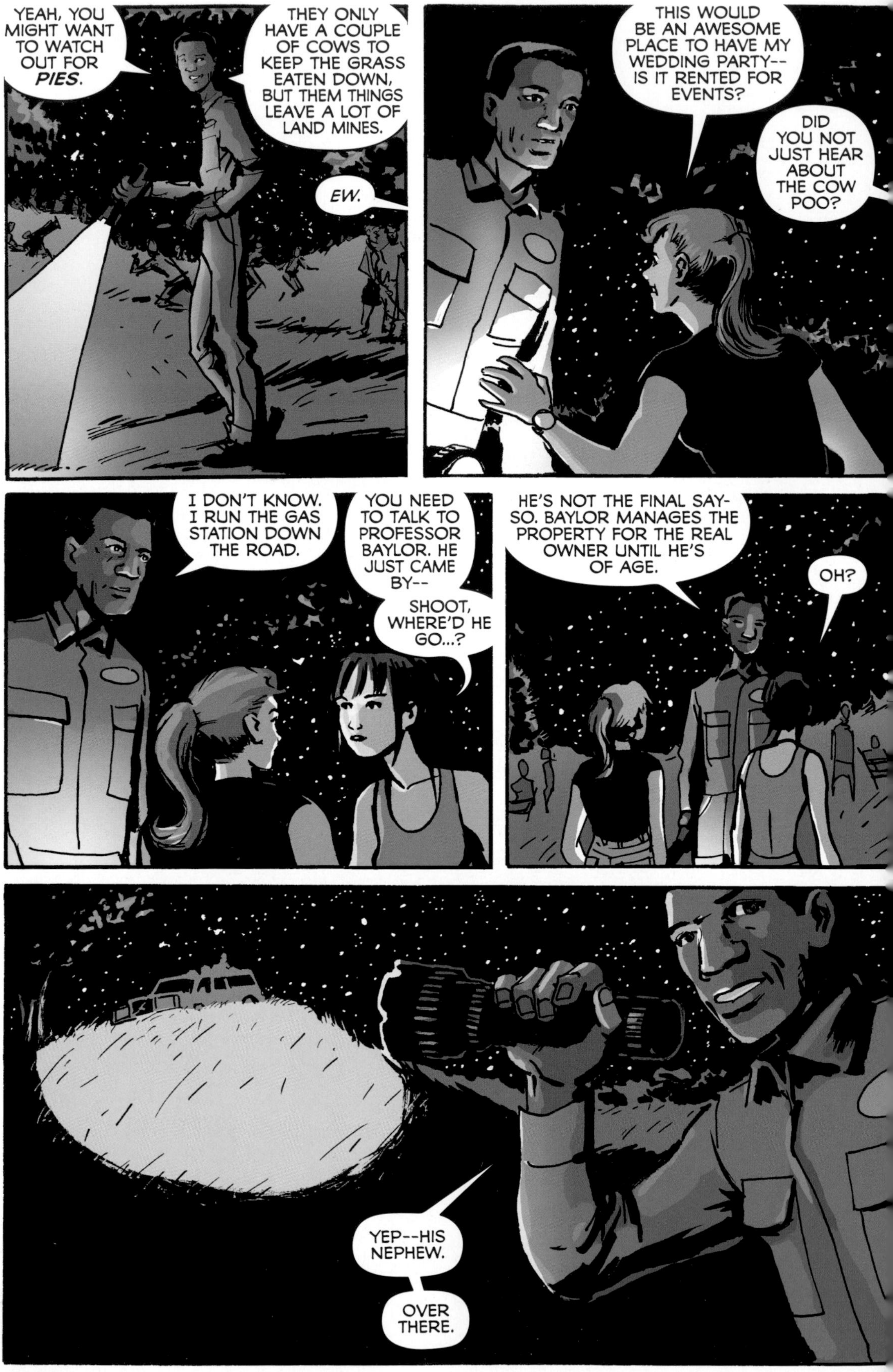
YEAH, YOU MIGHT WANT TO WATCH OUT FOR *PIES*.
THEY ONLY HAVE A COUPLE OF COWS TO KEEP THE GRASS EATEN DOWN, BUT THEM THINGS LEAVE A LOT OF LAND MINES.
EW.
THIS WOULD BE AN AWESOME PLACE TO HAVE MY WEDDING PARTY-- IS IT RENTED FOR EVENTS?
DID YOU NOT JUST HEAR ABOUT THE COW POO?
I DON'T KNOW. I RUN THE GAS STATION DOWN THE ROAD.
YOU NEED TO TALK TO PROFESSOR BAYLOR. HE JUST CAME BY--
SHOOT, WHERE'D HE GO...?
HE'S NOT THE FINAL SAY-SO. BAYLOR MANAGES THE PROPERTY FOR THE REAL OWNER UNTIL HE'S OF AGE.
OH?
YEP--HIS NEPHEW.
OVER THERE.

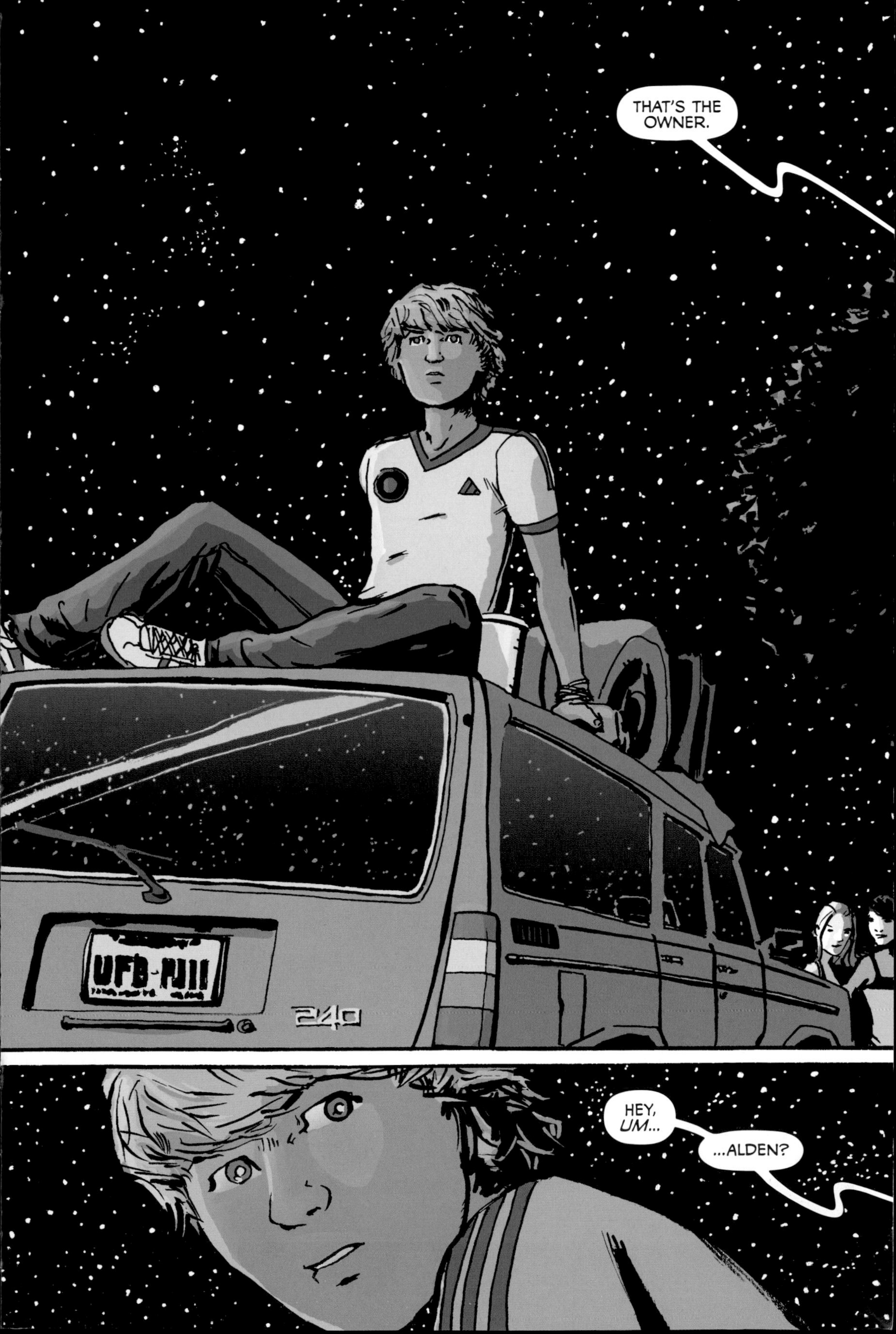
THAT'S THE OWNER.
HEY, UM...
...ALDEN?

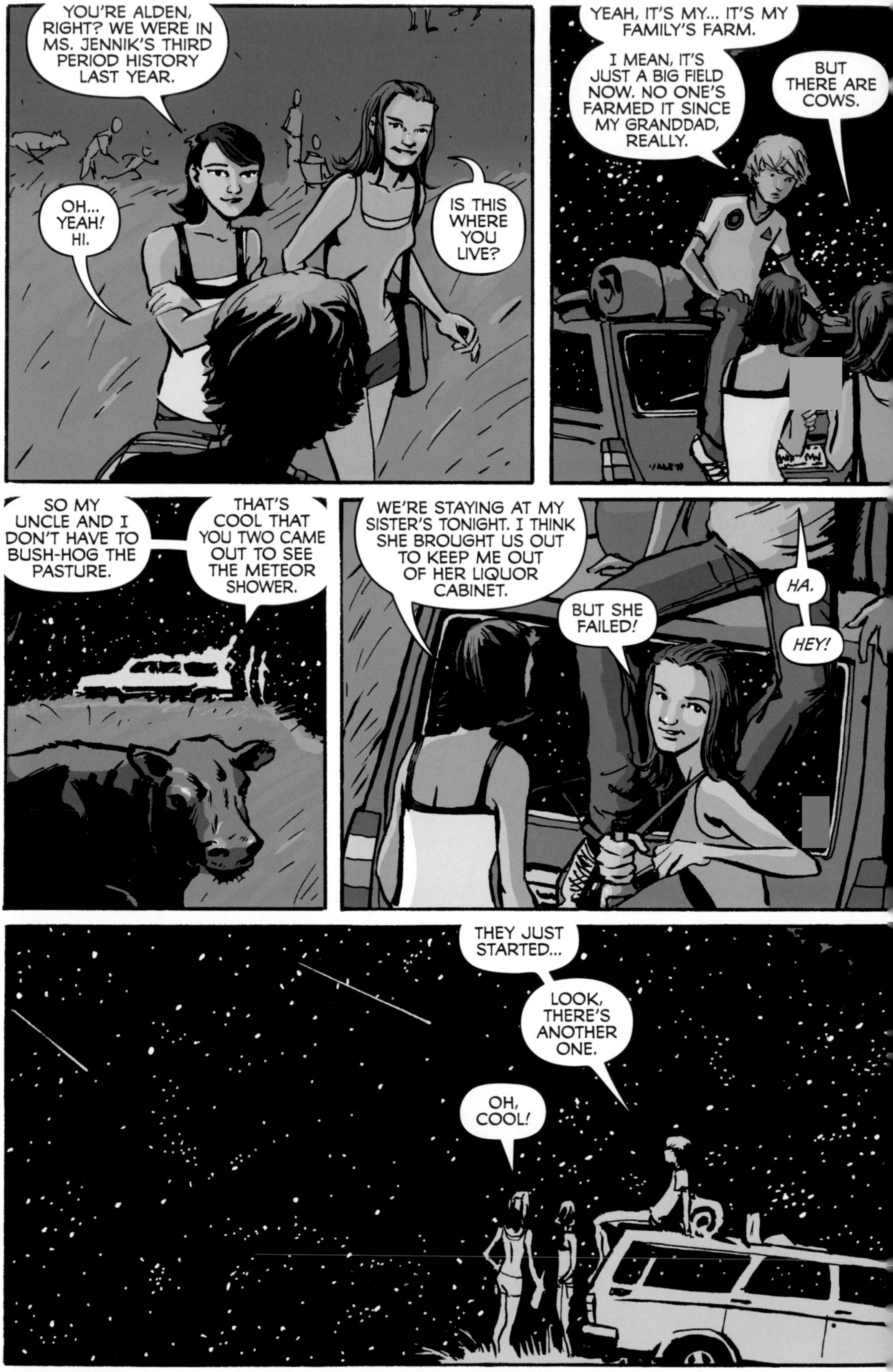
YOU'RE ALDEN, RIGHT? WE WERE IN MS. JENNIK'S THIRD PERIOD HISTORY LAST YEAR.
OH... YEAH! HI.
IS THIS WHERE YOU LIVE?
YEAH, IT'S MY... IT'S MY FAMILY'S FARM.
I MEAN, IT'S JUST A BIG FIELD NOW. NO ONE'S FARMED IT SINCE MY GRANDDAD, REALLY.
BUT THERE ARE COWS.
SO MY UNCLE AND I DON'T HAVE TO BUSH-HOG THE PASTURE.
THAT'S COOL THAT YOU TWO CAME OUT TO SEE THE METEOR SHOWER.
WE'RE STAYING AT MY SISTER'S TONIGHT. I THINK SHE BROUGHT US OUT TO KEEP ME OUT OF HER LIQUOR CABINET.
BUT SHE FAILED!
HA.
HEY!
THEY JUST STARTED...
LOOK, THERE'S ANOTHER ONE.
OH, COOL!

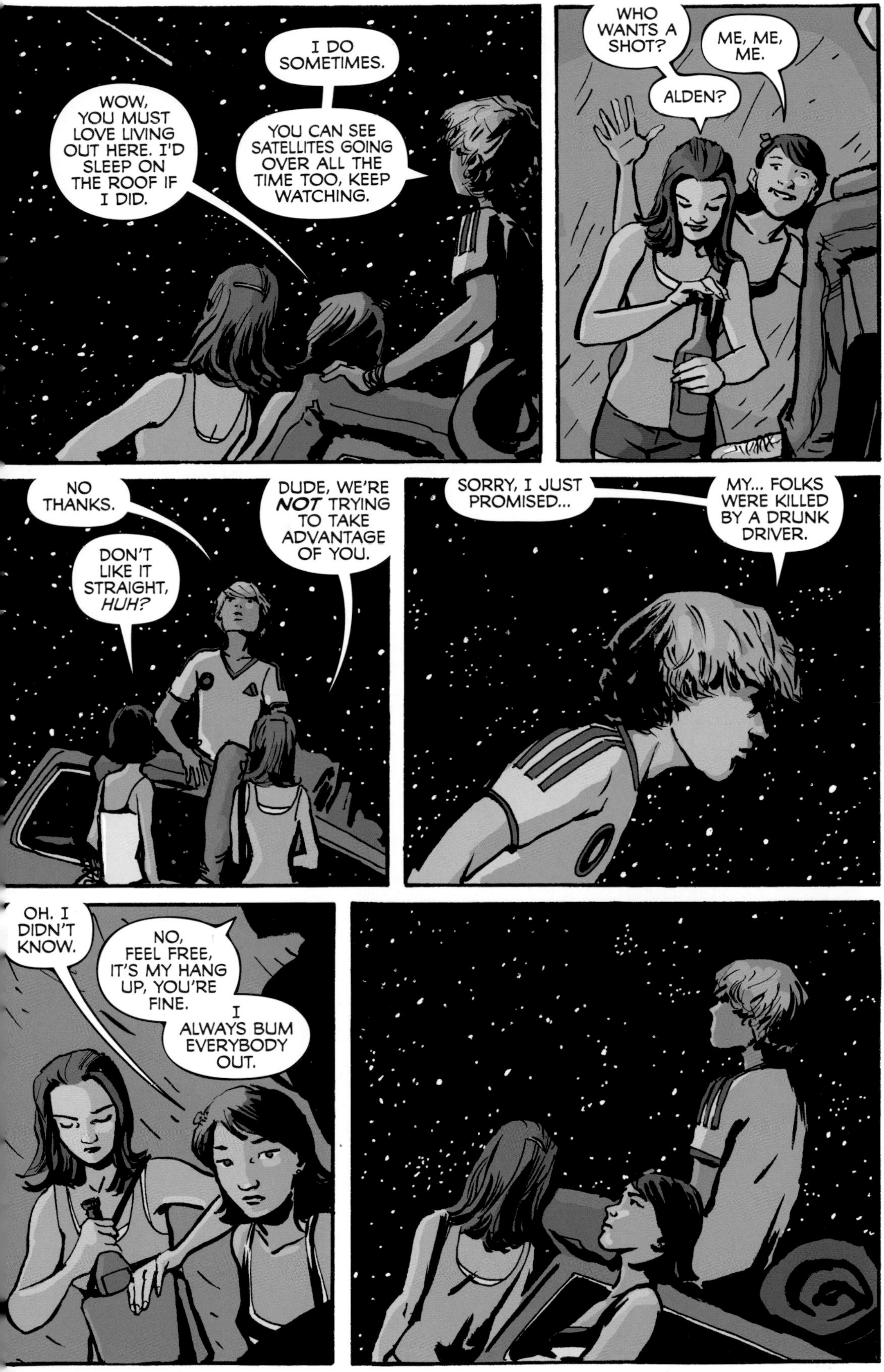
I DO SOMETIMES.
WOW, YOU MUST LOVE LIVING OUT HERE. I'D SLEEP ON THE ROOF IF I DID.
YOU CAN SEE SATELLITES GOING OVER ALL THE TIME TOO, KEEP WATCHING.
WHO WANTS A SHOT?
ME, ME, ME.
ALDEN?
NO THANKS.
DON'T LIKE IT STRAIGHT, *HUH?*
DUDE, WE'RE ***NOT*** TRYING TO TAKE ADVANTAGE OF YOU.
SORRY, I JUST PROMISED...
MY... FOLKS WERE KILLED BY A DRUNK DRIVER.
OH. I DIDN'T KNOW.
NO, FEEL FREE, IT'S MY HANG UP, YOU'RE FINE.
I ALWAYS BUM EVERYBODY OUT.

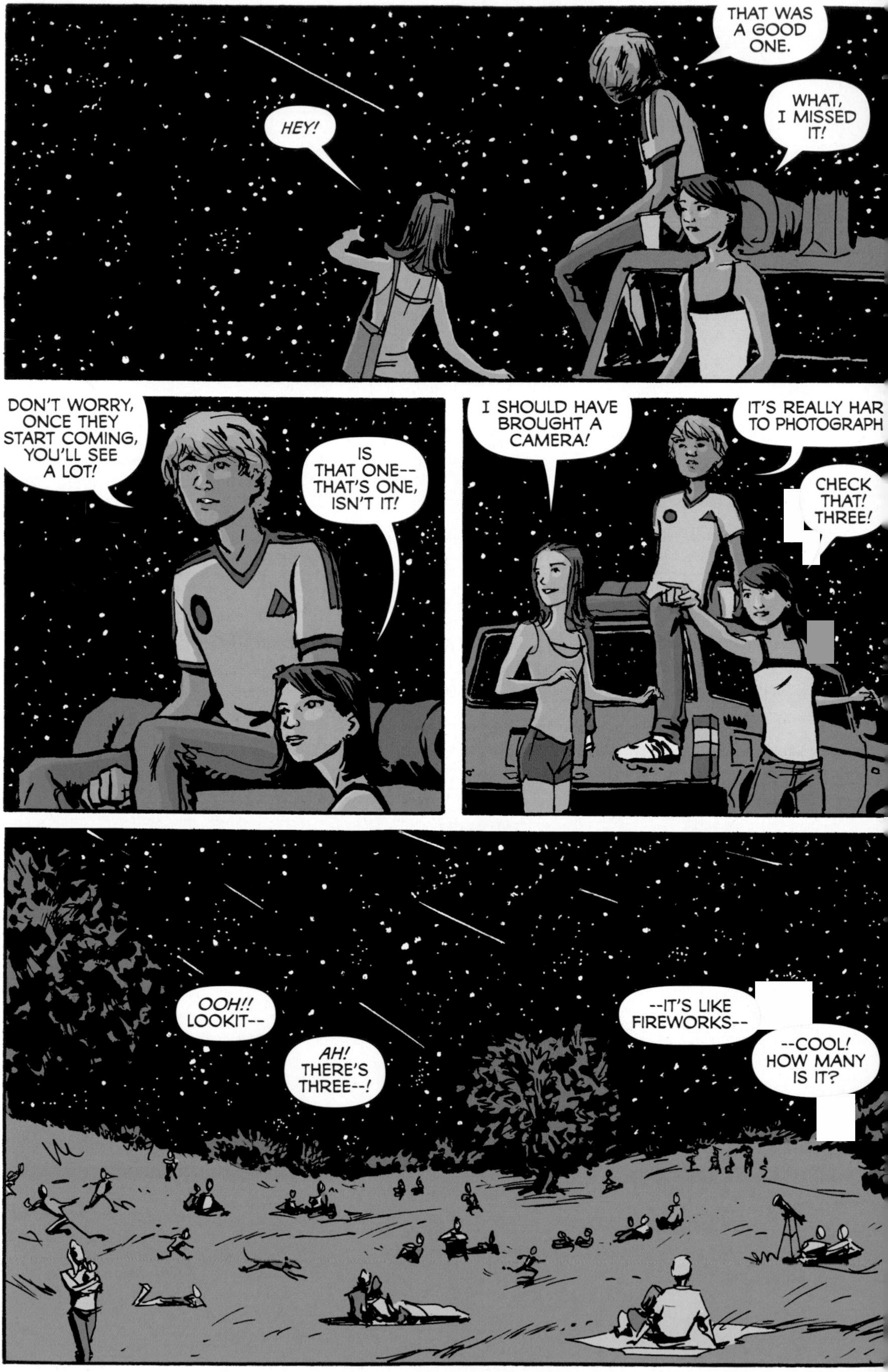

THAT WAS A GOOD ONE.
HEY!
WHAT, I MISSED IT!
DON'T WORRY, ONCE THEY START COMING, YOU'LL SEE A LOT!
IS THAT ONE-- THAT'S ONE, ISN'T IT!
I SHOULD HAVE BROUGHT A CAMERA!
IT'S REALLY HAR TO PHOTOGRAPH
CHECK THAT! THREE!
OOH!! LOOKIT--
AH! THERE'S THREE--!
--IT'S LIKE FIREWORKS--
--COOL! HOW MANY IS IT?

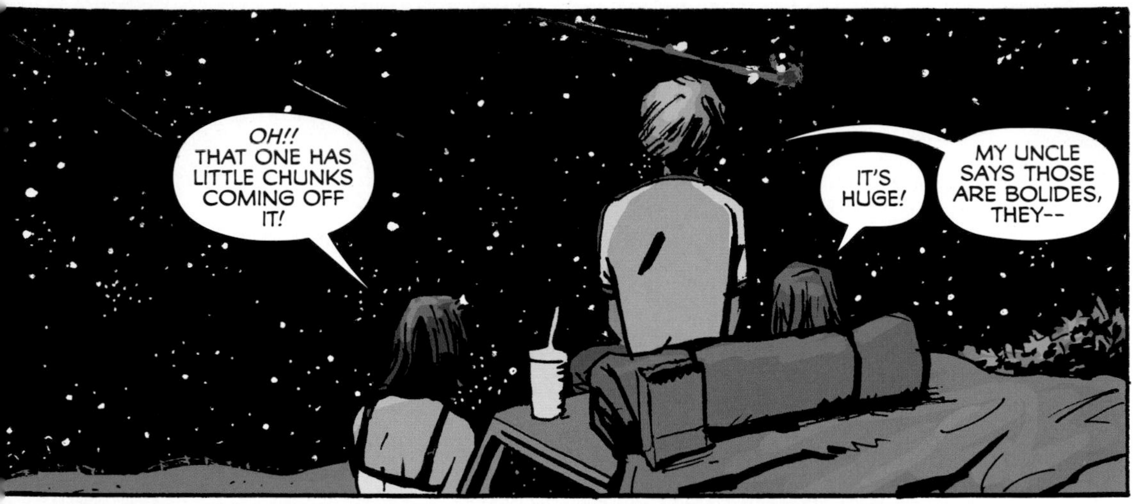
OH!! THAT ONE HAS LITTLE CHUNKS COMING OFF IT!
IT'S HUGE!
MY UNCLE SAYS THOSE ARE BOLIDES, THEY--

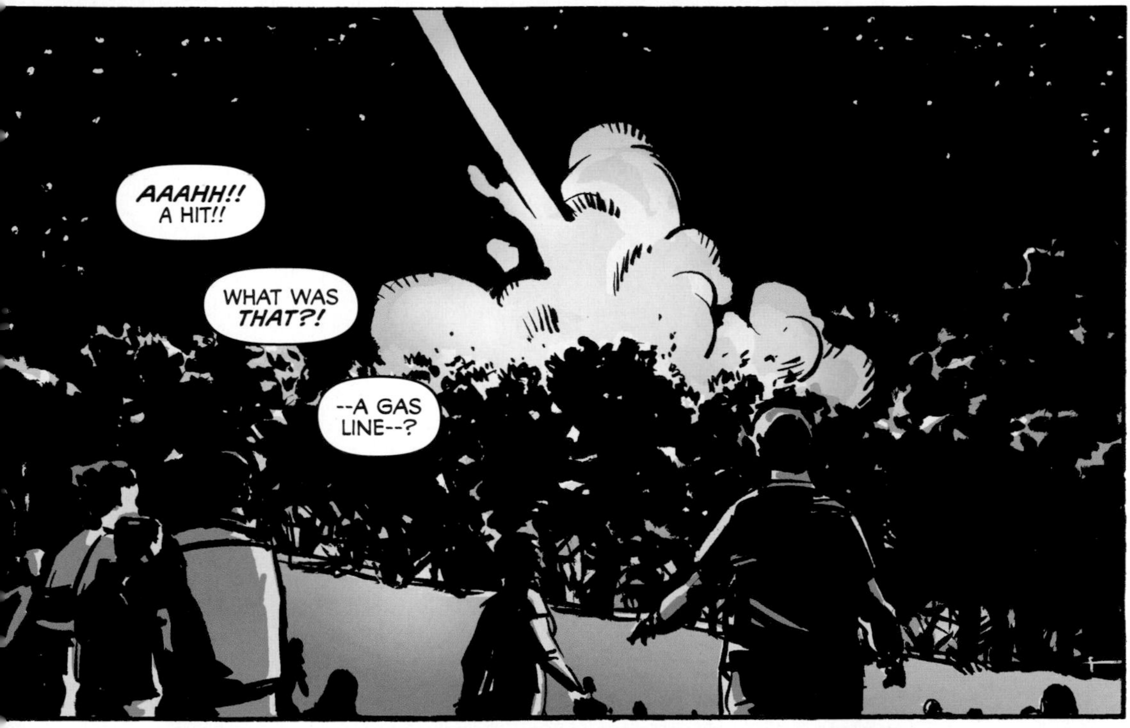
AAAHH!! A HIT!!
WHAT WAS THAT?!
--A GAS LINE--?

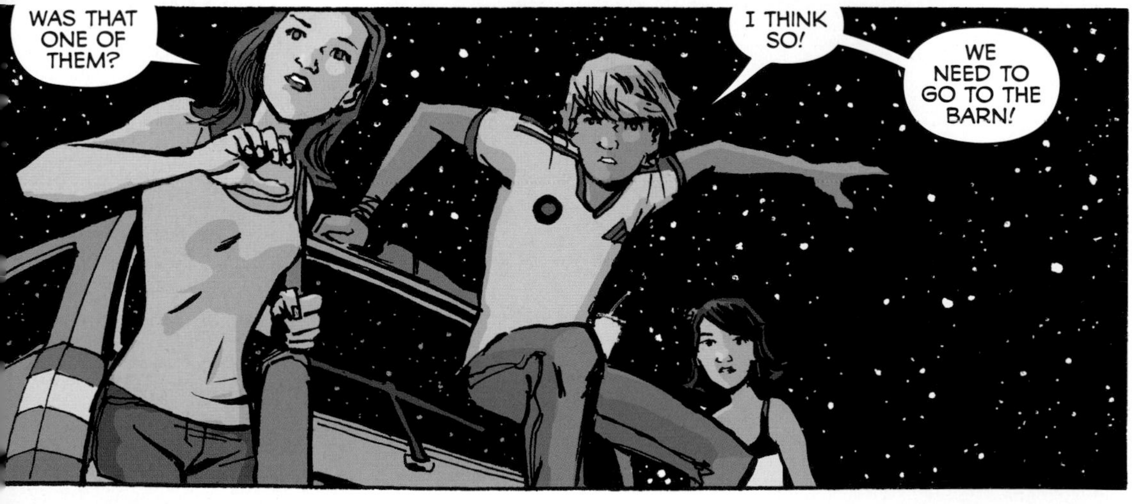
WAS THAT ONE OF THEM?
I THINK SO!
WE NEED TO GO TO THE BARN!

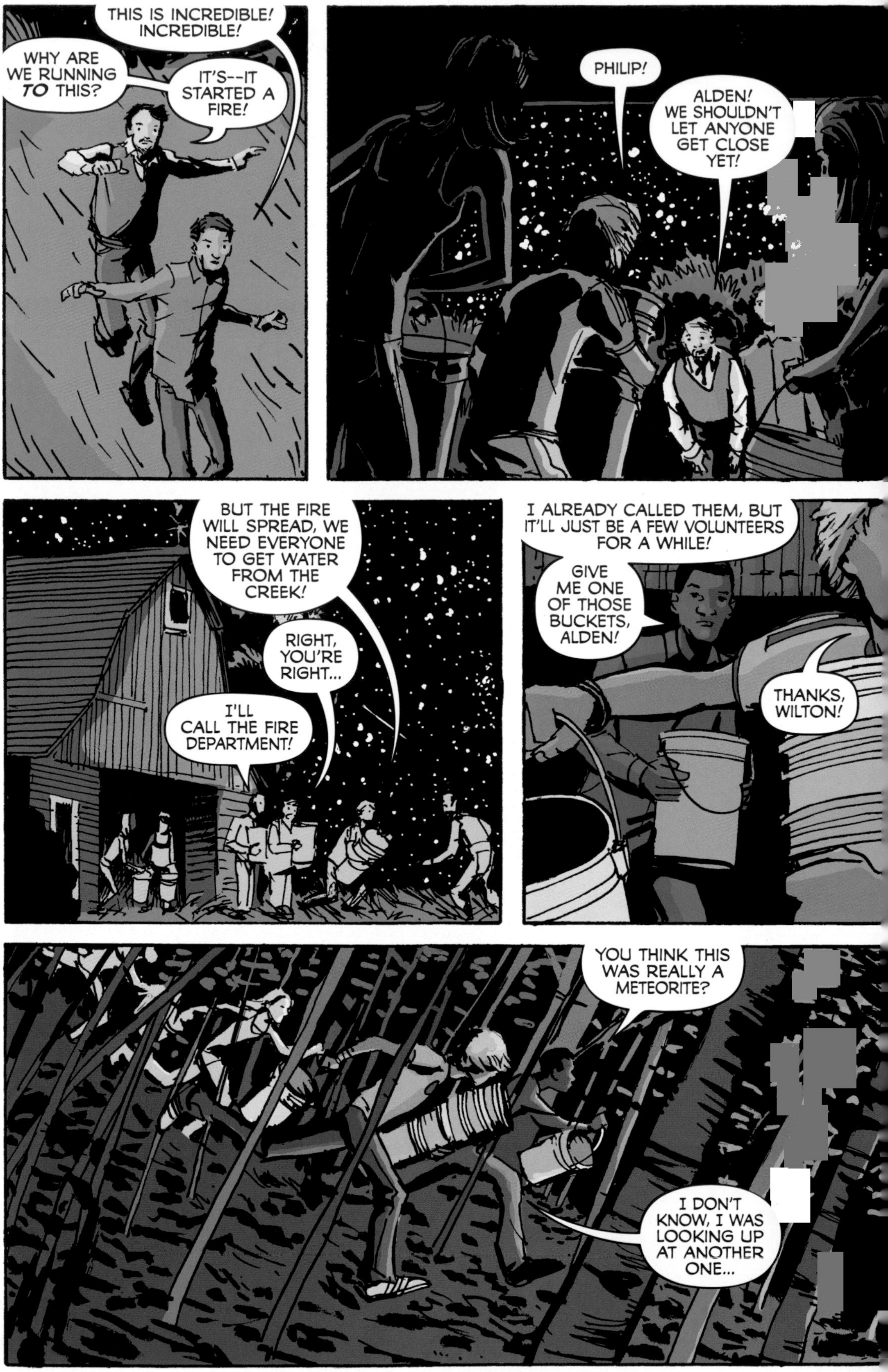
THIS IS INCREDIBLE! INCREDIBLE!
WHY ARE WE RUNNING *TO* THIS?
IT'S--IT STARTED A FIRE!
PHILIP!
ALDEN! WE SHOULDN'T LET ANYONE GET CLOSE YET!
BUT THE FIRE WILL SPREAD, WE NEED EVERYONE TO GET WATER FROM THE CREEK!
RIGHT, YOU'RE RIGHT...
I'LL CALL THE FIRE DEPARTMENT!
I ALREADY CALLED THEM, BUT IT'LL JUST BE A FEW VOLUNTEERS FOR A WHILE!
GIVE ME ONE OF THOSE BUCKETS, ALDEN!
THANKS, WILTON!
YOU THINK THIS WAS REALLY A METEORITE?
I DON'T KNOW, I WAS LOOKING UP AT ANOTHER ONE...

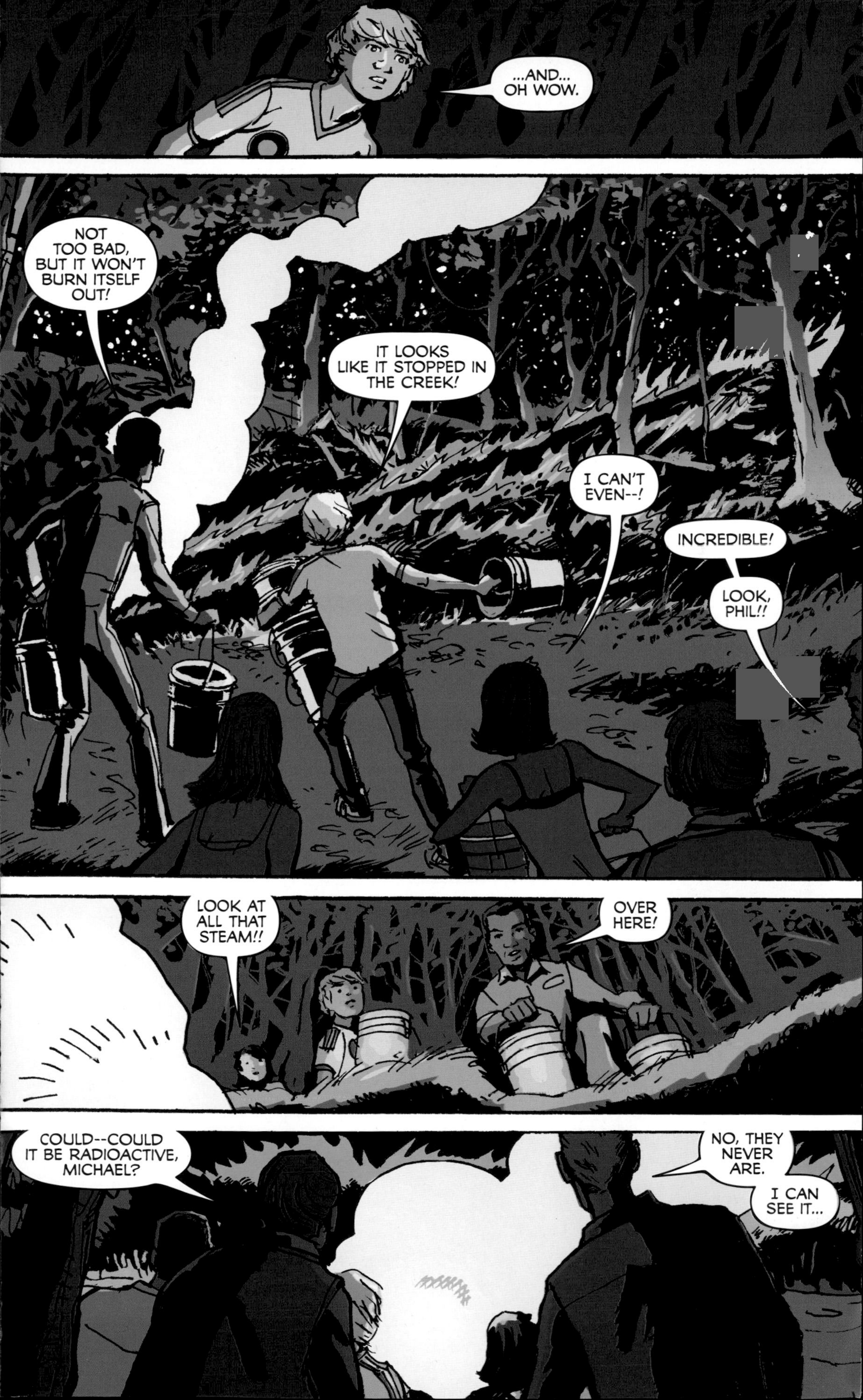
...AND... OH WOW.
NOT TOO BAD, BUT IT WON'T BURN ITSELF OUT!
IT LOOKS LIKE IT STOPPED IN THE CREEK!
I CAN'T EVEN--!
INCREDIBLE!
LOOK, PHIL!!
LOOK AT ALL THAT STEAM!!
OVER HERE!
COULD--COULD IT BE RADIOACTIVE, MICHAEL?
NO, THEY NEVER ARE.
I CAN SEE IT...

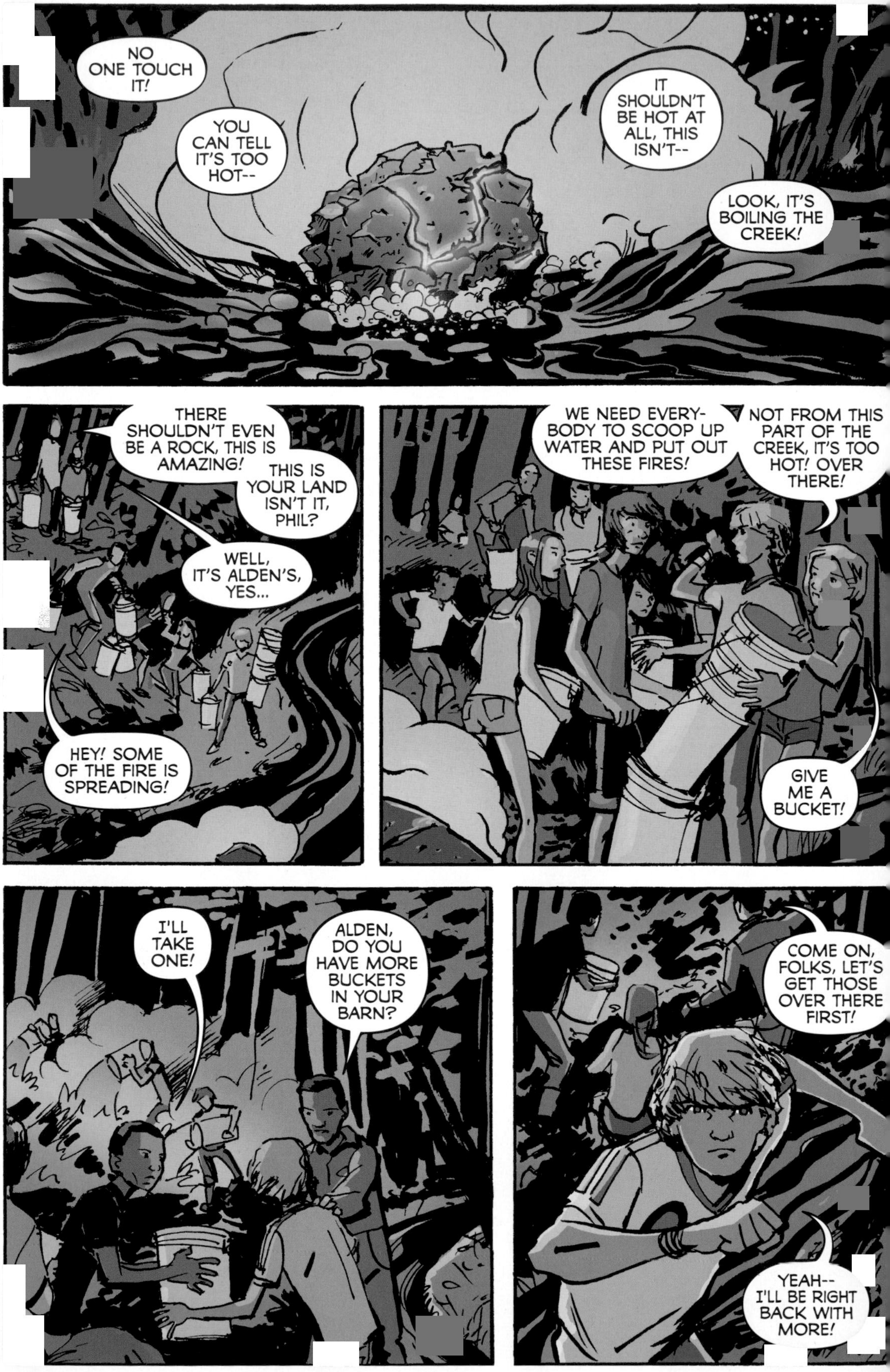
NO ONE TOUCH IT!
YOU CAN TELL IT'S TOO HOT--
IT SHOULDN'T BE HOT AT ALL, THIS ISN'T--
LOOK, IT'S BOILING THE CREEK!
THERE SHOULDN'T EVEN BE A ROCK, THIS IS AMAZING!
THIS IS YOUR LAND ISN'T IT, PHIL?
WELL, IT'S ALDEN'S, YES...
HEY! SOME OF THE FIRE IS SPREADING!
WE NEED EVERY-BODY TO SCOOP UP WATER AND PUT OUT THESE FIRES!
NOT FROM THIS PART OF THE CREEK, IT'S TOO HOT! OVER THERE!
GIVE ME A BUCKET!
I'LL TAKE ONE!
ALDEN, DO YOU HAVE MORE BUCKETS IN YOUR BARN?
COME ON, FOLKS, LET'S GET THOSE OVER THERE FIRST!
YEAH-- I'LL BE RIGHT BACK WITH MORE!

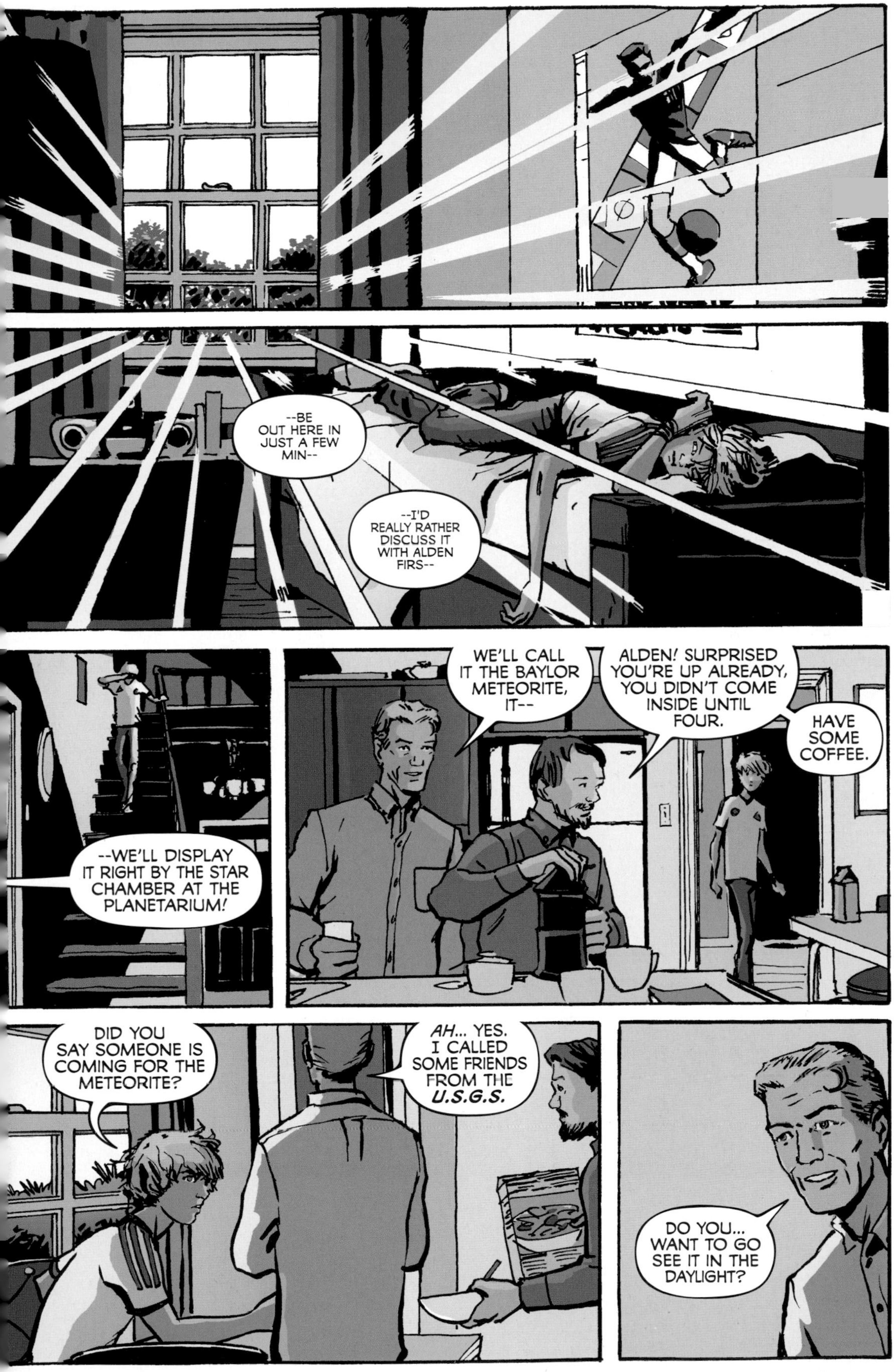
--BE OUT HERE IN JUST A FEW MIN--
--I'D REALLY RATHER DISCUSS IT WITH ALDEN FIRS--
--WE'LL DISPLAY IT RIGHT BY THE STAR CHAMBER AT THE PLANETARIUM!
WE'LL CALL IT THE BAYLOR METEORITE, IT--
ALDEN! SURPRISED YOU'RE UP ALREADY, YOU DIDN'T COME INSIDE UNTIL FOUR.
HAVE SOME COFFEE.
DID YOU SAY SOMEONE IS COMING FOR THE METEORITE?
AH... YES. I CALLED SOME FRIENDS FROM THE U.S.G.S.
DO YOU... WANT TO GO SEE IT IN THE DAYLIGHT?

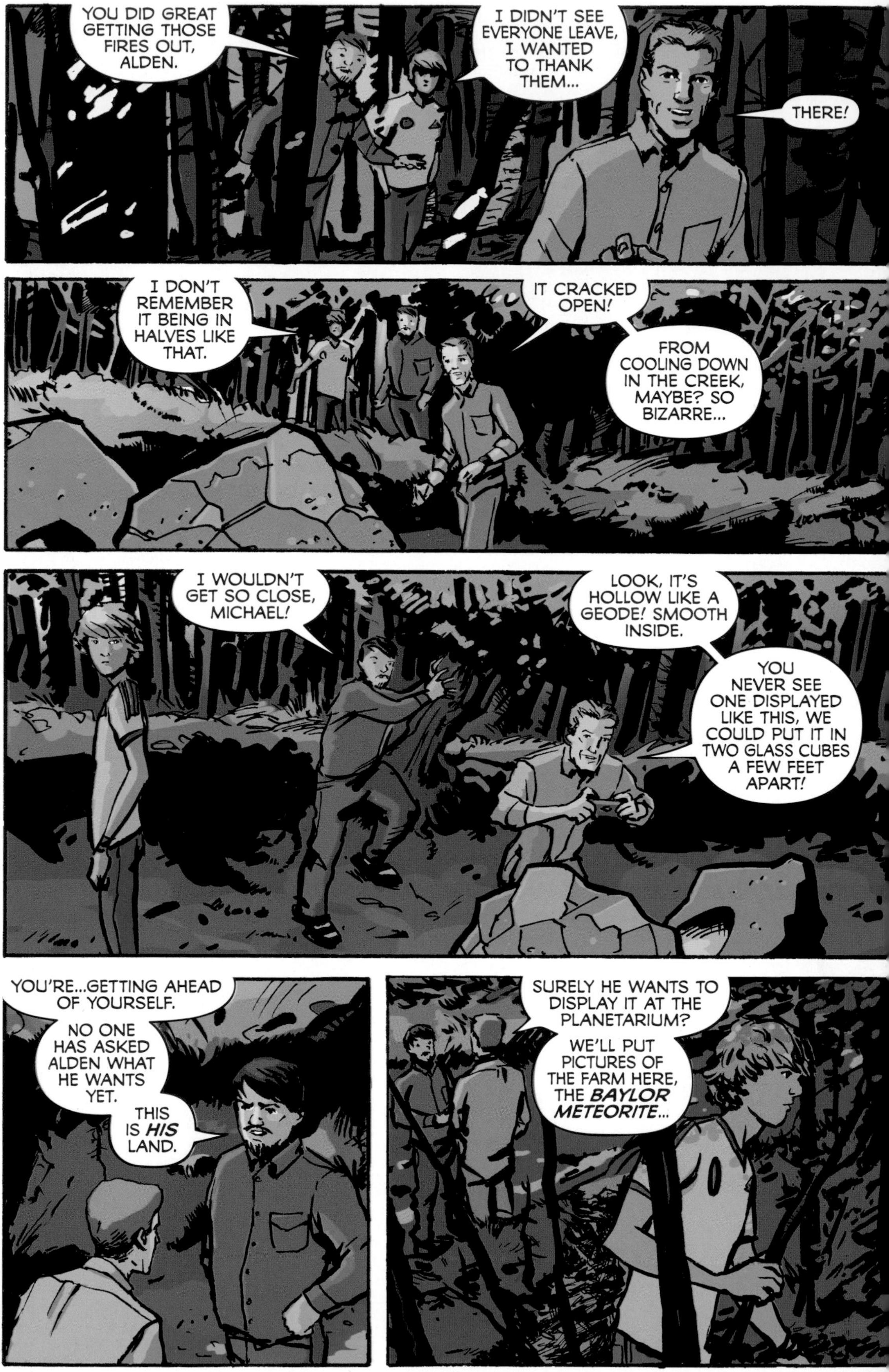
YOU DID GREAT GETTING THOSE FIRES OUT, ALDEN.
I DIDN'T SEE EVERYONE LEAVE, I WANTED TO THANK THEM...
THERE!
I DON'T REMEMBER IT BEING IN HALVES LIKE THAT.
IT CRACKED OPEN!
FROM COOLING DOWN IN THE CREEK, MAYBE? SO BIZARRE...
I WOULDN'T GET SO CLOSE, MICHAEL!
LOOK, IT'S HOLLOW LIKE A GEODE! SMOOTH INSIDE.
YOU NEVER SEE ONE DISPLAYED LIKE THIS, WE COULD PUT IT IN TWO GLASS CUBES A FEW FEET APART!
YOU'RE...GETTING AHEAD OF YOURSELF.
NO ONE HAS ASKED ALDEN WHAT HE WANTS YET.
THIS IS *HIS* LAND.
SURELY HE WANTS TO DISPLAY IT AT THE PLANETARIUM?
WE'LL PUT PICTURES OF THE FARM HERE, THE ***BAYLOR METEORITE***...

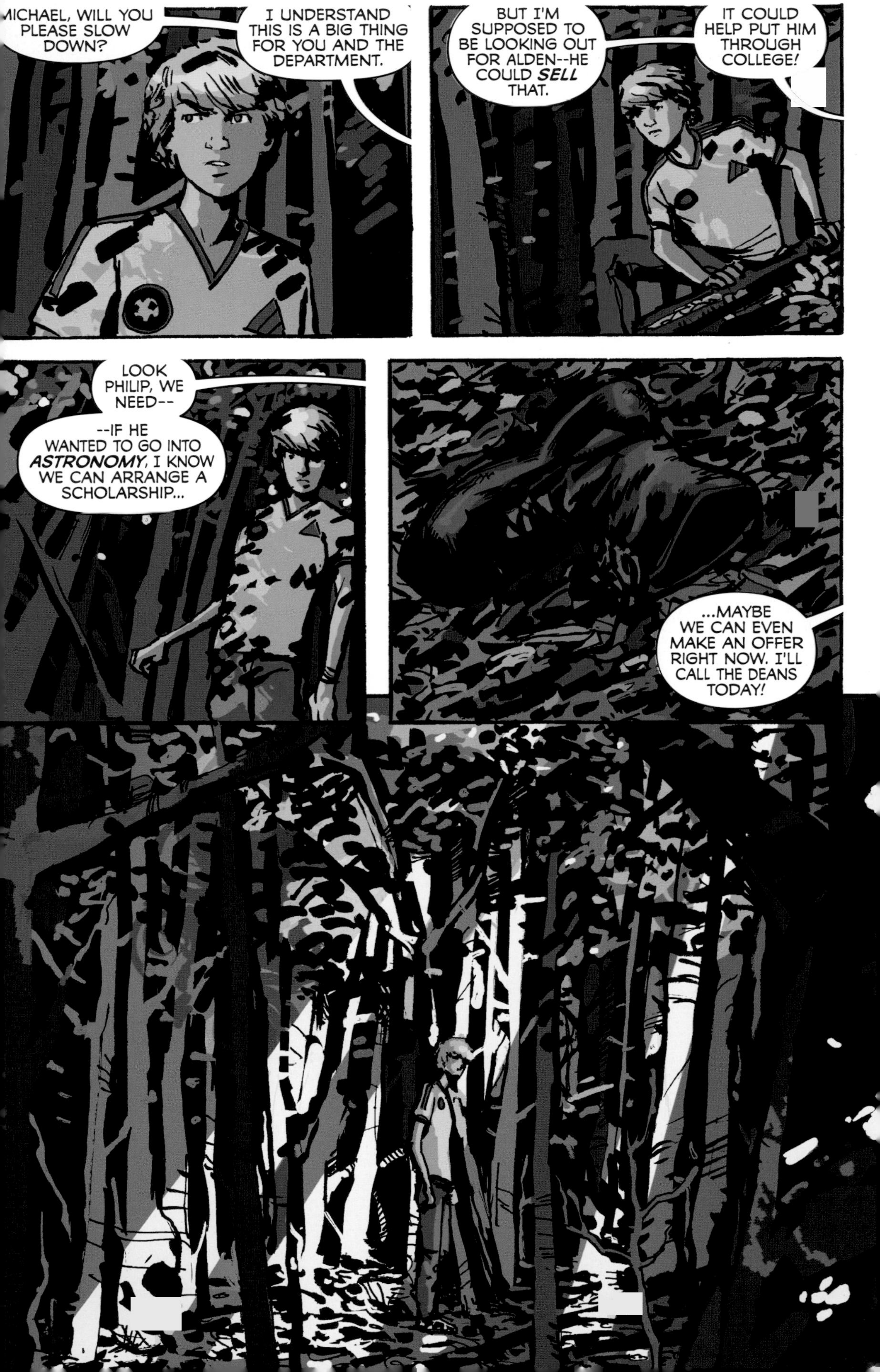
MICHAEL, WILL YOU PLEASE SLOW DOWN?
I UNDERSTAND THIS IS A BIG THING FOR YOU AND THE DEPARTMENT.
BUT I'M SUPPOSED TO BE LOOKING OUT FOR ALDEN--HE COULD SELL THAT.
IT COULD HELP PUT HIM THROUGH COLLEGE!
LOOK PHILIP, WE NEED--
--IF HE WANTED TO GO INTO ASTRONOMY, I KNOW WE CAN ARRANGE A SCHOLARSHIP...
...MAYBE WE CAN EVEN MAKE AN OFFER RIGHT NOW. I'LL CALL THE DEANS TODAY!

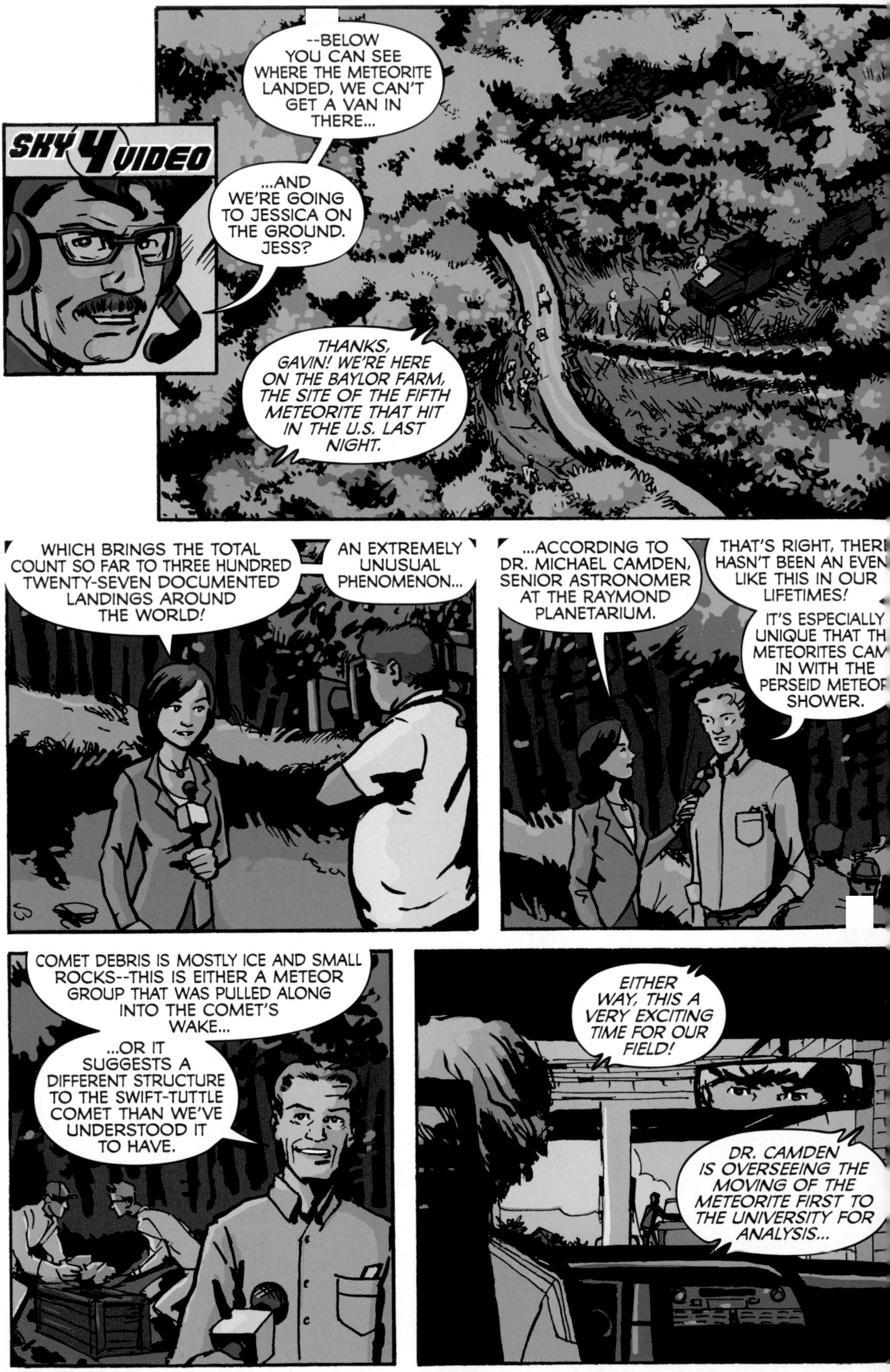
SKY 4 VIDEO
--BELOW YOU CAN SEE WHERE THE METEORITE LANDED, WE CAN'T GET A VAN IN THERE...
...AND WE'RE GOING TO JESSICA ON THE GROUND. JESS?
THANKS, GAVIN! WE'RE HERE ON THE BAYLOR FARM, THE SITE OF THE FIFTH METEORITE THAT HIT IN THE U.S. LAST NIGHT.
WHICH BRINGS THE TOTAL COUNT SO FAR TO THREE HUNDRED TWENTY-SEVEN DOCUMENTED LANDINGS AROUND THE WORLD!
AN EXTREMELY UNUSUAL PHENOMENON...
...ACCORDING TO DR. MICHAEL CAMDEN, SENIOR ASTRONOMER AT THE RAYMOND PLANETARIUM.
THAT'S RIGHT, THER HASN'T BEEN AN EVEN LIKE THIS IN OUR LIFETIMES!
IT'S ESPECIALLY UNIQUE THAT TH METEORITES CAM IN WITH THE PERSEID METEOR SHOWER.
COMET DEBRIS IS MOSTLY ICE AND SMALL ROCKS--THIS IS EITHER A METEOR GROUP THAT WAS PULLED ALONG INTO THE COMET'S WAKE...
...OR IT SUGGESTS A DIFFERENT STRUCTURE TO THE SWIFT-TUTTLE COMET THAN WE'VE UNDERSTOOD IT TO HAVE.
EITHER WAY, THIS A VERY EXCITING TIME FOR OUR FIELD!
DR. CAMDEN IS OVERSEEING THE MOVING OF THE METEORITE FIRST TO THE UNIVERSITY FOR ANALYSIS...

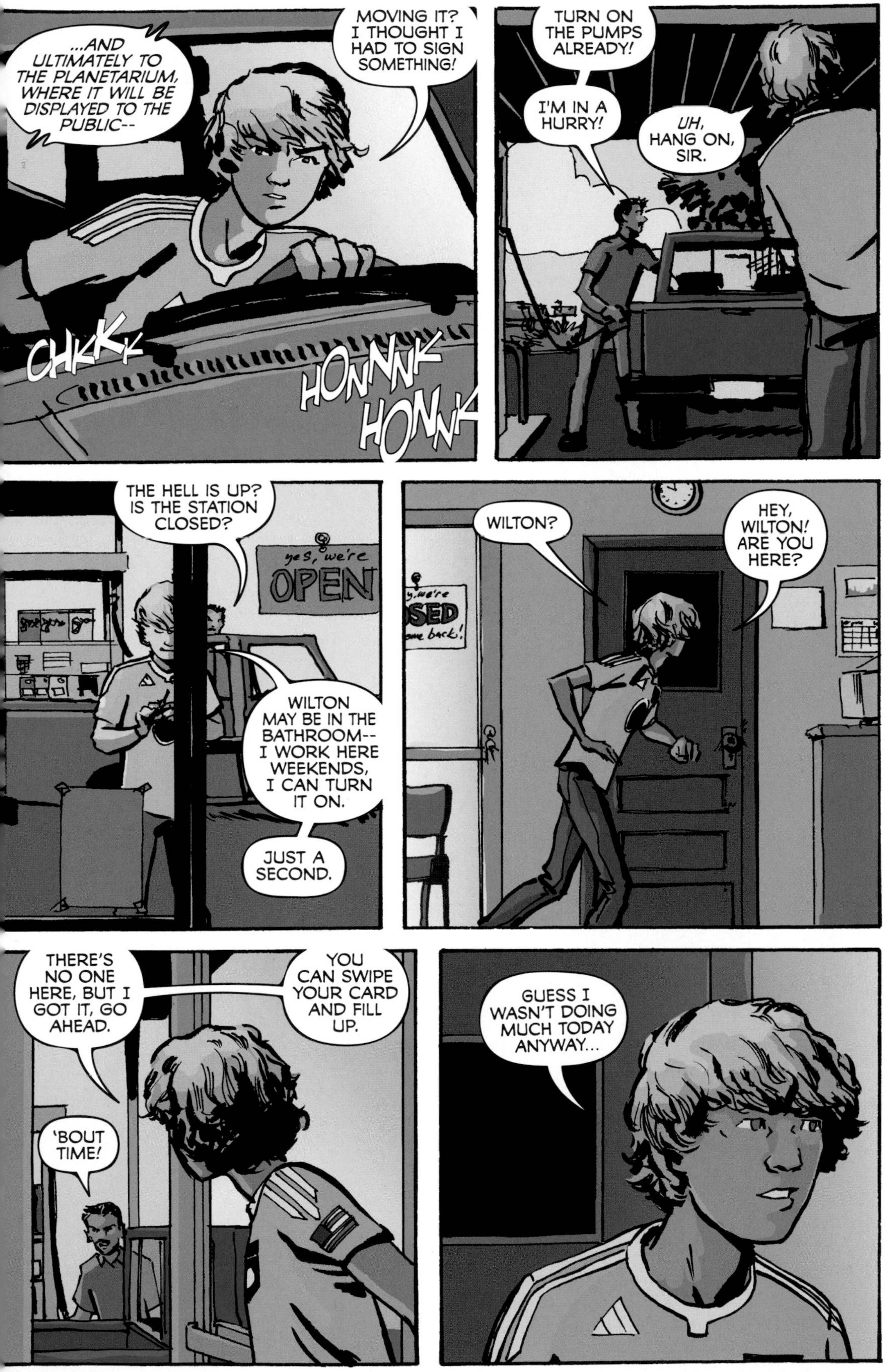
...AND ULTIMATELY TO THE PLANETARIUM, WHERE IT WILL BE DISPLAYED TO THE PUBLIC--
MOVING IT? I THOUGHT I HAD TO SIGN SOMETHING!
CHKKK
HONNNK HONNK
TURN ON THE PUMPS ALREADY!
I'M IN A HURRY!
UH, HANG ON, SIR.
THE HELL IS UP? IS THE STATION CLOSED?
yes, we're OPEN
WILTON MAY BE IN THE BATHROOM-- I WORK HERE WEEKENDS, I CAN TURN IT ON.
JUST A SECOND.
WILTON?
HEY, WILTON! ARE YOU HERE?
THERE'S NO ONE HERE, BUT I GOT IT, GO AHEAD.
YOU CAN SWIPE YOUR CARD AND FILL UP.
'BOUT TIME!
GUESS I WASN'T DOING MUCH TODAY ANYWAY...

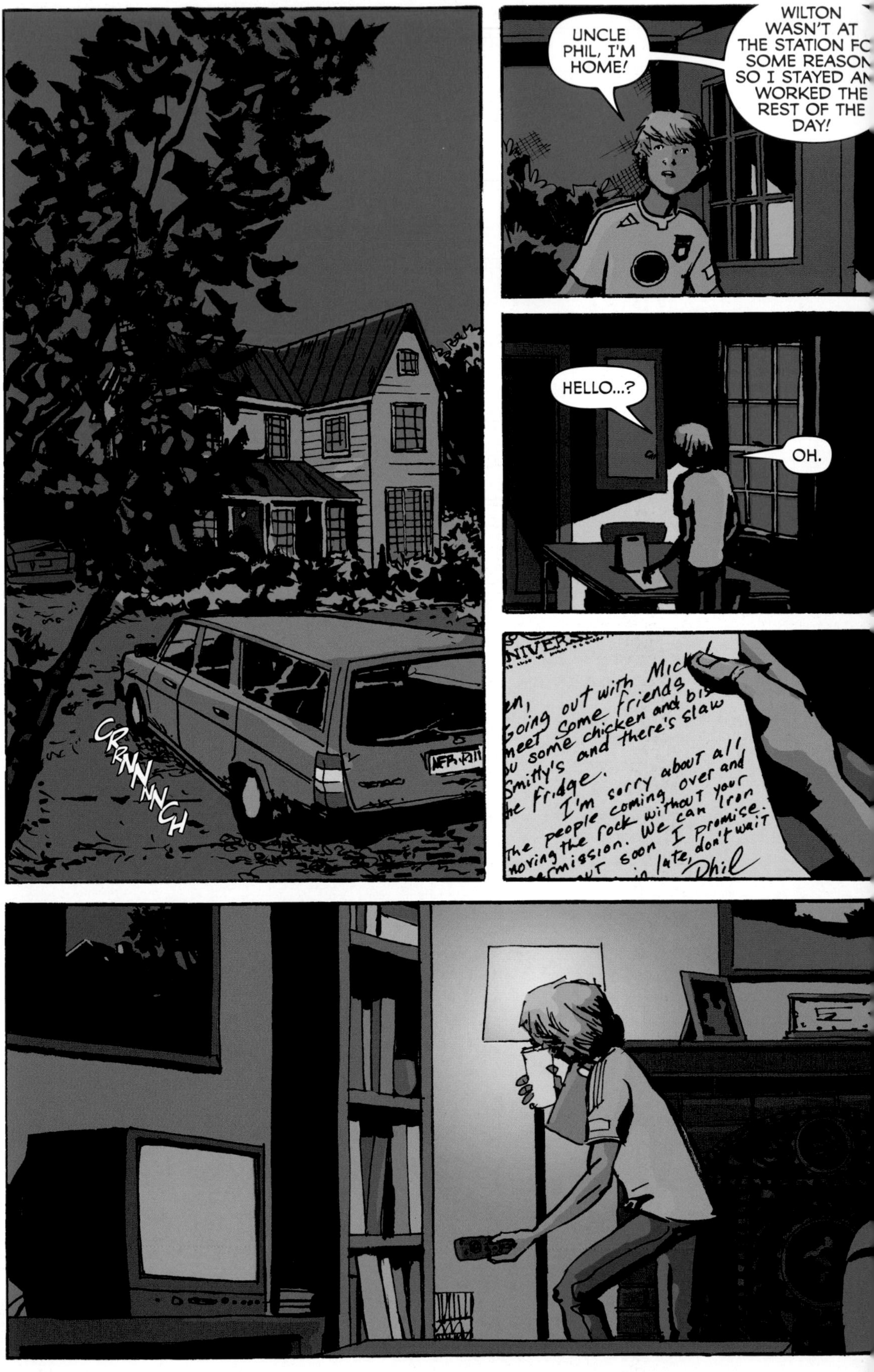
CRRNNNNCH
UNCLE PHIL, I'M HOME!
WILTON WASN'T AT THE STATION FO SOME REASON SO I STAYED AN WORKED THE REST OF THE DAY!
HELLO...?
OH.
en,
Going out with Mick
meet some friends
u some chicken and bis
Smitty's and there's slaw
the fridge.
I'm sorry about all
the people coming over and
moving the rock without your
permission. We can iron
out soon I promise.
in late, don't wait
Phil

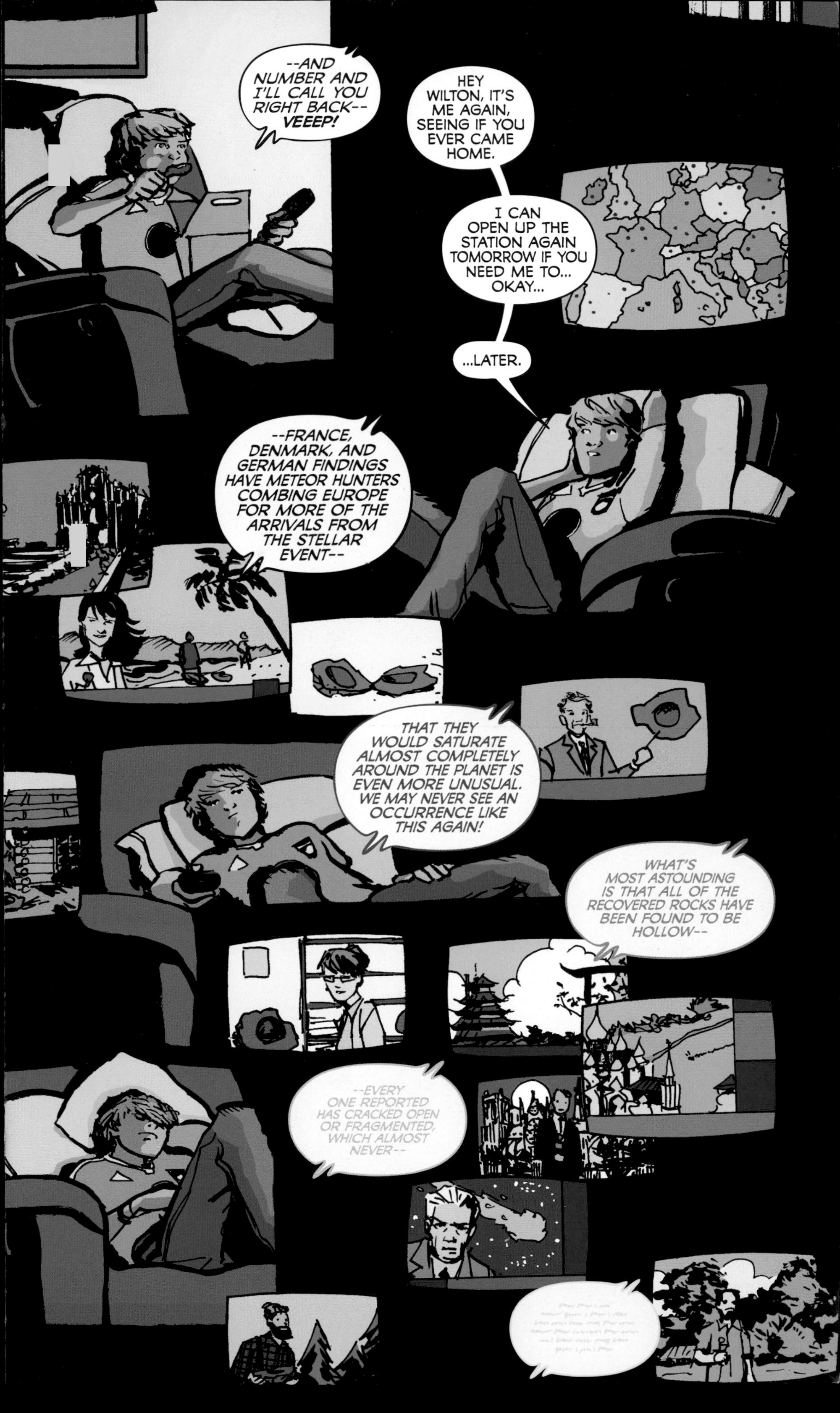
--AND NUMBER AND I'LL CALL YOU RIGHT BACK-- VEEEP!
HEY WILTON, IT'S ME AGAIN, SEEING IF YOU EVER CAME HOME.
I CAN OPEN UP THE STATION AGAIN TOMORROW IF YOU NEED ME TO... OKAY...
...LATER.
--FRANCE, DENMARK, AND GERMAN FINDINGS HAVE METEOR HUNTERS COMBING EUROPE FOR MORE OF THE ARRIVALS FROM THE STELLAR EVENT--
THAT THEY WOULD SATURATE ALMOST COMPLETELY AROUND THE PLANET IS EVEN MORE UNUSUAL. WE MAY NEVER SEE AN OCCURRENCE LIKE THIS AGAIN!
WHAT'S MOST ASTOUNDING IS THAT ALL OF THE RECOVERED ROCKS HAVE BEEN FOUND TO BE HOLLOW--
--EVERY ONE REPORTED HAS CRACKED OPEN OR FRAGMENTED, WHICH ALMOST NEVER--

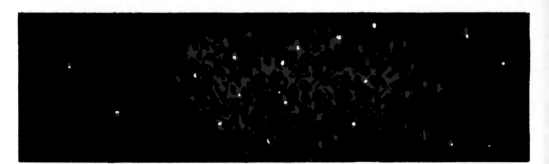

ALDEN.

ALDEN.

ALDEN,
I'M STILL
HERE.

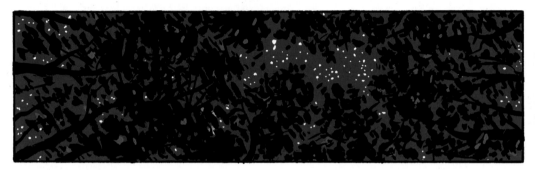

ALDEN.

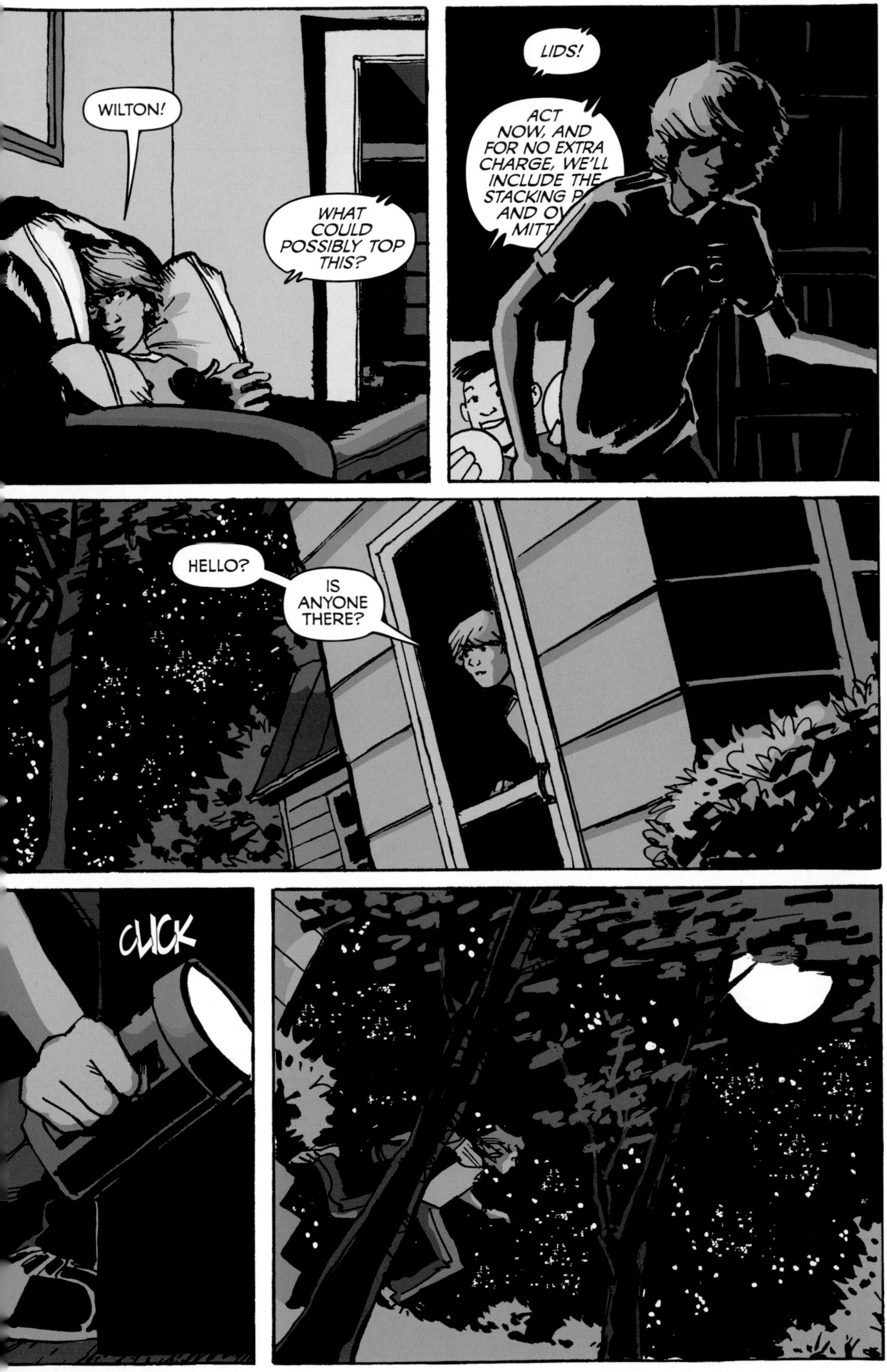
WILTON!
WHAT COULD POSSIBLY TOP THIS?
LIDS!
ACT NOW, AND FOR NO EXTRA CHARGE, WE'LL INCLUDE THE STACKING P AND OV MITT
HELLO?
IS ANYONE THERE?
CLICK

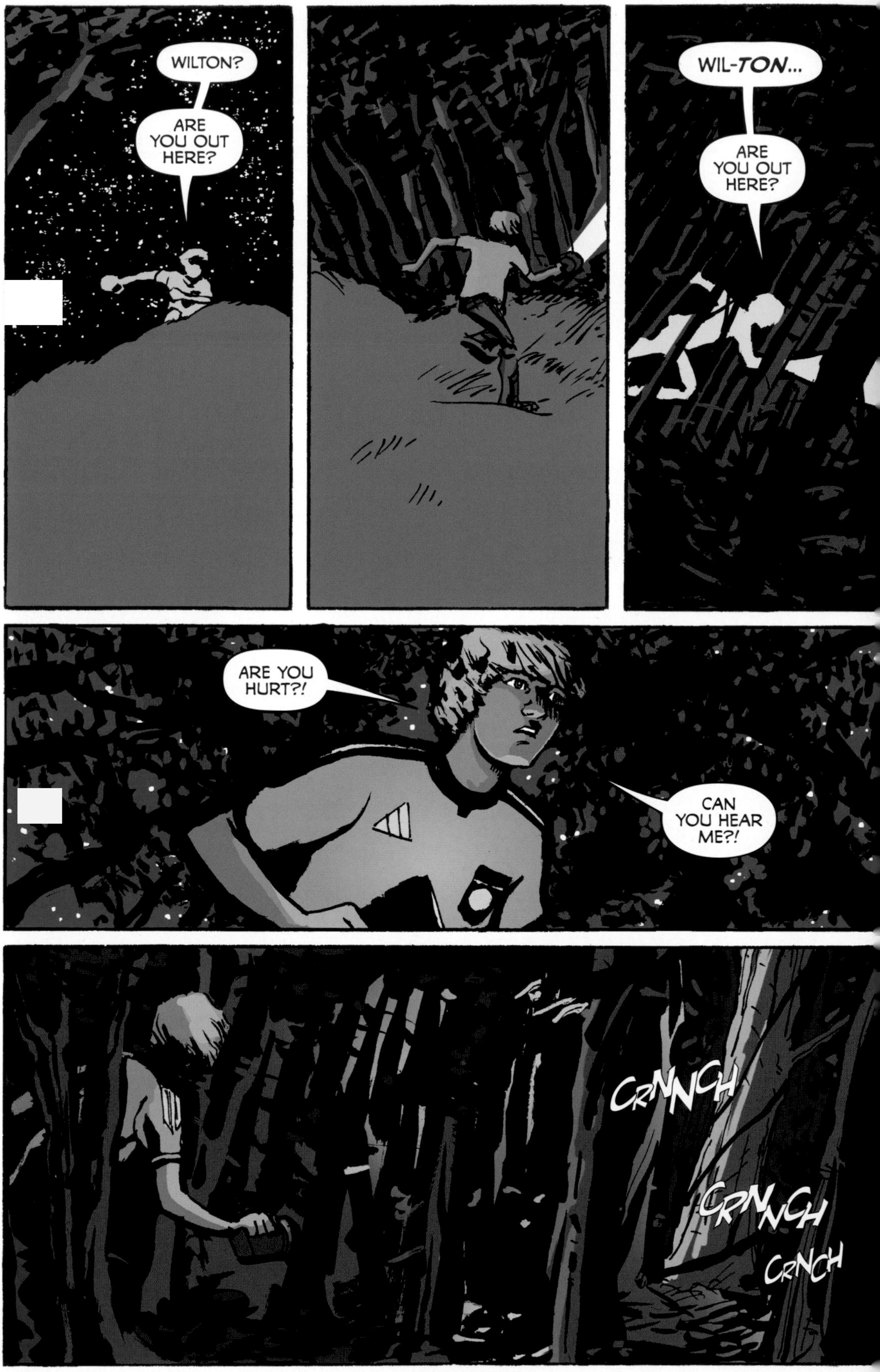
WILTON?
ARE YOU OUT HERE?
WIL-TON...
ARE YOU OUT HERE?
ARE YOU HURT?!
CAN YOU HEAR ME?!
CRNNCH
CRNNCH
CRNCH

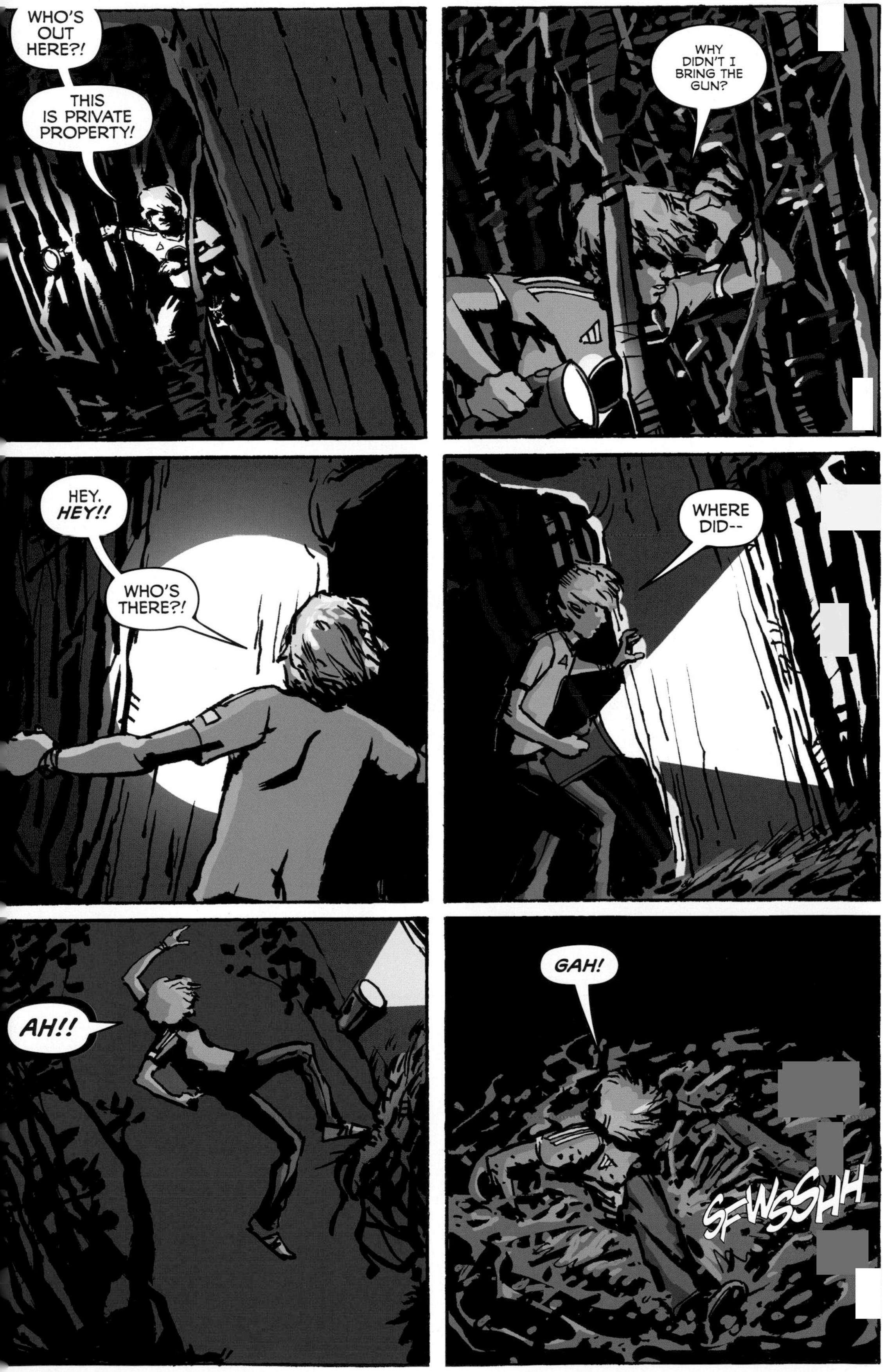
WHO'S OUT HERE?!
THIS IS PRIVATE PROPERTY!
WHY DIDN'T I BRING THE GUN?
HEY. *HEY!!*
WHO'S THERE?!
WHERE DID--
AH!!
GAH!
SFWSSHH

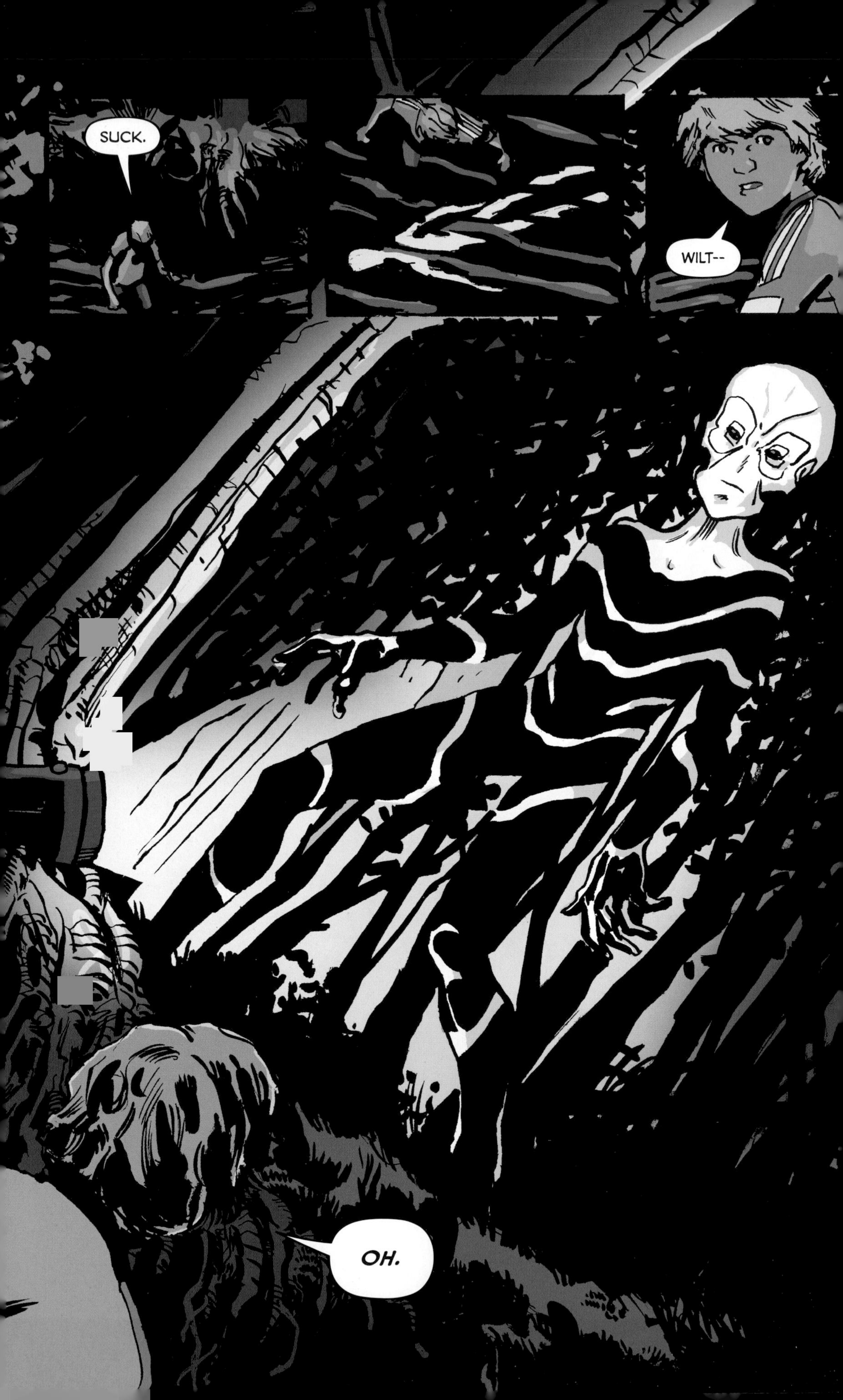
SUCK.
WILT--
OH.

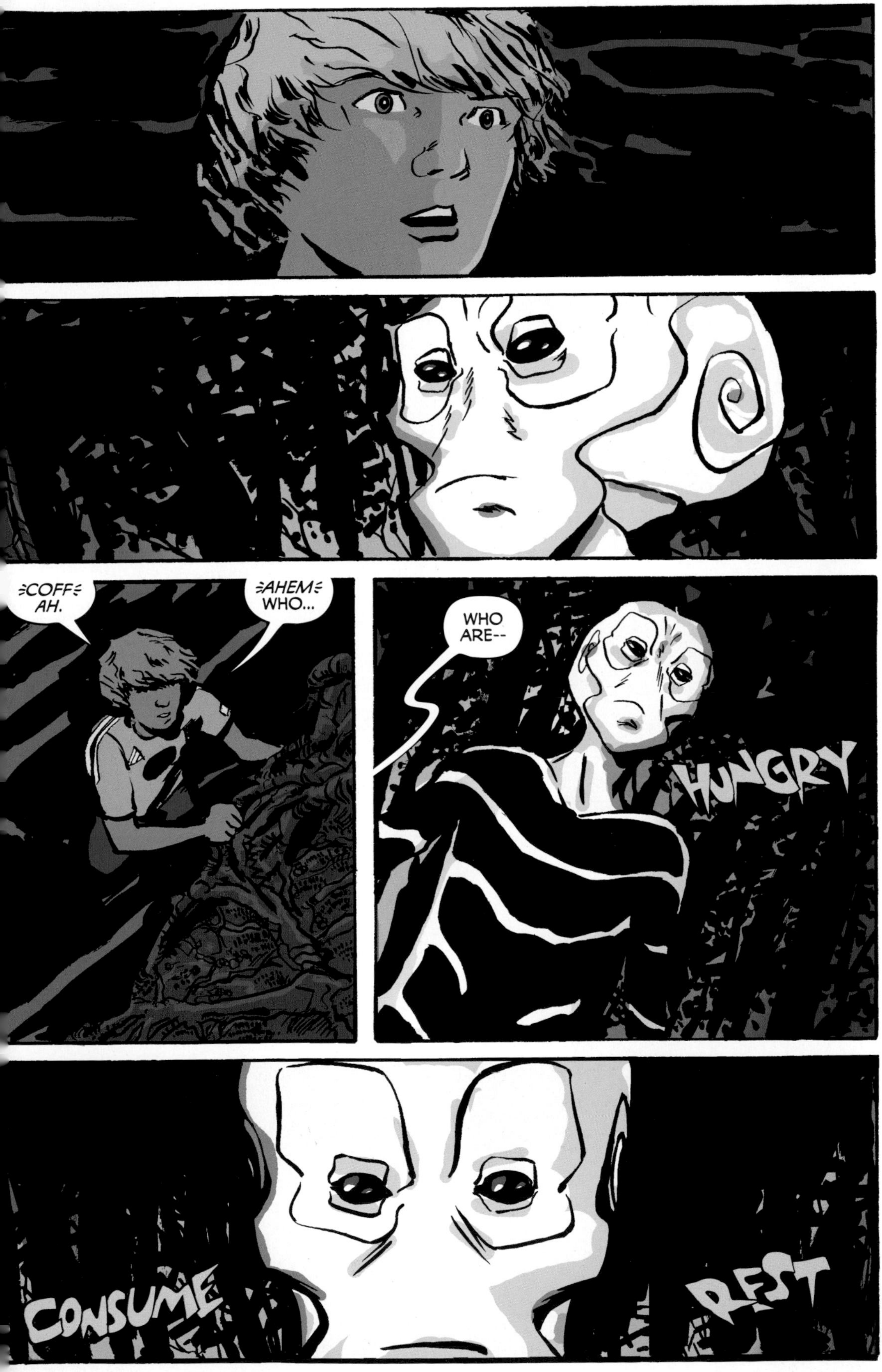
≈COFF≈
AH.
≈AHEM≈
WHO...
WHO
ARE--
HUNGRY
CONSUME
REST

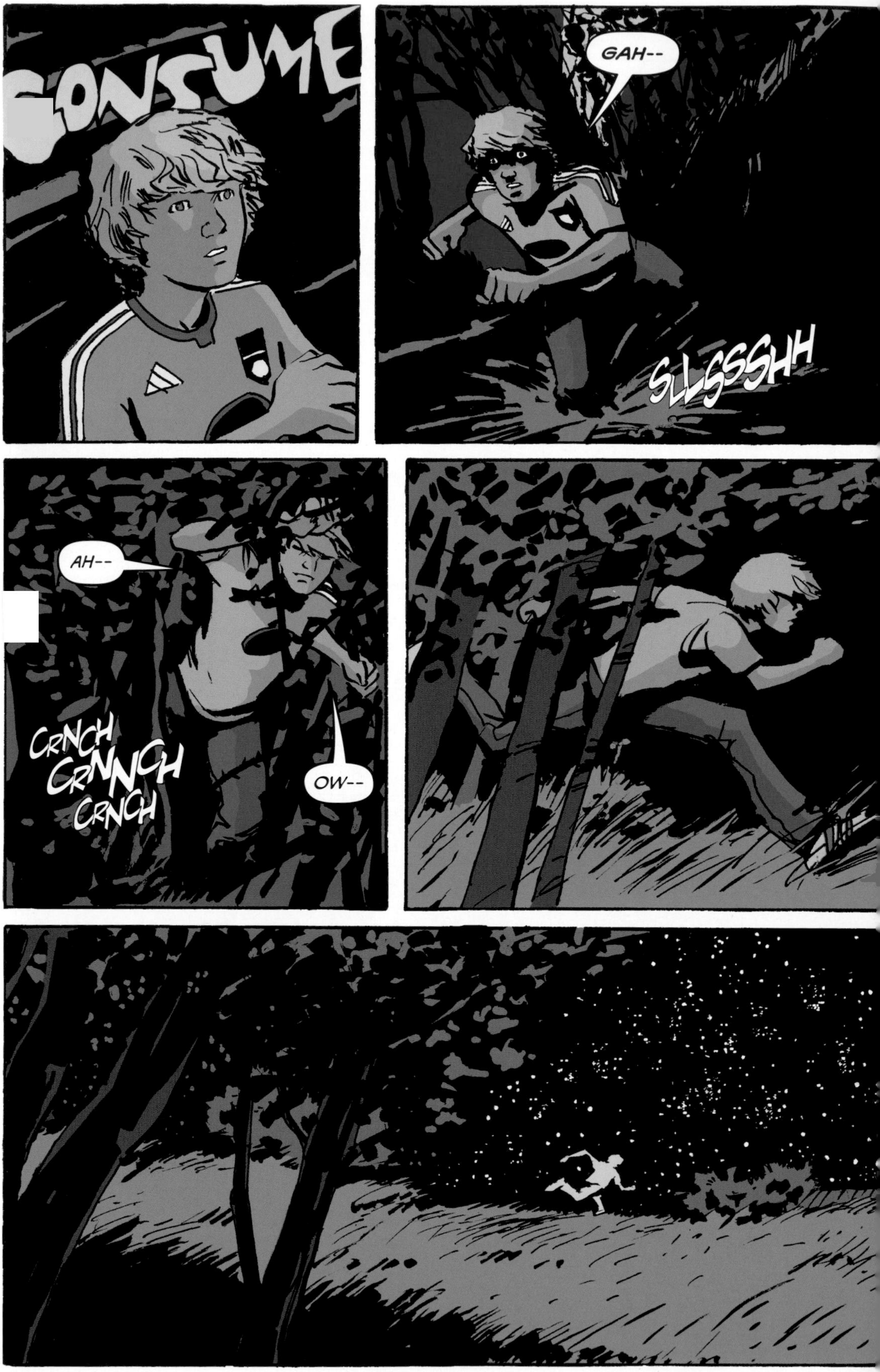
CONSUME
GAH--
SLLSSSHH
AH--
CRNCH
CRNNCH
CRNCH
OW--

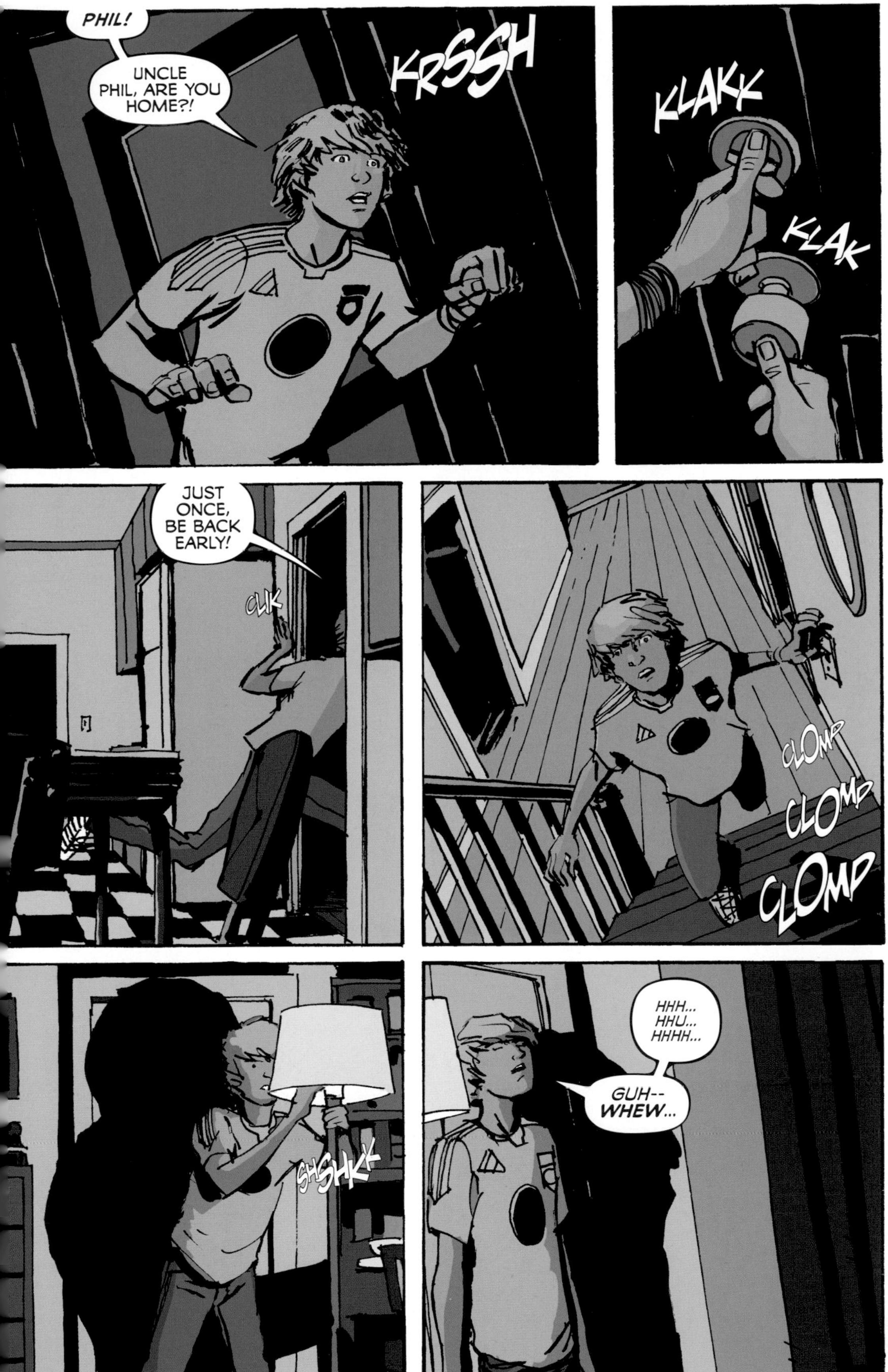
PHIL!
UNCLE PHIL, ARE YOU HOME?!
KRSSH
KLAKK
KLAK
JUST ONCE, BE BACK EARLY!
CLIK
CLOMP
CLOMP
CLOMP
SHSHKK
HHH... HHU... HHHH...
GUH-- WHEW...

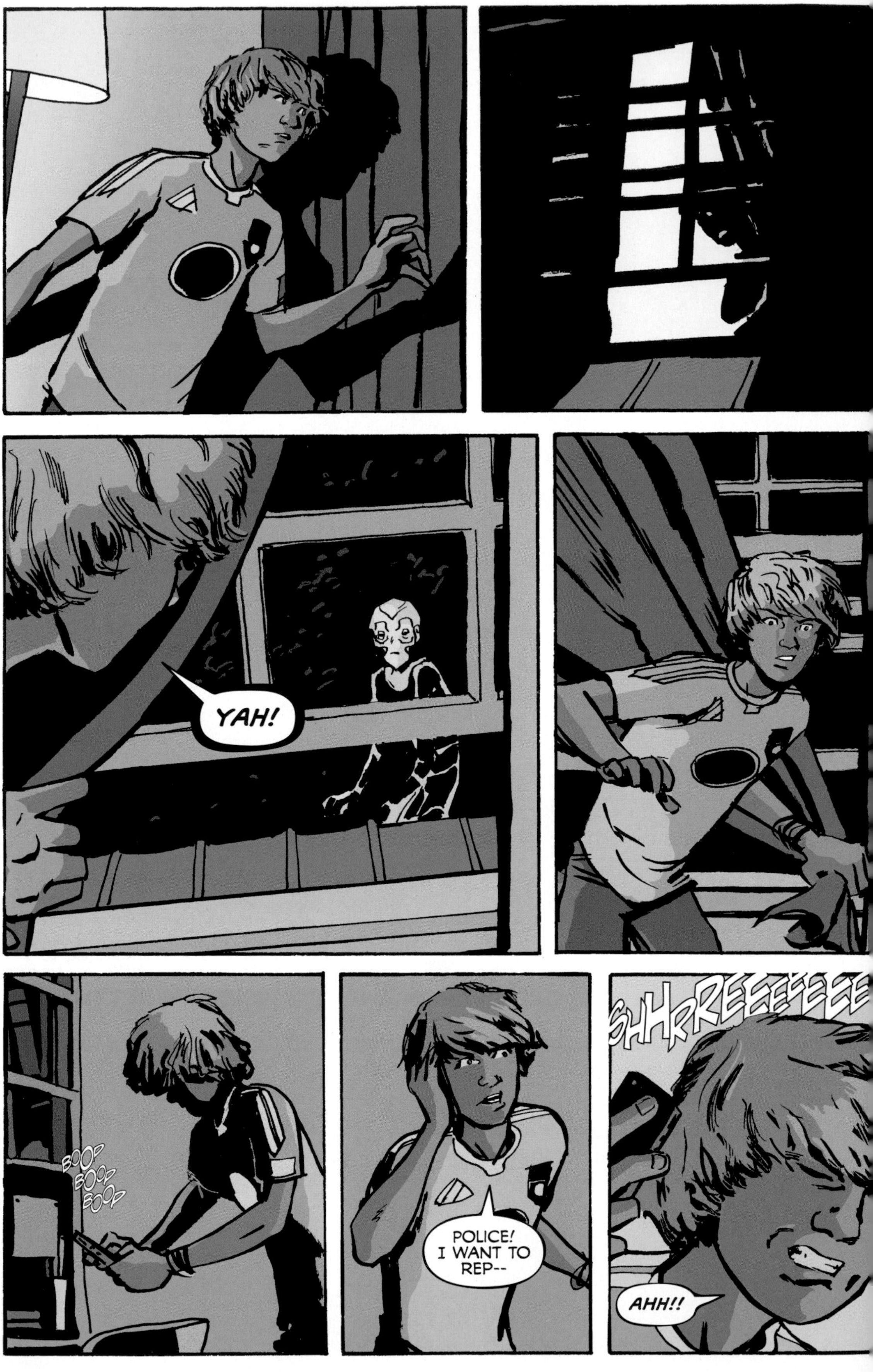
YAH!
BOOP
BOOP
BOOP
POLICE! I WANT TO REP--
SHHRREEEEEEEE
AHH!!

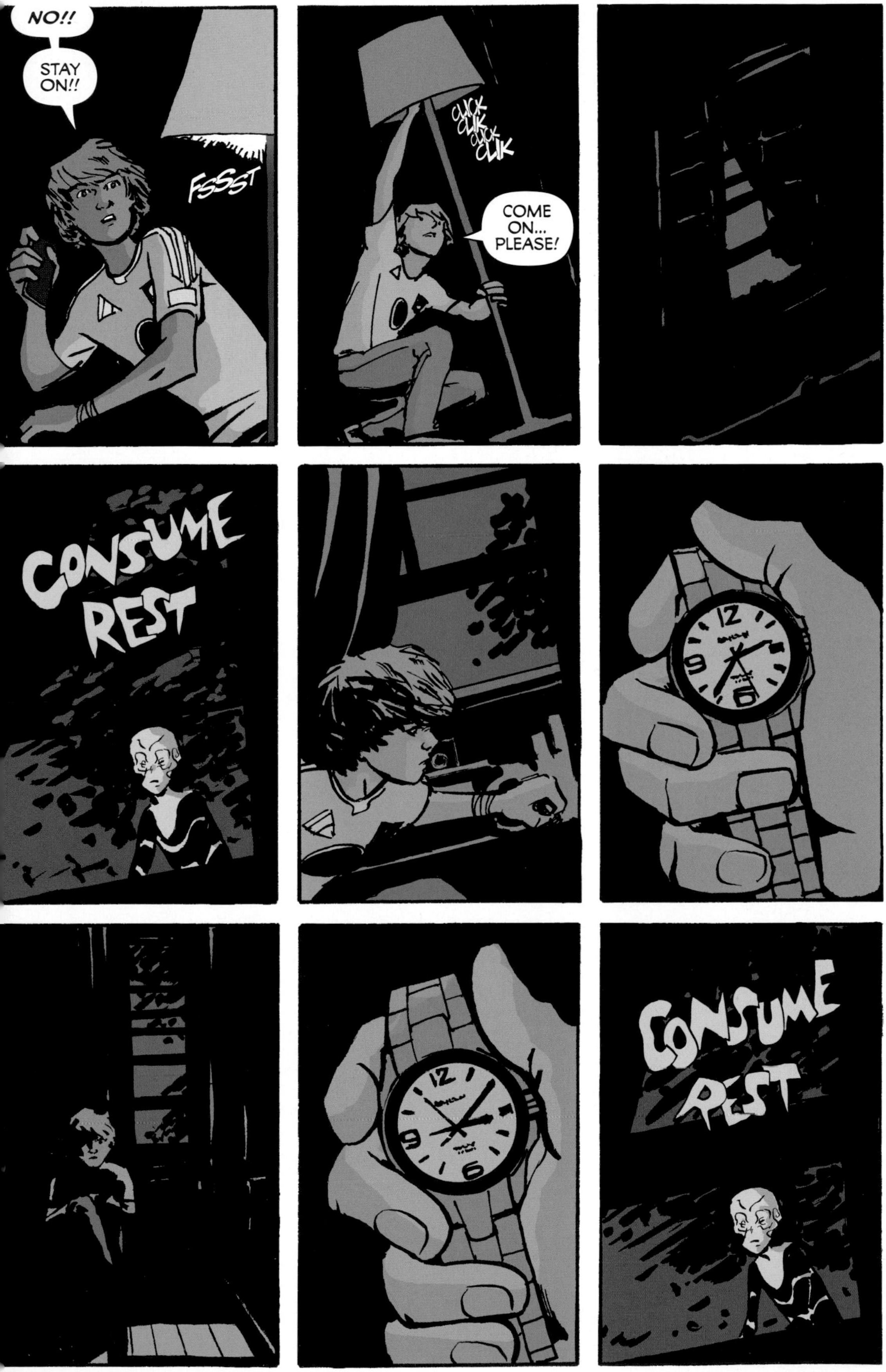
NO!!
STAY ON!!
FSSST
CLICK CLIK CLICK CLIK
COME ON... PLEASE!
CONSUME REST
CONSUME REST

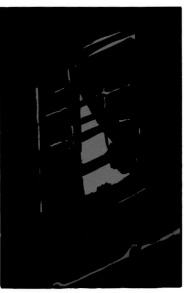

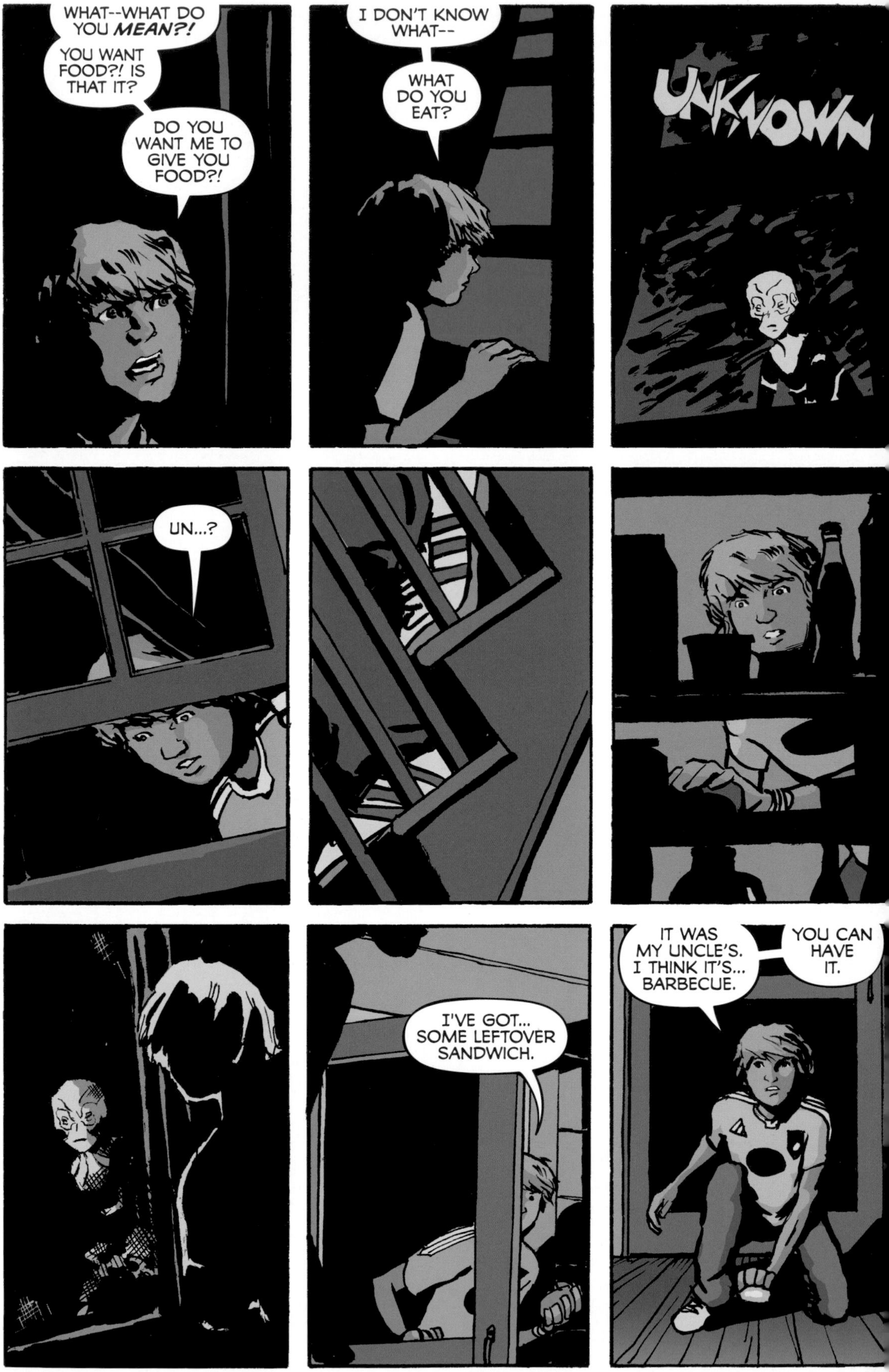
WHAT--WHAT DO YOU *MEAN?!*
YOU WANT FOOD?! IS THAT IT?
DO YOU WANT ME TO GIVE YOU FOOD?!
I DON'T KNOW WHAT--
WHAT DO YOU EAT?
UNKNOWN
UN...?
I'VE GOT... SOME LEFTOVER SANDWICH.
IT WAS MY UNCLE'S. I THINK IT'S... BARBECUE.
YOU CAN HAVE IT.

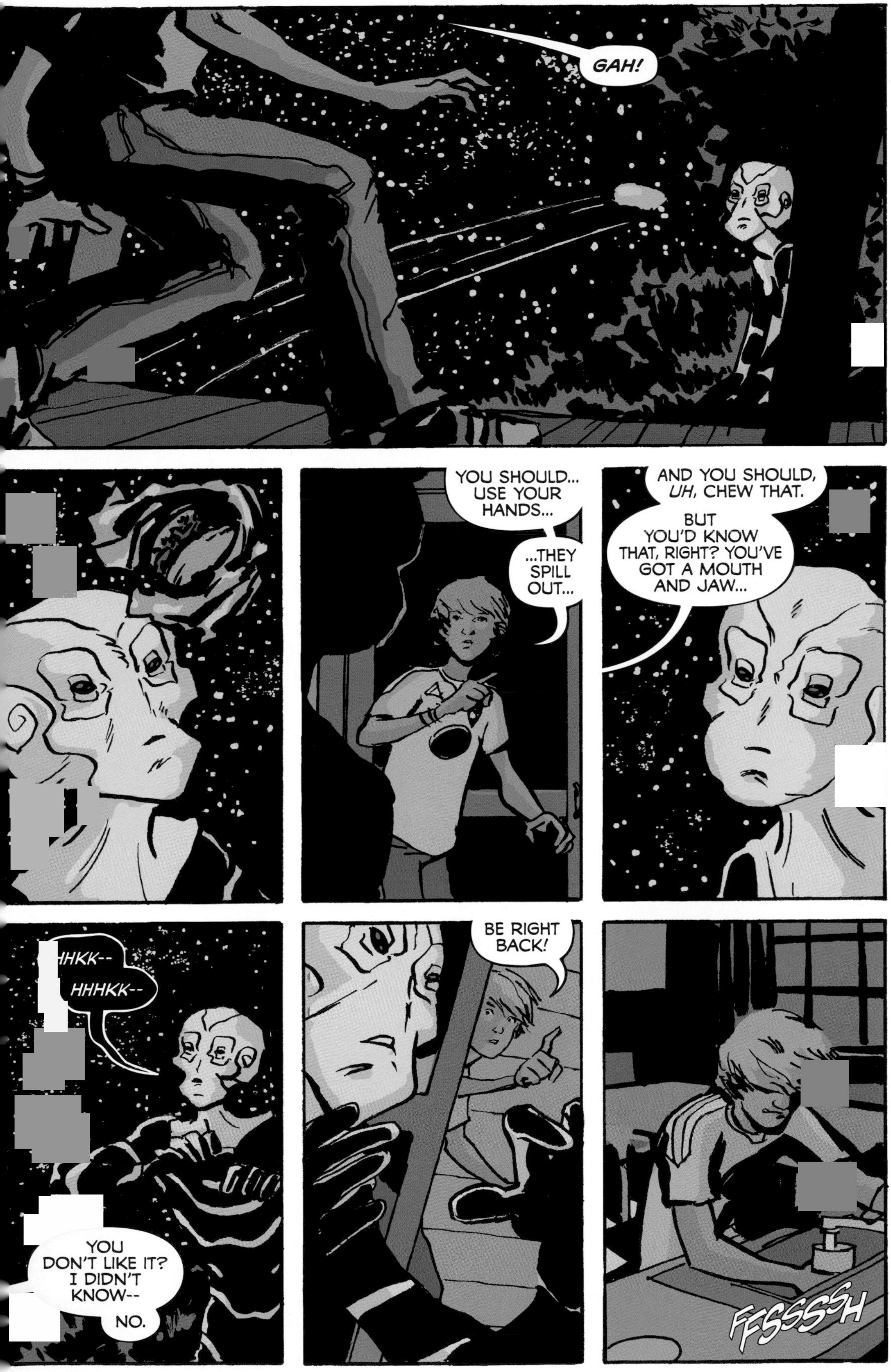
GAH!
YOU SHOULD... USE YOUR HANDS...
...THEY SPILL OUT...
AND YOU SHOULD, *UH,* CHEW THAT.
BUT YOU'D KNOW THAT, RIGHT? YOU'VE GOT A MOUTH AND JAW...
HHKK--
HHHKK--
YOU DON'T LIKE IT? I DIDN'T KNOW--
NO.
BE RIGHT BACK!
FFSSSSH

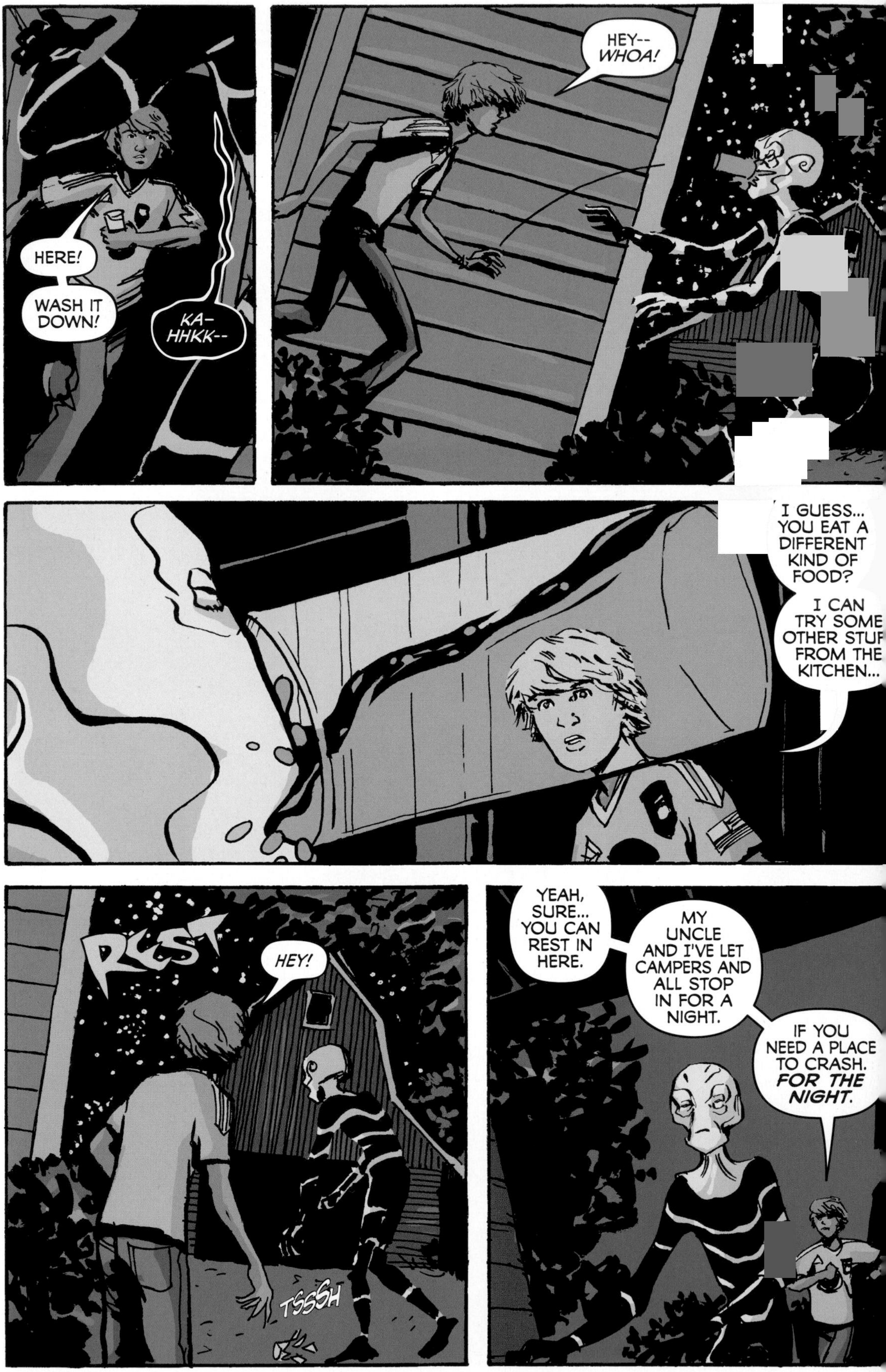
HERE!
WASH IT DOWN!
KA-HHKK--
HEY-- *WHOA!*
I GUESS... YOU EAT A DIFFERENT KIND OF FOOD?
I CAN TRY SOME OTHER STUF FROM THE KITCHEN...
RUST
HEY!
TSSSH
YEAH, SURE... YOU CAN REST IN HERE.
MY UNCLE AND I'VE LET CAMPERS AND ALL STOP IN FOR A NIGHT.
IF YOU NEED A PLACE TO CRASH. ***FOR THE NIGHT.***

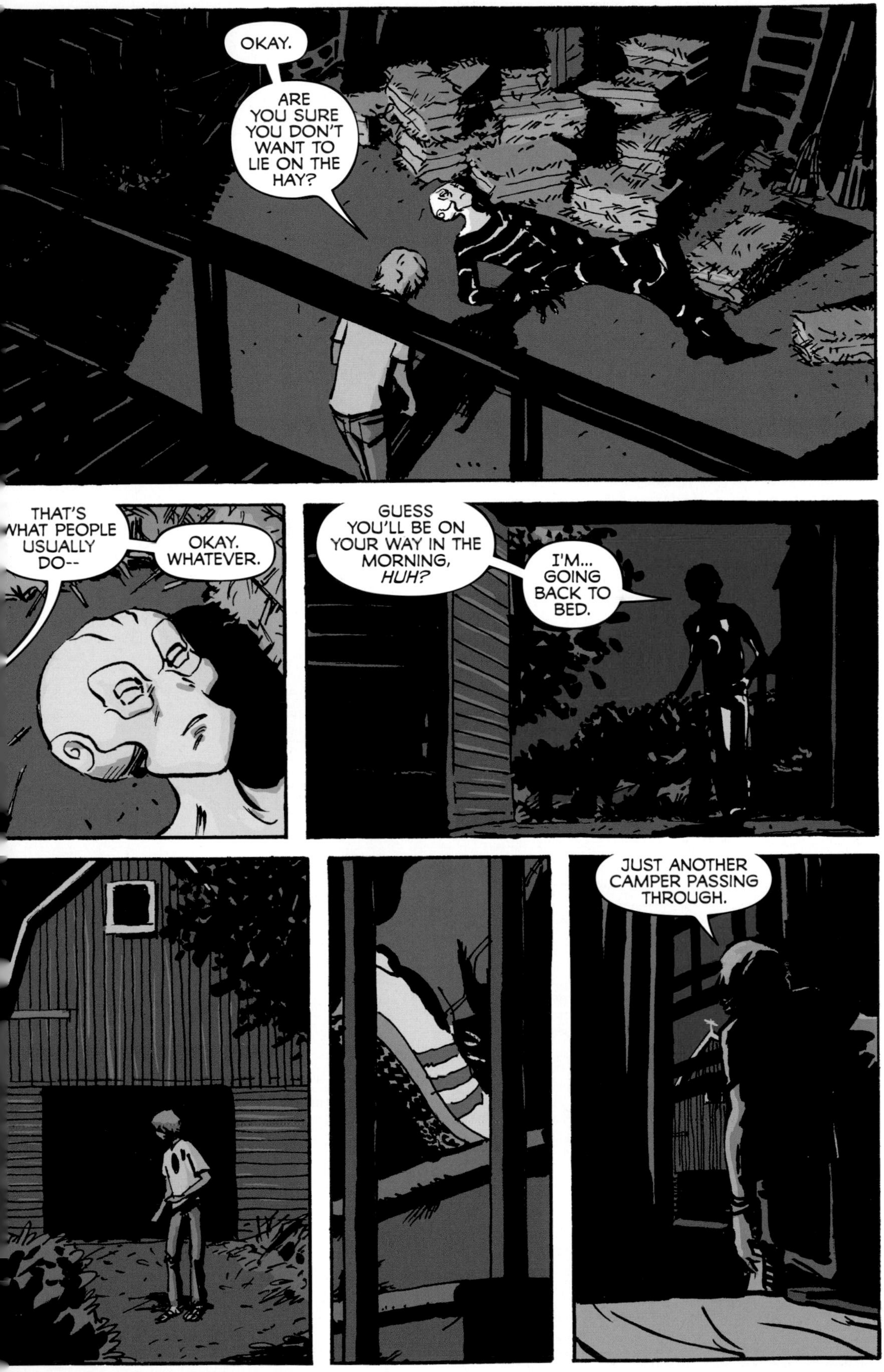
OKAY.
ARE YOU SURE YOU DON'T WANT TO LIE ON THE HAY?
THAT'S WHAT PEOPLE USUALLY DO--
OKAY. WHATEVER.
GUESS YOU'LL BE ON YOUR WAY IN THE MORNING, *HUH?*
I'M... GOING BACK TO BED.
JUST ANOTHER CAMPER PASSING THROUGH.

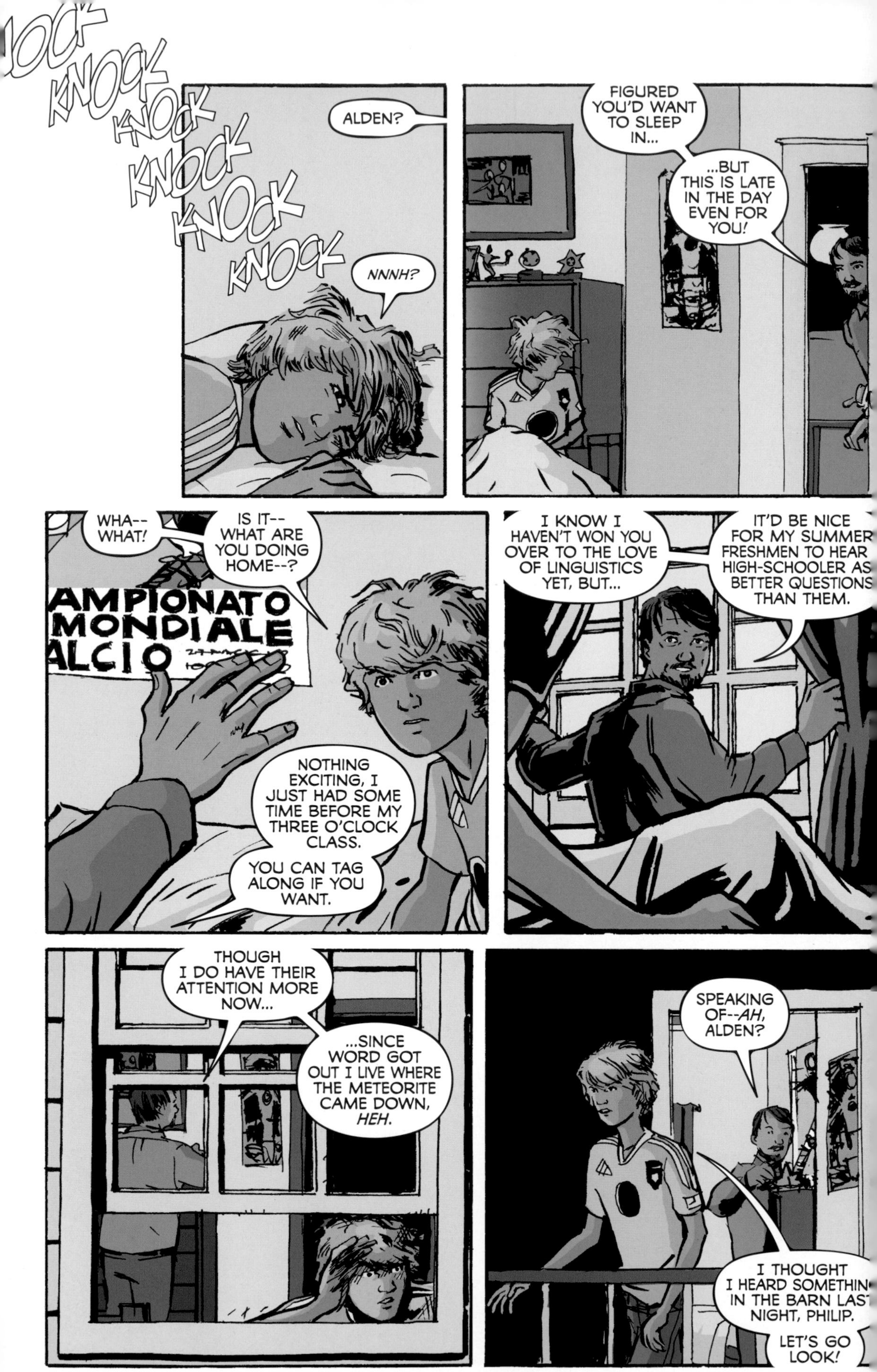
KNOCK
KNOCK
KNOCK
KNOCK
KNOCK
KNOCK
ALDEN?
NNNH?
FIGURED YOU'D WANT TO SLEEP IN...
...BUT THIS IS LATE IN THE DAY EVEN FOR YOU!
WHA-- WHAT!
IS IT-- WHAT ARE YOU DOING HOME--?
AMPIONATO MONDIALE ALCIO
NOTHING EXCITING, I JUST HAD SOME TIME BEFORE MY THREE O'CLOCK CLASS.
YOU CAN TAG ALONG IF YOU WANT.
I KNOW I HAVEN'T WON YOU OVER TO THE LOVE OF LINGUISTICS YET, BUT...
IT'D BE NICE FOR MY SUMMER FRESHMEN TO HEAR HIGH-SCHOOLER AS BETTER QUESTIONS THAN THEM.
THOUGH I DO HAVE THEIR ATTENTION MORE NOW...
...SINCE WORD GOT OUT I LIVE WHERE THE METEORITE CAME DOWN, *HEH*.
SPEAKING OF--*AH*, ALDEN?
I THOUGHT I HEARD SOMETHIN IN THE BARN LAST NIGHT, PHILIP.
LET'S GO LOOK!

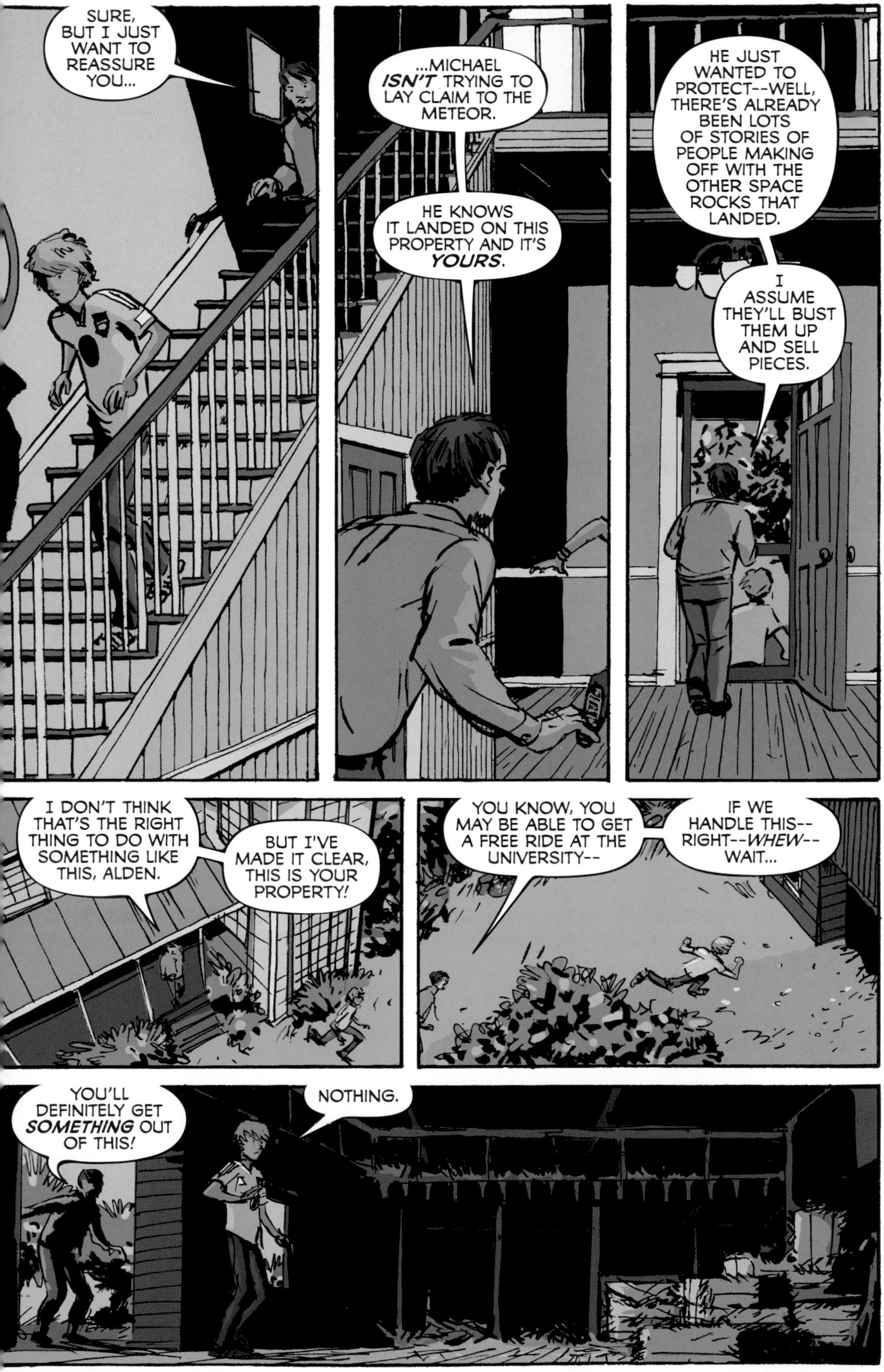
SURE, BUT I JUST WANT TO REASSURE YOU...
...MICHAEL ISN'T TRYING TO LAY CLAIM TO THE METEOR.
HE KNOWS IT LANDED ON THIS PROPERTY AND IT'S YOURS.
HE JUST WANTED TO PROTECT--WELL, THERE'S ALREADY BEEN LOTS OF STORIES OF PEOPLE MAKING OFF WITH THE OTHER SPACE ROCKS THAT LANDED.
I ASSUME THEY'LL BUST THEM UP AND SELL PIECES.
I DON'T THINK THAT'S THE RIGHT THING TO DO WITH SOMETHING LIKE THIS, ALDEN.
BUT I'VE MADE IT CLEAR, THIS IS YOUR PROPERTY!
YOU KNOW, YOU MAY BE ABLE TO GET A FREE RIDE AT THE UNIVERSITY--
IF WE HANDLE THIS-- RIGHT--WHEW-- WAIT...
YOU'LL DEFINITELY GET SOMETHING OUT OF THIS!
NOTHING.

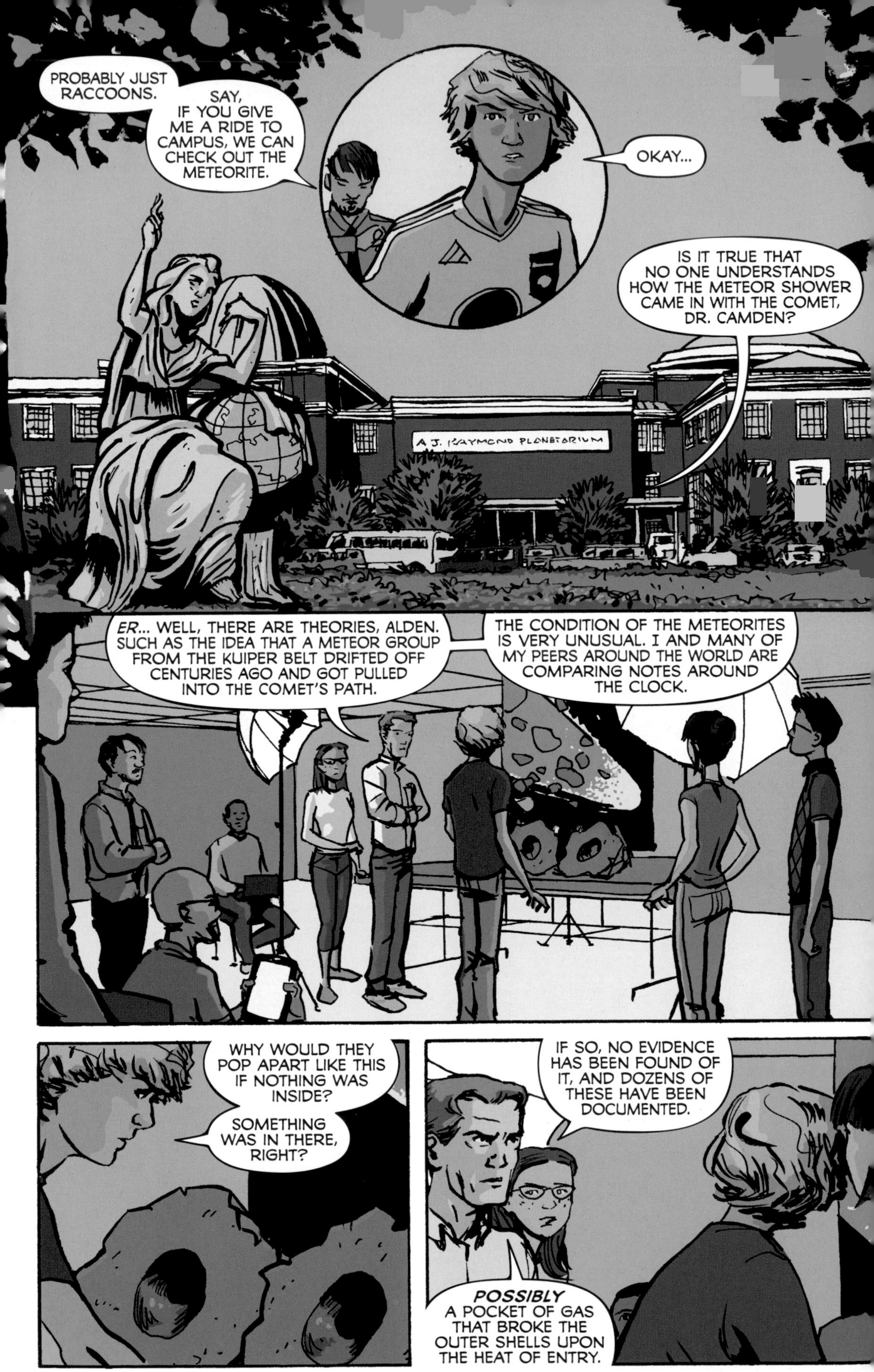
PROBABLY JUST RACCOONS.
SAY, IF YOU GIVE ME A RIDE TO CAMPUS, WE CAN CHECK OUT THE METEORITE.
OKAY...
IS IT TRUE THAT NO ONE UNDERSTANDS HOW THE METEOR SHOWER CAME IN WITH THE COMET, DR. CAMDEN?
A.J. RAYMOND PLANETARIUM
ER... WELL, THERE ARE THEORIES, ALDEN. SUCH AS THE IDEA THAT A METEOR GROUP FROM THE KUIPER BELT DRIFTED OFF CENTURIES AGO AND GOT PULLED INTO THE COMET'S PATH.
THE CONDITION OF THE METEORITES IS VERY UNUSUAL. I AND MANY OF MY PEERS AROUND THE WORLD ARE COMPARING NOTES AROUND THE CLOCK.
WHY WOULD THEY POP APART LIKE THIS IF NOTHING WAS INSIDE?
SOMETHING WAS IN THERE, RIGHT?
IF SO, NO EVIDENCE HAS BEEN FOUND OF IT, AND DOZENS OF THESE HAVE BEEN DOCUMENTED.
POSSIBLY A POCKET OF GAS THAT BROKE THE OUTER SHELLS UPON THE HEAT OF ENTRY.

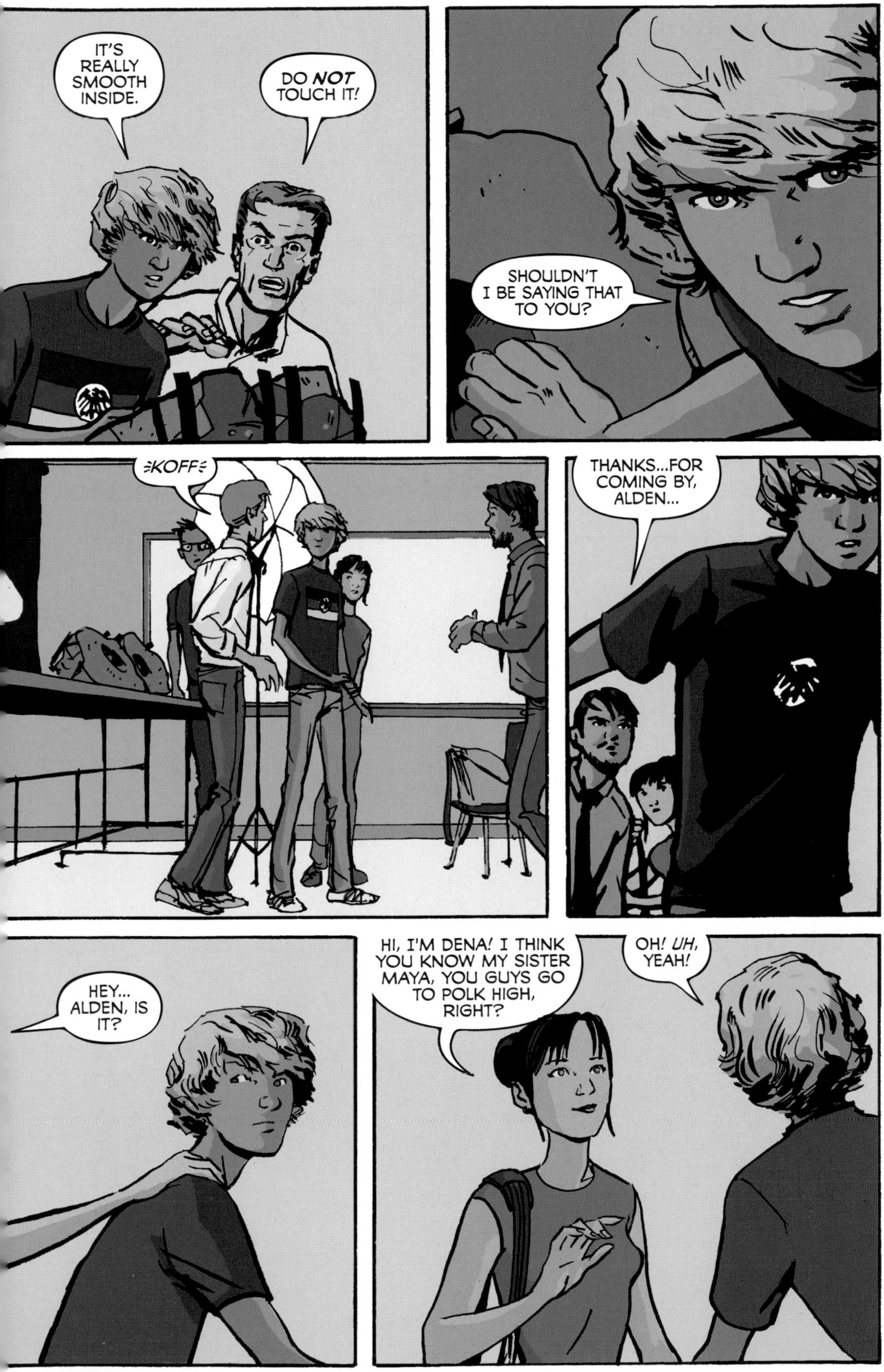
IT'S REALLY SMOOTH INSIDE.
DO *NOT* TOUCH IT!
SHOULDN'T I BE SAYING THAT TO YOU?
KOFF
THANKS...FOR COMING BY, ALDEN...
HEY... ALDEN, IS IT?
HI, I'M DENA! I THINK YOU KNOW MY SISTER MAYA, YOU GUYS GO TO POLK HIGH, RIGHT?
OH! *UH*, YEAH!

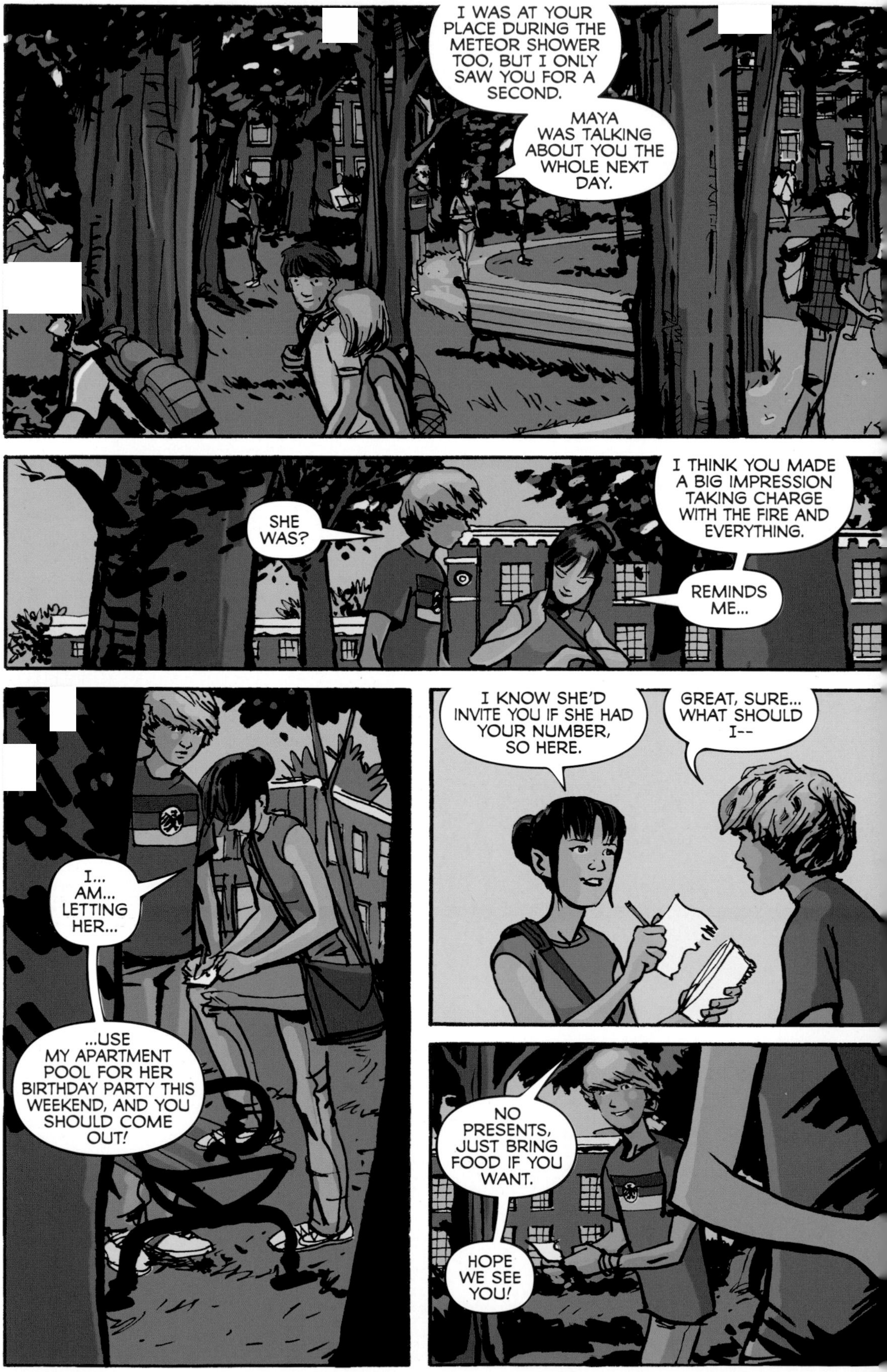
I WAS AT YOUR PLACE DURING THE METEOR SHOWER TOO, BUT I ONLY SAW YOU FOR A SECOND.
MAYA WAS TALKING ABOUT YOU THE WHOLE NEXT DAY.
SHE WAS?
I THINK YOU MADE A BIG IMPRESSION TAKING CHARGE WITH THE FIRE AND EVERYTHING.
REMINDS ME...
I... AM... LETTING HER...
...USE MY APARTMENT POOL FOR HER BIRTHDAY PARTY THIS WEEKEND, AND YOU SHOULD COME OUT!
I KNOW SHE'D INVITE YOU IF SHE HAD YOUR NUMBER, SO HERE.
GREAT, SURE... WHAT SHOULD I--
NO PRESENTS, JUST BRING FOOD IF YOU WANT.
HOPE WE SEE YOU!

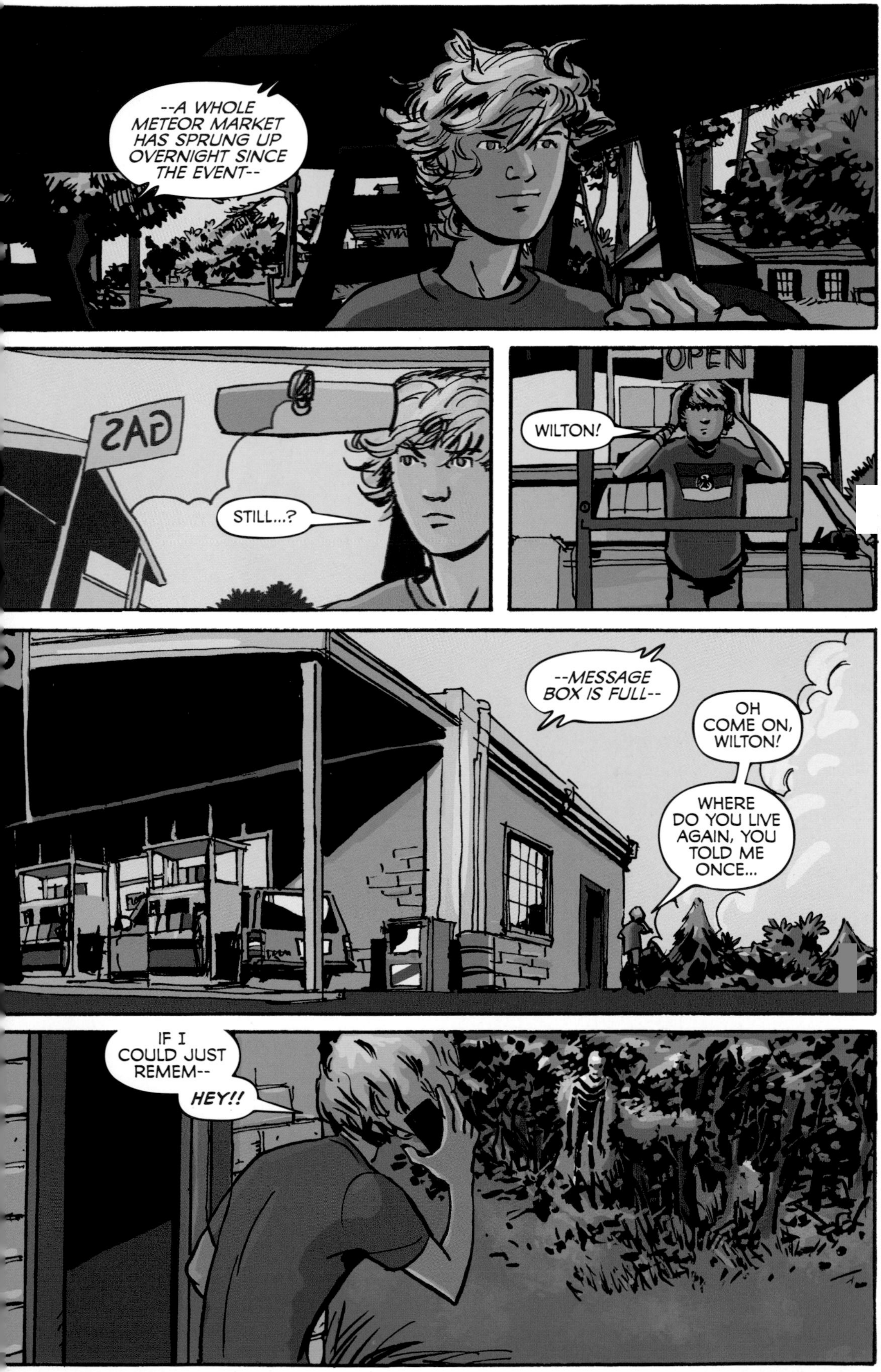
--A WHOLE METEOR MARKET HAS SPRUNG UP OVERNIGHT SINCE THE EVENT--
GAS
STILL...?
OPEN
WILTON!
--MESSAGE BOX IS FULL--
OH COME ON, WILTON!
WHERE DO YOU LIVE AGAIN, YOU TOLD ME ONCE...
IF I COULD JUST REMEM--
HEY!!

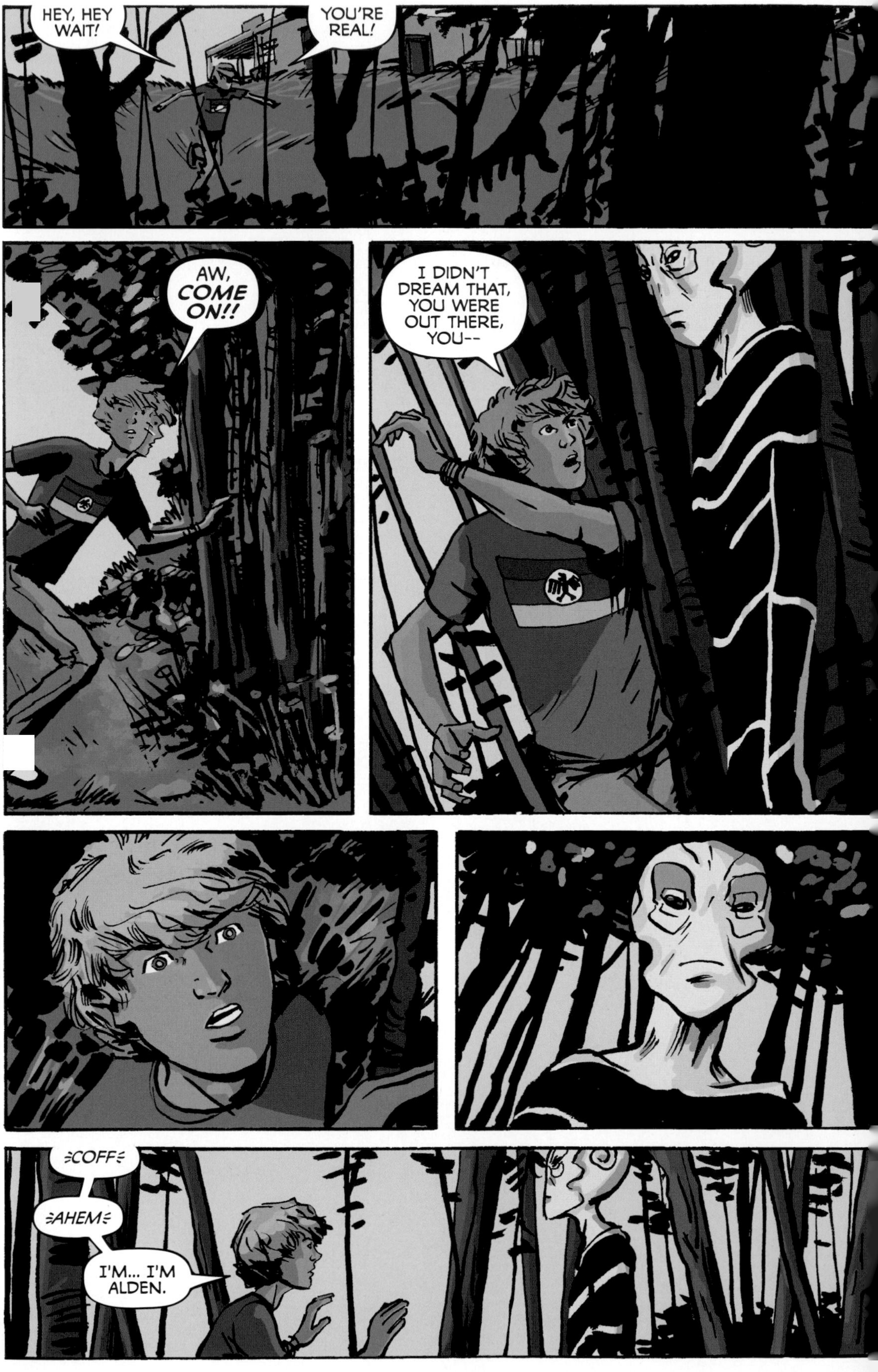
HEY, HEY WAIT!
YOU'RE REAL!
AW, COME ON!!
I DIDN'T DREAM THAT, YOU WERE OUT THERE, YOU--
COFF
AHEM
I'M... I'M ALDEN.

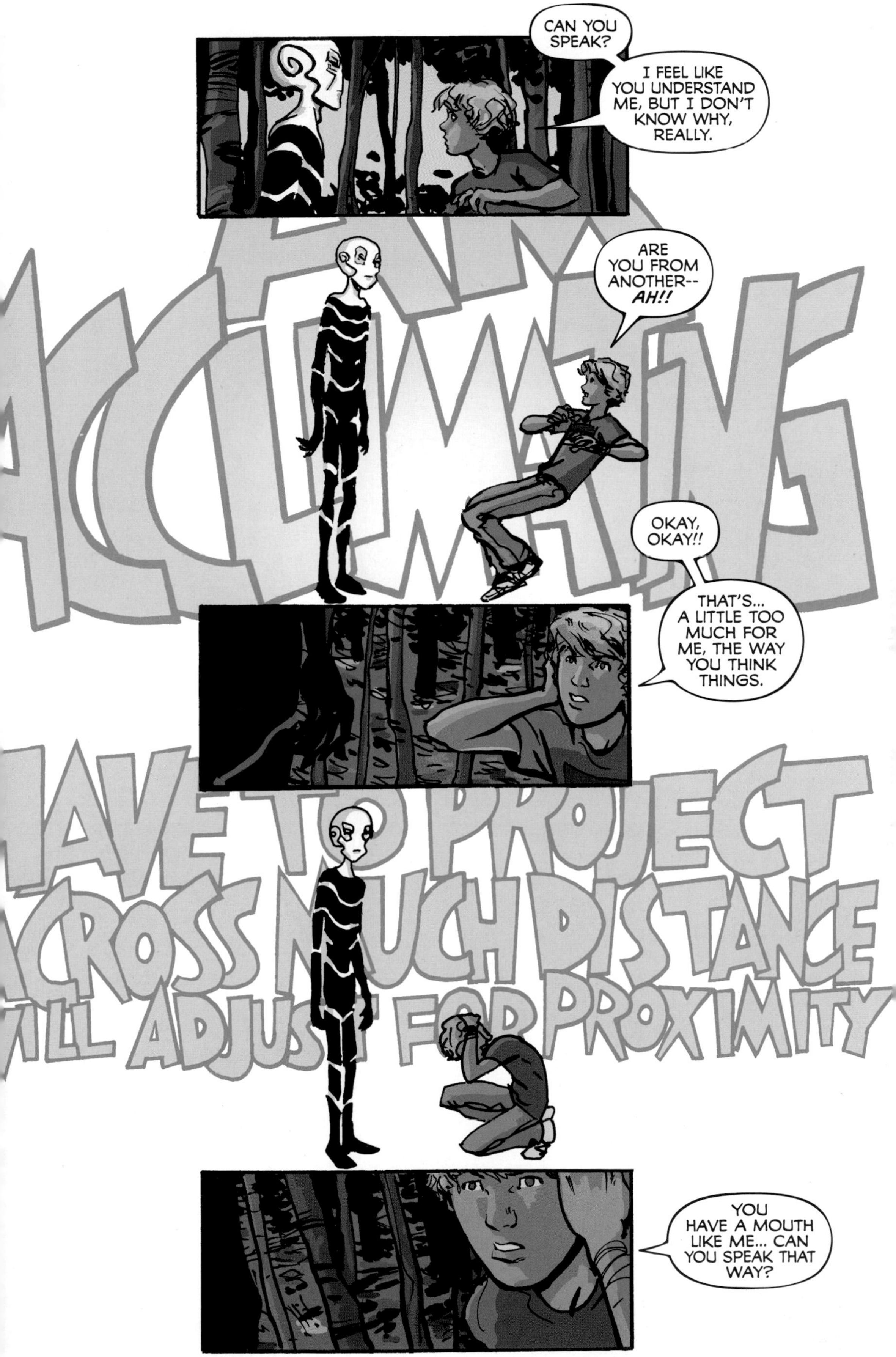
CAN YOU SPEAK?
I FEEL LIKE YOU UNDERSTAND ME, BUT I DON'T KNOW WHY, REALLY.
ACCLIMATING
ARE YOU FROM ANOTHER-- *AH!!*
OKAY, OKAY!!
THAT'S... A LITTLE TOO MUCH FOR ME, THE WAY YOU THINK THINGS.
HAVE TO PROJECT
ACROSS MUCH DISTANCE
WILL ADJUST FOR PROXIMITY
YOU HAVE A MOUTH LIKE ME... CAN YOU SPEAK THAT WAY?

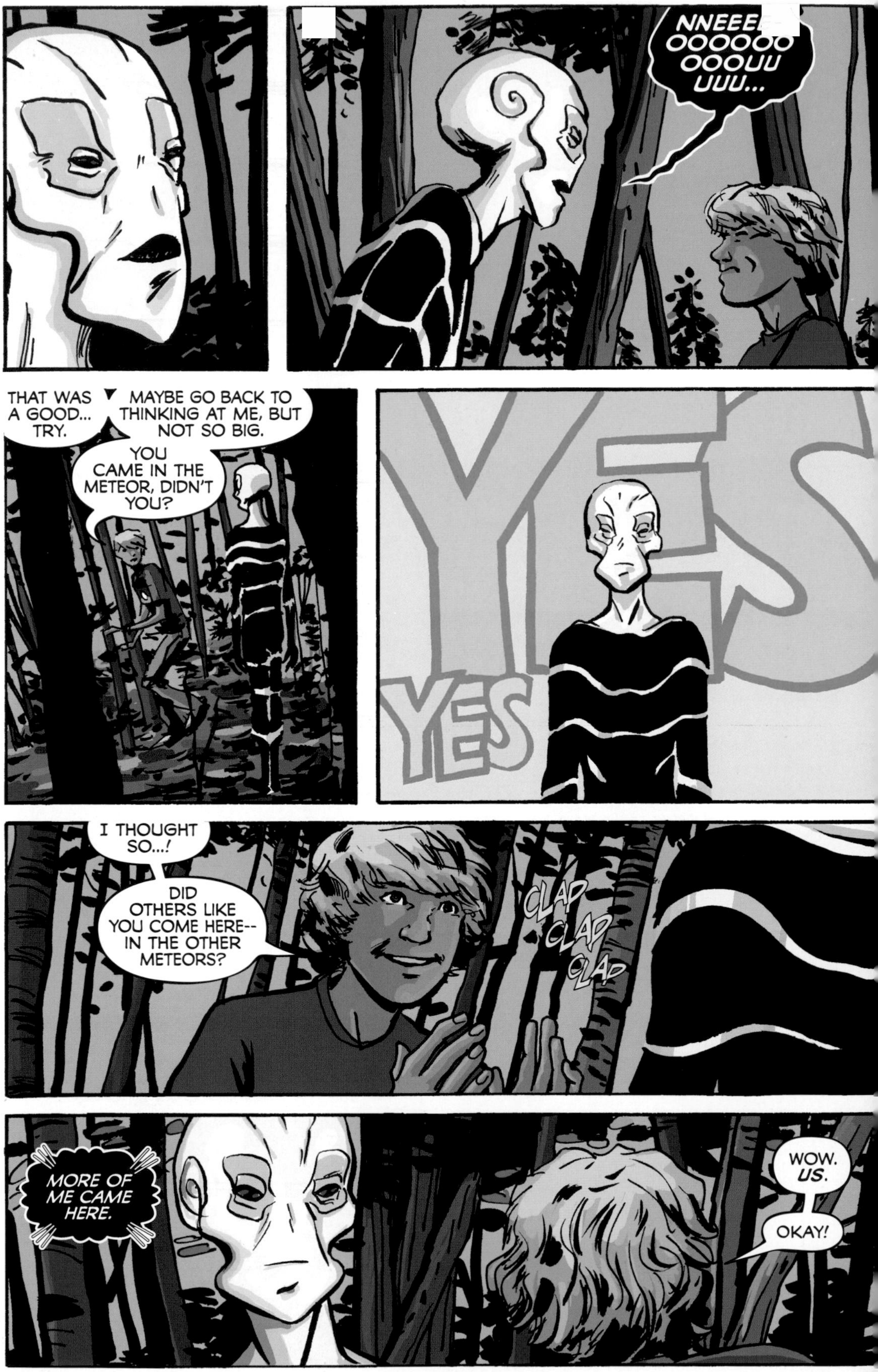

NNEEEE OOOOOO OOOUU UUU...
THAT WAS A GOOD... TRY.
MAYBE GO BACK TO THINKING AT ME, BUT NOT SO BIG.
YOU CAME IN THE METEOR, DIDN'T YOU?
YES
YES
I THOUGHT SO...!
DID OTHERS LIKE YOU COME HERE-- IN THE OTHER METEORS?
CLAP CLAP CLAP
MORE OF ME CAME HERE.
WOW. *US.*
OKAY!

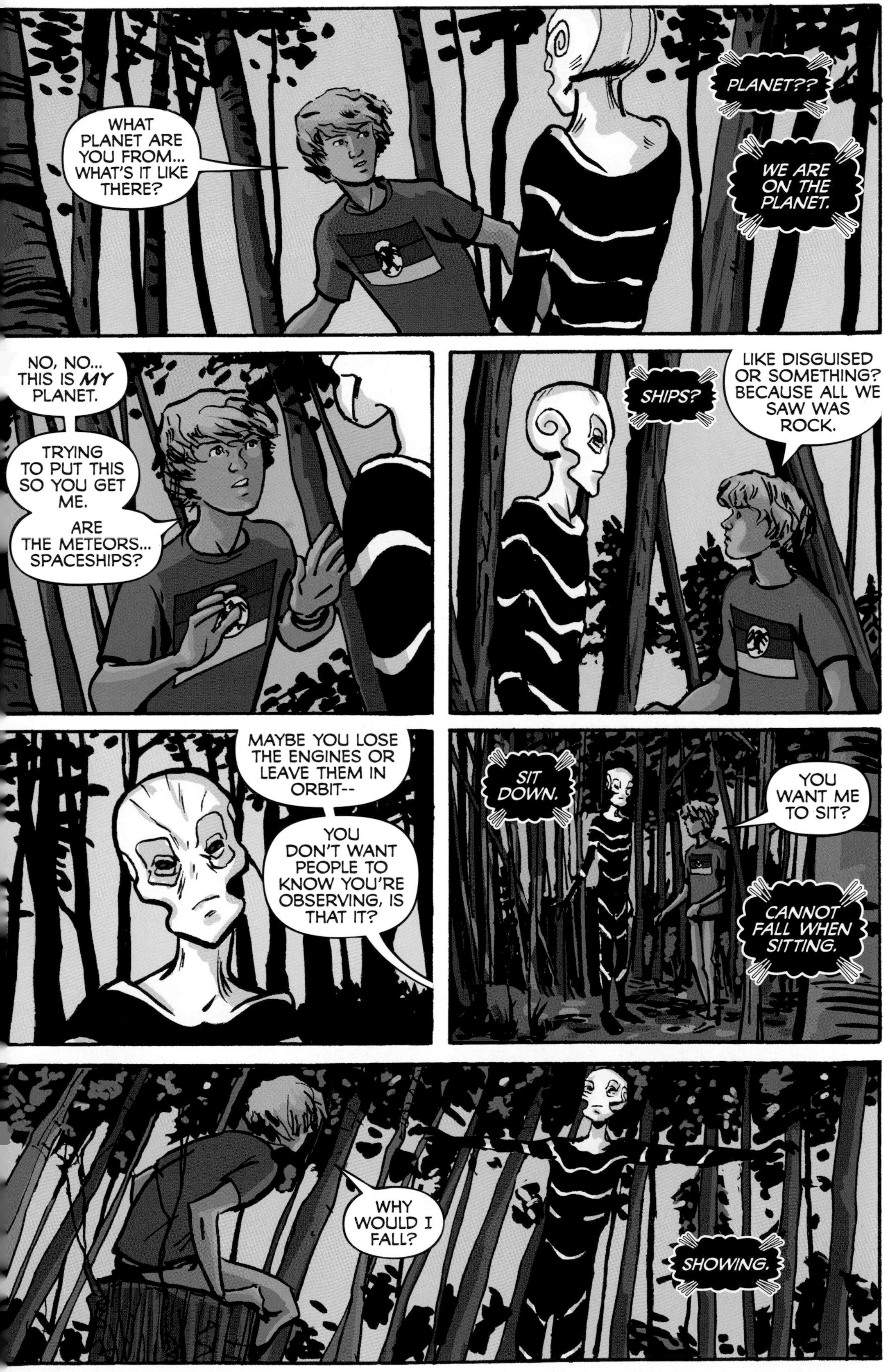
WHAT PLANET ARE YOU FROM... WHAT'S IT LIKE THERE?
PLANET??
WE ARE ON THE PLANET.
NO, NO... THIS IS *MY* PLANET.
TRYING TO PUT THIS SO YOU GET ME.
ARE THE METEORS... SPACESHIPS?
SHIPS?
LIKE DISGUISED OR SOMETHING? BECAUSE ALL WE SAW WAS ROCK.
MAYBE YOU LOSE THE ENGINES OR LEAVE THEM IN ORBIT--
YOU DON'T WANT PEOPLE TO KNOW YOU'RE OBSERVING, IS THAT IT?
SIT DOWN.
YOU WANT ME TO SIT?
CANNOT FALL WHEN SITTING.
WHY WOULD I FALL?
SHOWING.

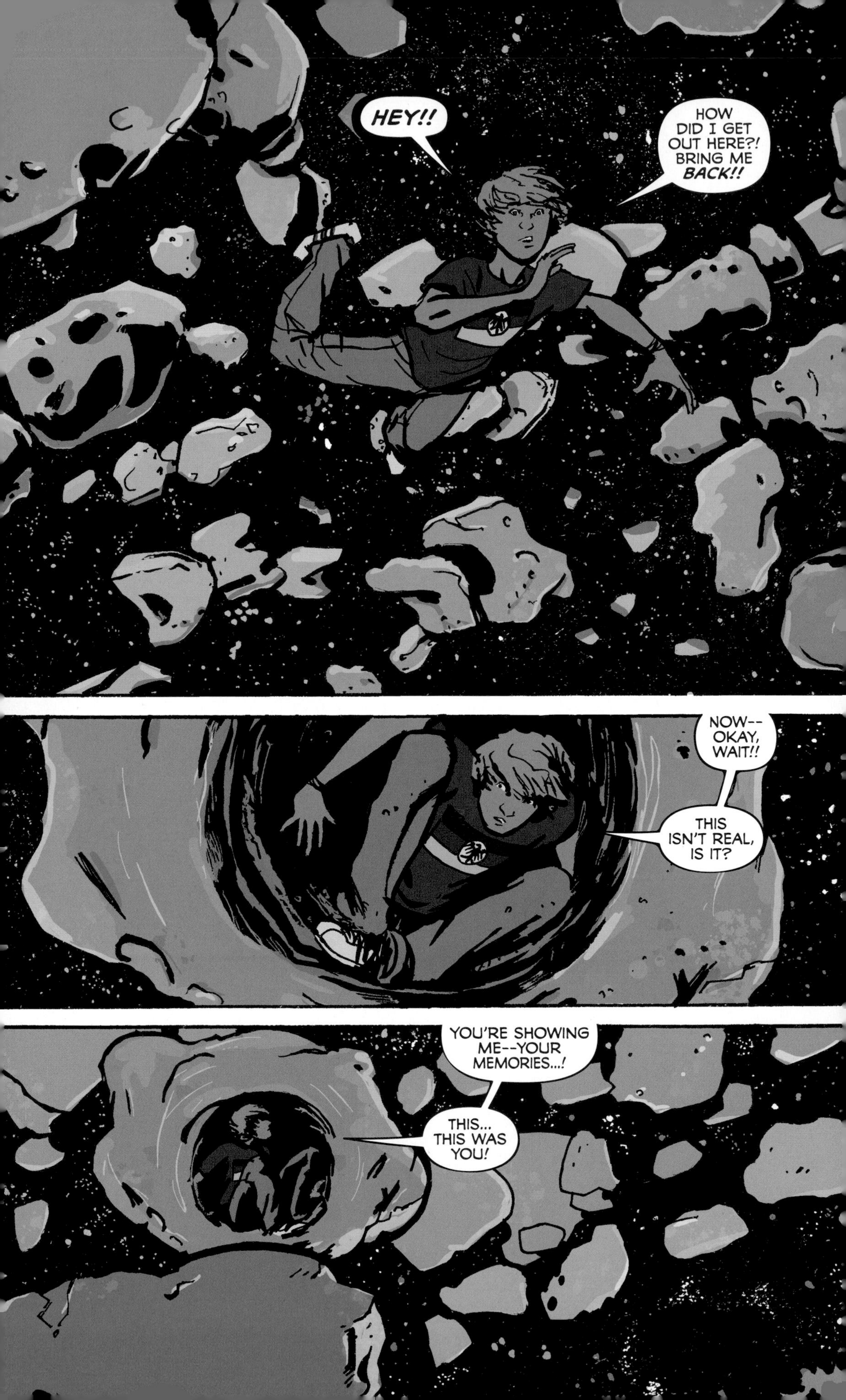
HEY!!
HOW DID I GET OUT HERE?! BRING ME *BACK!!*
NOW-- OKAY, WAIT!!
THIS ISN'T REAL, IS IT?
YOU'RE SHOWING ME--YOUR MEMORIES...!
THIS... THIS WAS YOU!

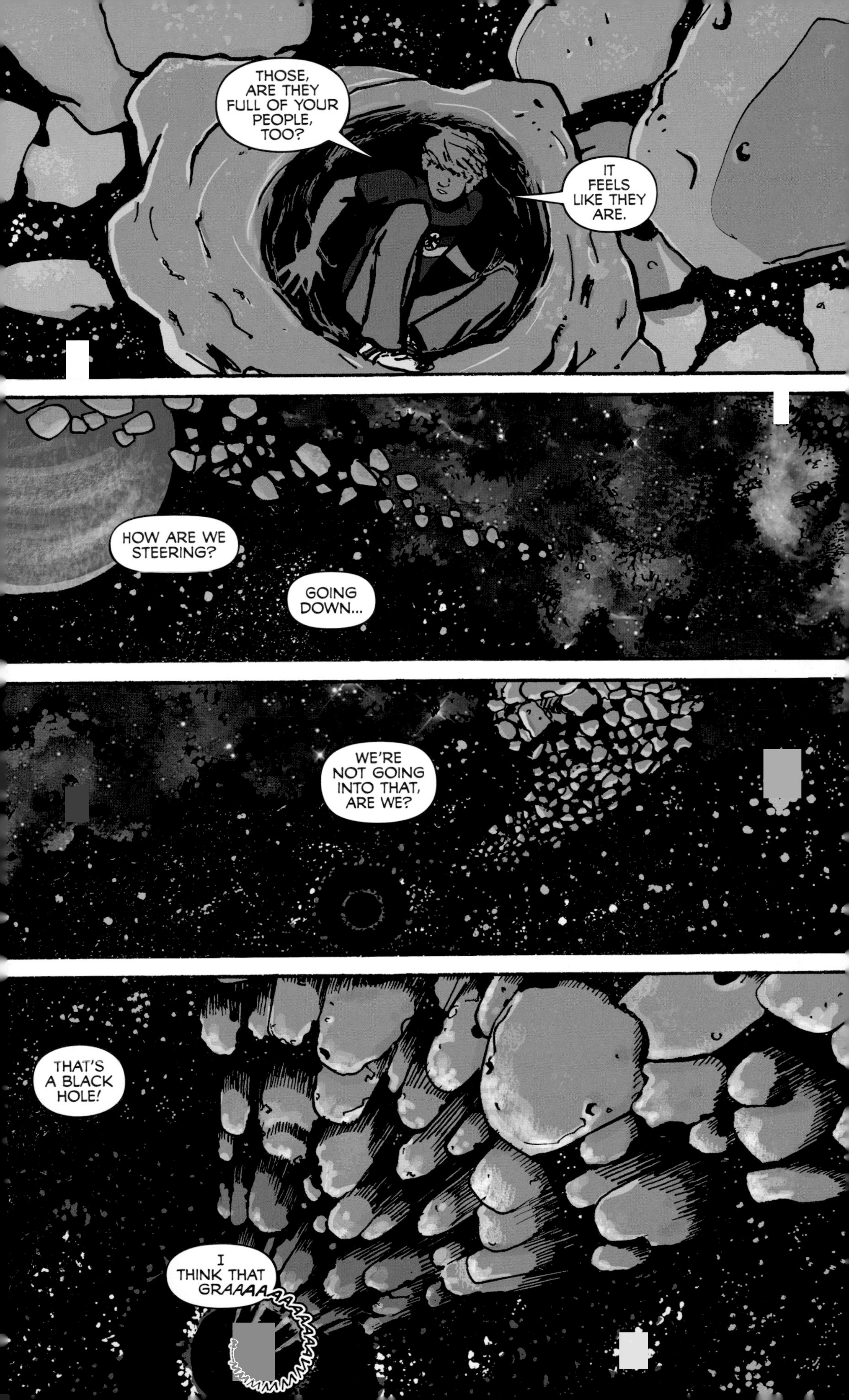
THOSE, ARE THEY FULL OF YOUR PEOPLE, TOO?
IT FEELS LIKE THEY ARE.
HOW ARE WE STEERING?
GOING DOWN...
WE'RE NOT GOING INTO THAT, ARE WE?
THAT'S A BLACK HOLE!
I THINK THAT GRAAAAAAAAAAAAAA

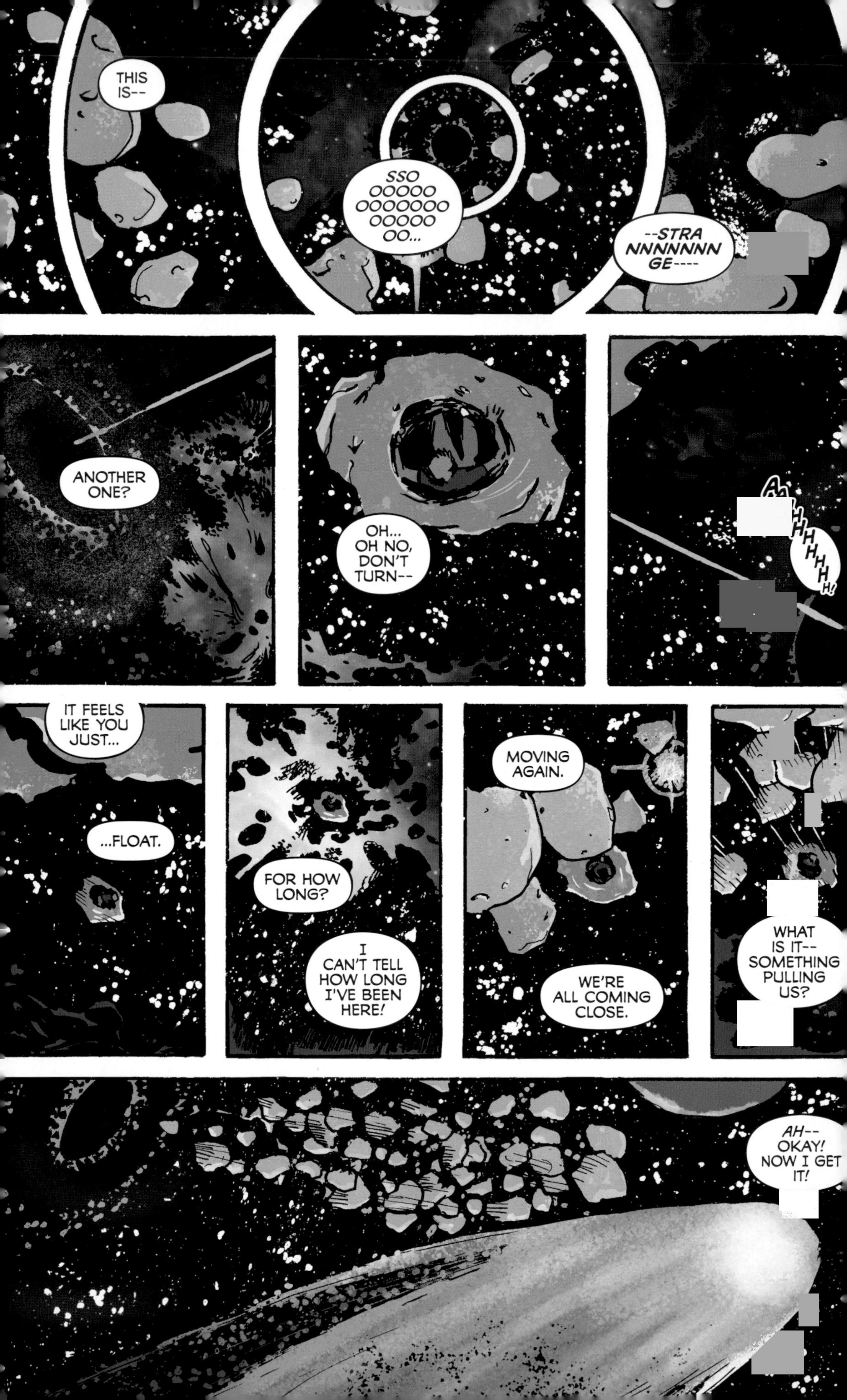
THIS IS--
SSOOOOOOOOOOOOOOOOOOOOO...
--STRANNNNNNNGE----
ANOTHER ONE?
OH... OH NO, DON'T TURN--
IT FEELS LIKE YOU JUST...
...FLOAT.
FOR HOW LONG?
I CAN'T TELL HOW LONG I'VE BEEN HERE!
MOVING AGAIN.
WE'RE ALL COMING CLOSE.
WHAT IS IT-- SOMETHING PULLING US?
AH-- OKAY! NOW I GET IT!

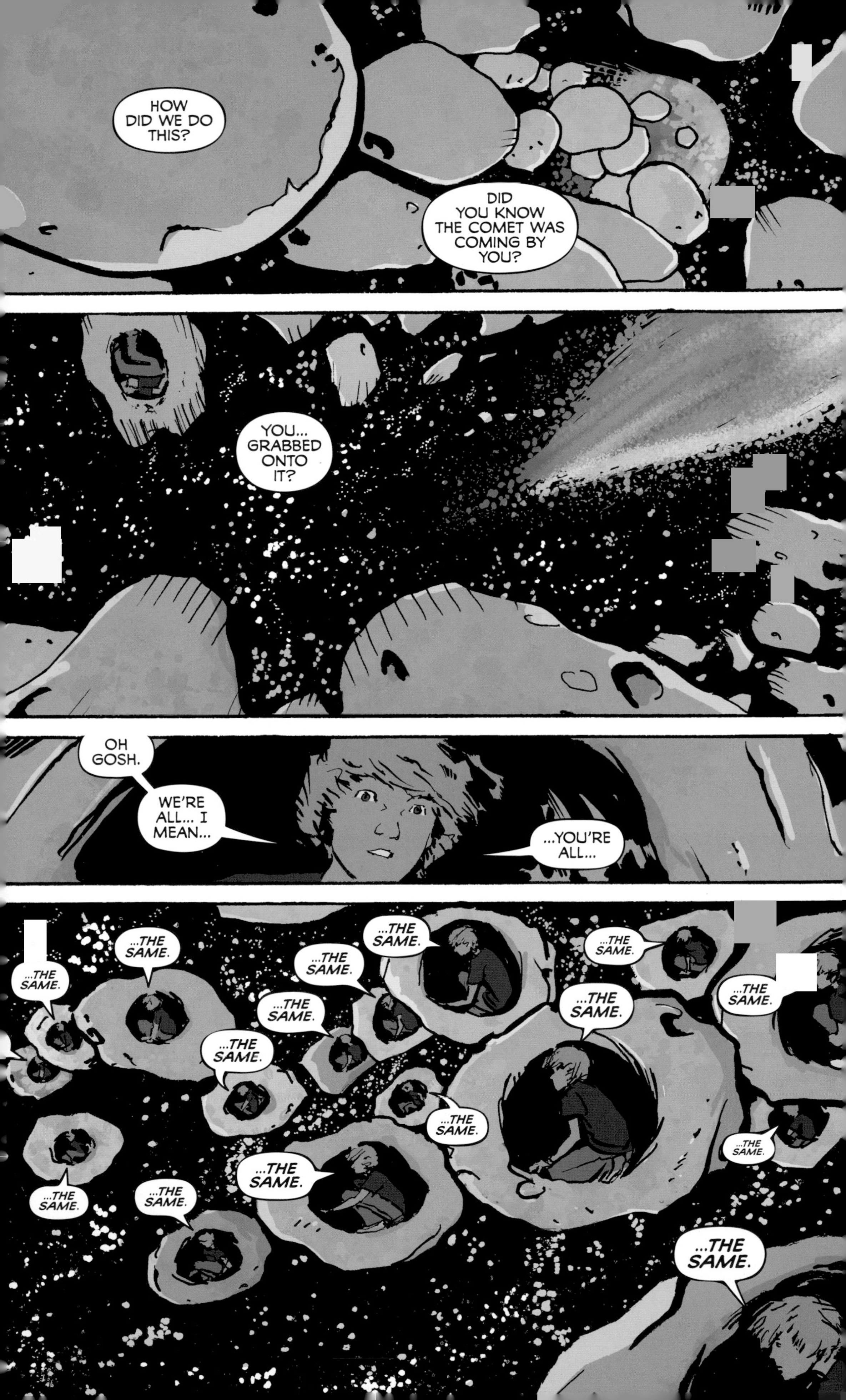
HOW DID WE DO THIS?
DID YOU KNOW THE COMET WAS COMING BY YOU?
YOU... GRABBED ONTO IT?
OH GOSH.
WE'RE ALL... I MEAN...
...YOU'RE ALL...
...THE SAME.
...THE SAME.
...THE SAME.
...THE SAME.
...THE SAME.
...THE SAME.
...THE SAME.
...THE SAME.
...THE SAME.
...THE SAME.
...THE SAME.
...THE SAME.
...THE SAME.
...THE SAME.
...THE SAME.

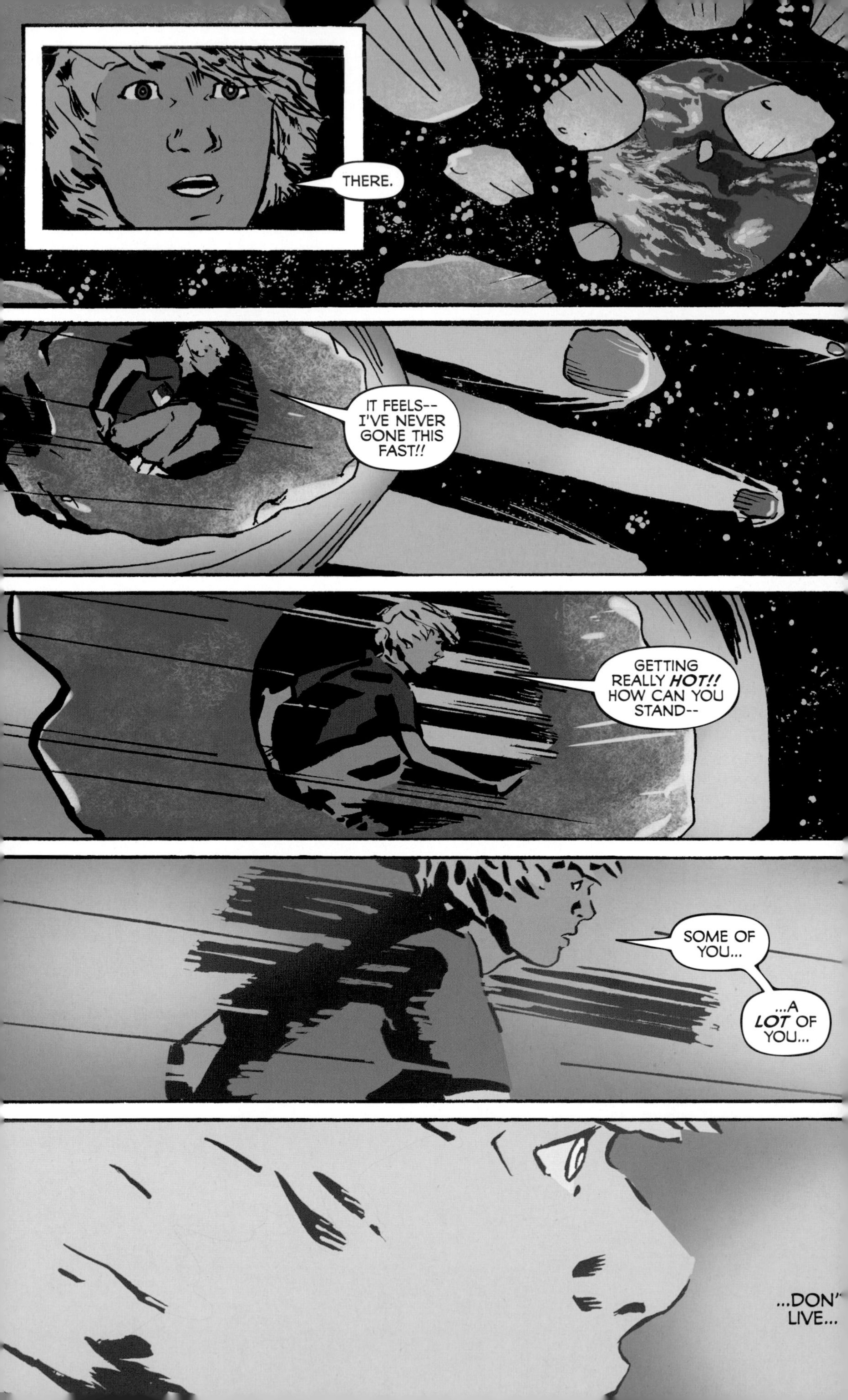
THERE.
IT FEELS-- I'VE NEVER GONE THIS FAST!!
GETTING REALLY HOT!! HOW CAN YOU STAND--
SOME OF YOU...
...A LOT OF YOU...
...DON' LIVE...

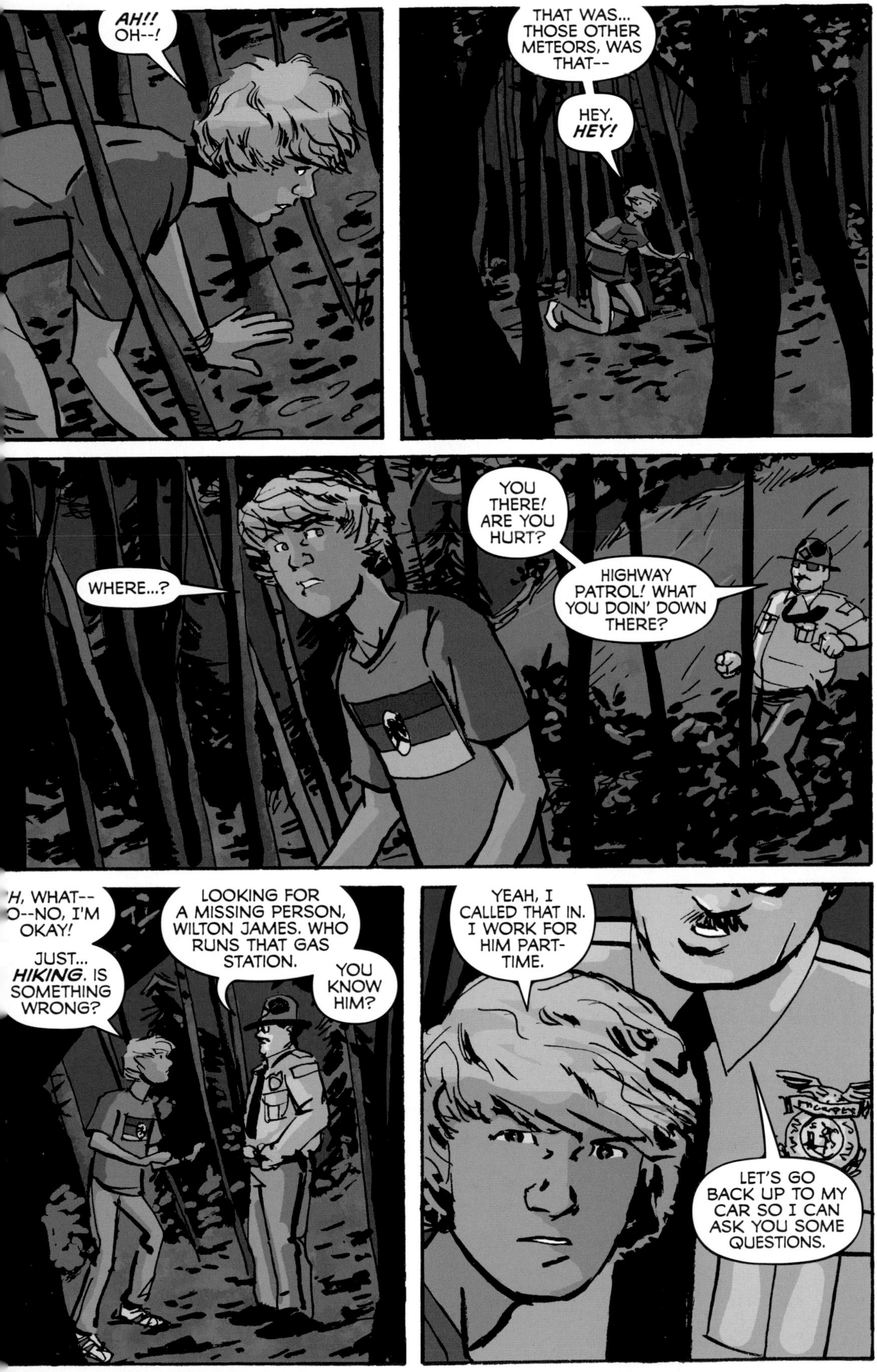

AH!! OH--!
THAT WAS... THOSE OTHER METEORS, WAS THAT--
HEY. HEY!
WHERE...?
YOU THERE! ARE YOU HURT?
HIGHWAY PATROL! WHAT YOU DOIN' DOWN THERE?
H, WHAT-- O--NO, I'M OKAY!
JUST... HIKING. IS SOMETHING WRONG?
LOOKING FOR A MISSING PERSON, WILTON JAMES. WHO RUNS THAT GAS STATION.
YOU KNOW HIM?
YEAH, I CALLED THAT IN. I WORK FOR HIM PART-TIME.
LET'S GO BACK UP TO MY CAR SO I CAN ASK YOU SOME QUESTIONS.

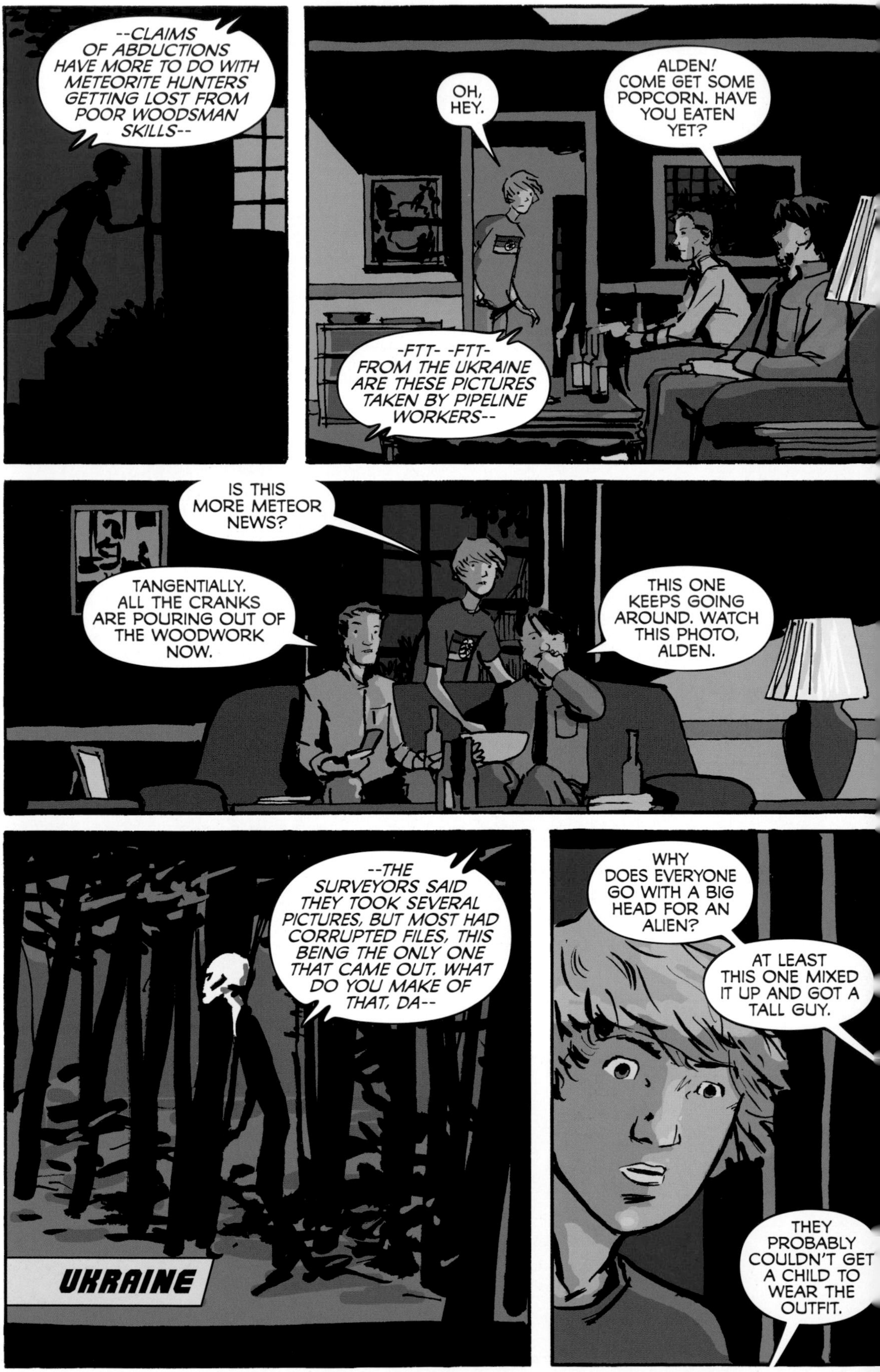
--CLAIMS OF ABDUCTIONS HAVE MORE TO DO WITH METEORITE HUNTERS GETTING LOST FROM POOR WOODSMAN SKILLS--
OH, HEY.
ALDEN! COME GET SOME POPCORN. HAVE YOU EATEN YET?
-FTT- -FTT- FROM THE UKRAINE ARE THESE PICTURES TAKEN BY PIPELINE WORKERS--
IS THIS MORE METEOR NEWS?
TANGENTIALLY. ALL THE CRANKS ARE POURING OUT OF THE WOODWORK NOW.
THIS ONE KEEPS GOING AROUND. WATCH THIS PHOTO, ALDEN.
--THE SURVEYORS SAID THEY TOOK SEVERAL PICTURES, BUT MOST HAD CORRUPTED FILES, THIS BEING THE ONLY ONE THAT CAME OUT. WHAT DO YOU MAKE OF THAT, DA--
UKRAINE
WHY DOES EVERYONE GO WITH A BIG HEAD FOR AN ALIEN?
AT LEAST THIS ONE MIXED IT UP AND GOT A TALL GUY.
THEY PROBABLY COULDN'T GET A CHILD TO WEAR THE OUTFIT.

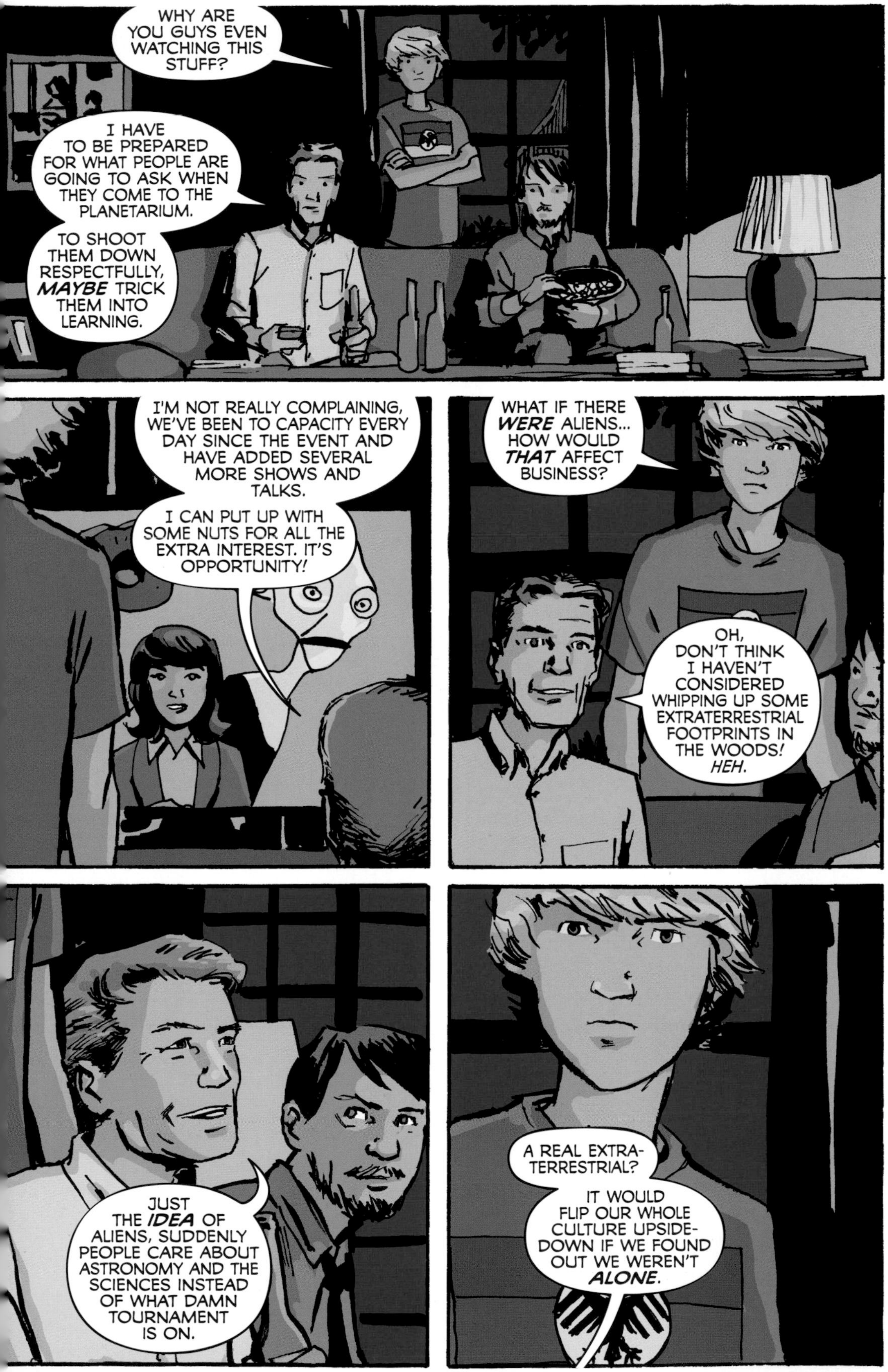
WHY ARE YOU GUYS EVEN WATCHING THIS STUFF?
I HAVE TO BE PREPARED FOR WHAT PEOPLE ARE GOING TO ASK WHEN THEY COME TO THE PLANETARIUM.
TO SHOOT THEM DOWN RESPECTFULLY, *MAYBE* TRICK THEM INTO LEARNING.
I'M NOT REALLY COMPLAINING, WE'VE BEEN TO CAPACITY EVERY DAY SINCE THE EVENT AND HAVE ADDED SEVERAL MORE SHOWS AND TALKS.
I CAN PUT UP WITH SOME NUTS FOR ALL THE EXTRA INTEREST. IT'S OPPORTUNITY!
WHAT IF THERE *WERE* ALIENS... HOW WOULD *THAT* AFFECT BUSINESS?
OH, DON'T THINK I HAVEN'T CONSIDERED WHIPPING UP SOME EXTRATERRESTRIAL FOOTPRINTS IN THE WOODS! *HEH*.
JUST THE *IDEA* OF ALIENS, SUDDENLY PEOPLE CARE ABOUT ASTRONOMY AND THE SCIENCES INSTEAD OF WHAT DAMN TOURNAMENT IS ON.
A REAL EXTRA-TERRESTRIAL?
IT WOULD FLIP OUR WHOLE CULTURE UPSIDE-DOWN IF WE FOUND OUT WE WEREN'T *ALONE*.

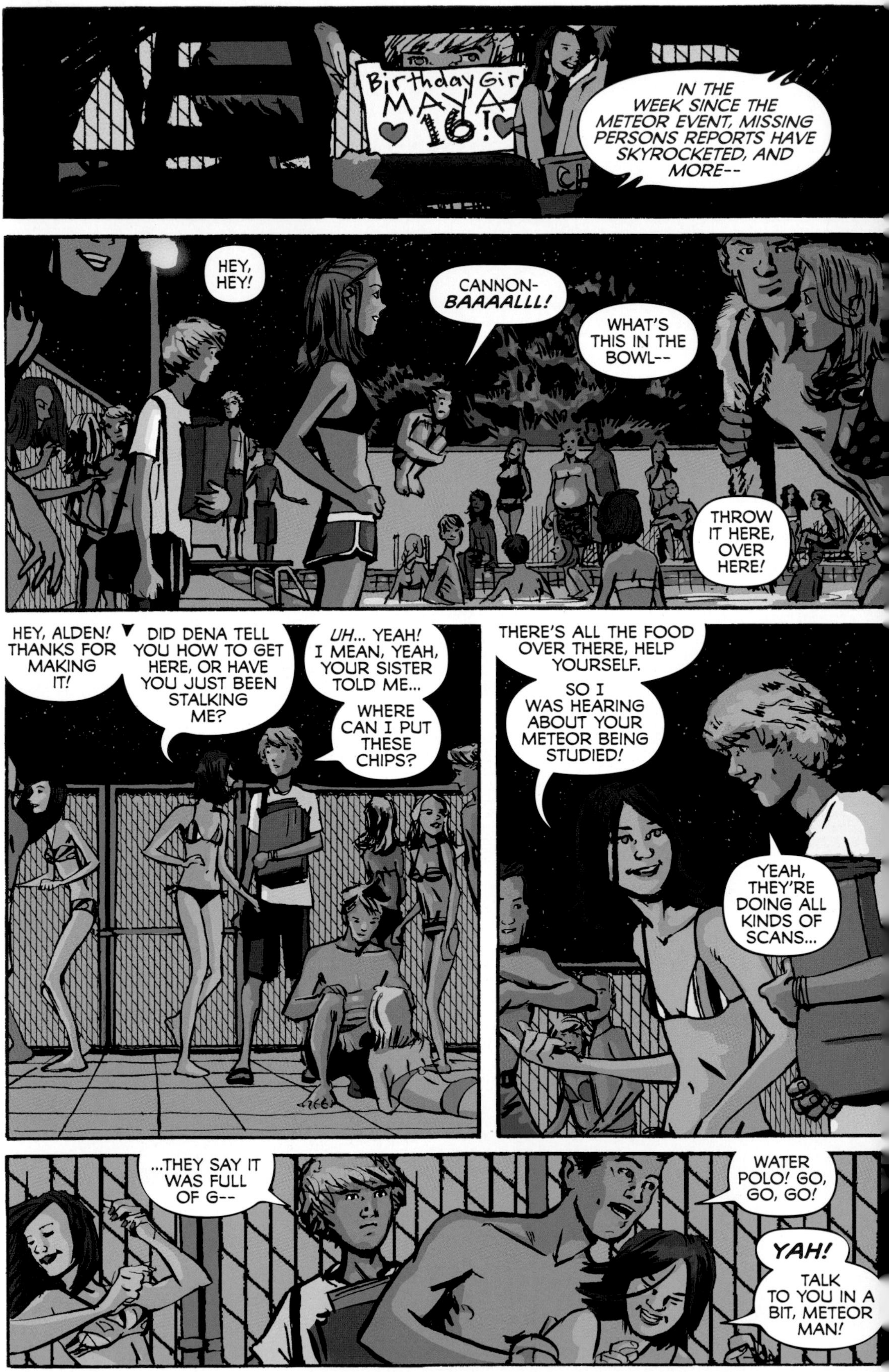
Birthday Girl MAYA 16!
IN THE WEEK SINCE THE METEOR EVENT, MISSING PERSONS REPORTS HAVE SKYROCKETED, AND MORE--
HEY, HEY!
CANNON-BAAAALLL!
WHAT'S THIS IN THE BOWL--
THROW IT HERE, OVER HERE!
HEY, ALDEN! THANKS FOR MAKING IT!
DID DENA TELL YOU HOW TO GET HERE, OR HAVE YOU JUST BEEN STALKING ME?
UH... YEAH! I MEAN, YEAH, YOUR SISTER TOLD ME...
WHERE CAN I PUT THESE CHIPS?
THERE'S ALL THE FOOD OVER THERE, HELP YOURSELF.
SO I WAS HEARING ABOUT YOUR METEOR BEING STUDIED!
YEAH, THEY'RE DOING ALL KINDS OF SCANS...
...THEY SAY IT WAS FULL OF G--
WATER POLO! GO, GO, GO!
YAH!
TALK TO YOU IN A BIT, METEOR MAN!

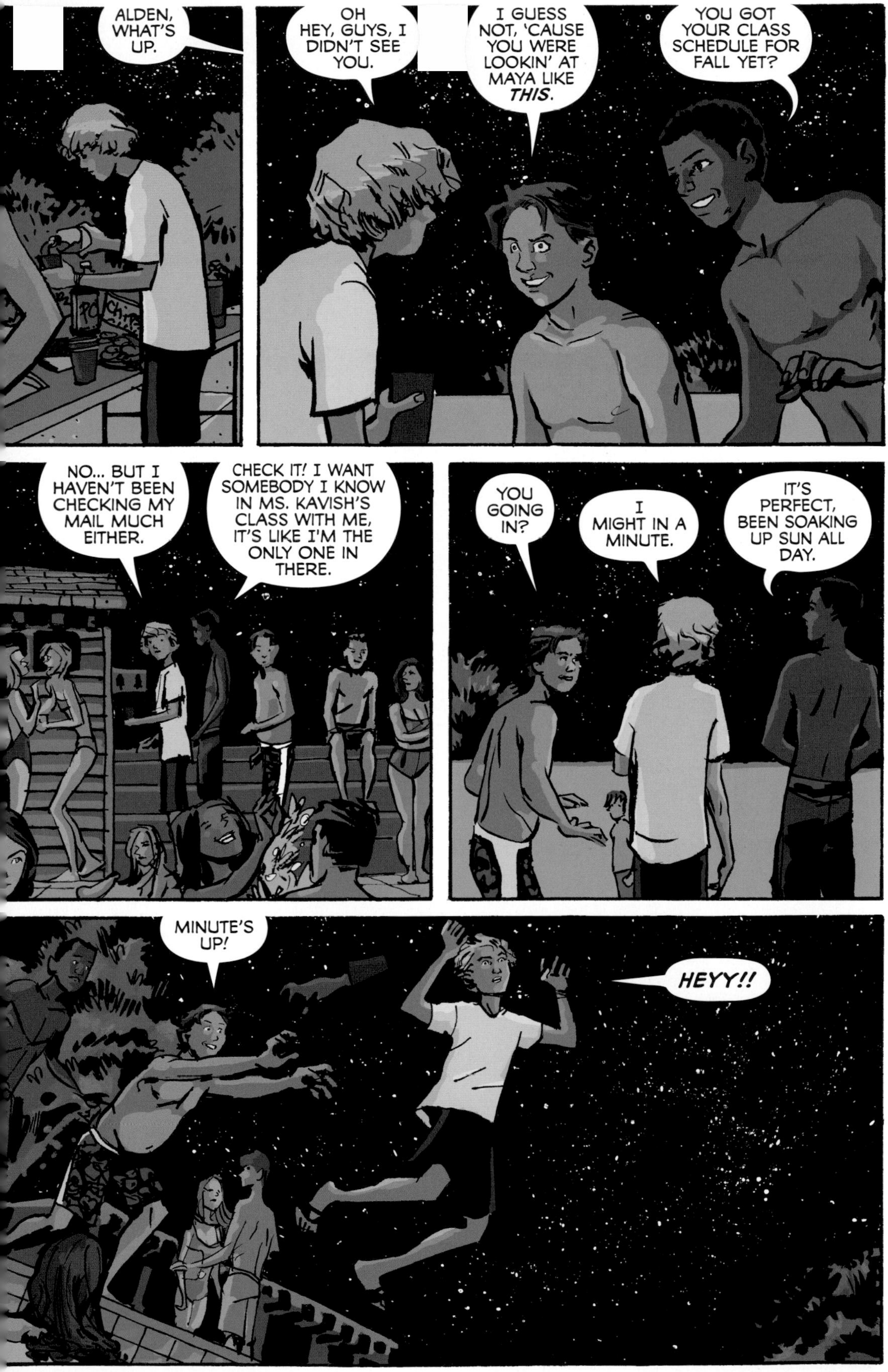
ALDEN, WHAT'S UP.
OH HEY, GUYS, I DIDN'T SEE YOU.
I GUESS NOT, 'CAUSE YOU WERE LOOKIN' AT MAYA LIKE *THIS*.
YOU GOT YOUR CLASS SCHEDULE FOR FALL YET?
NO... BUT I HAVEN'T BEEN CHECKING MY MAIL MUCH EITHER.
CHECK IT! I WANT SOMEBODY I KNOW IN MS. KAVISH'S CLASS WITH ME, IT'S LIKE I'M THE ONLY ONE IN THERE.
YOU GOING IN?
I MIGHT IN A MINUTE.
IT'S PERFECT, BEEN SOAKING UP SUN ALL DAY.
MINUTE'S UP!
HEYY!!

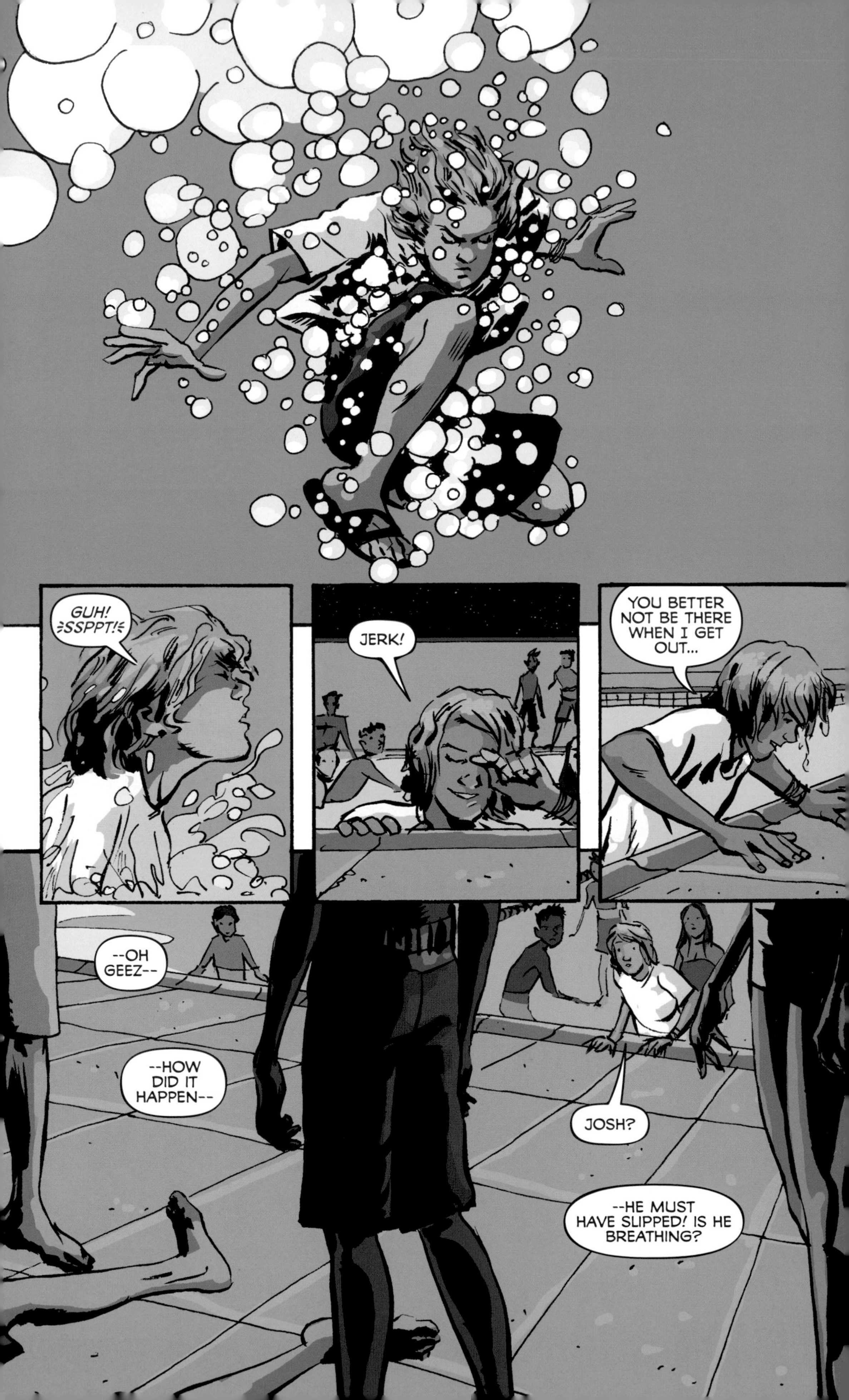
GUH!
SSPPT!
JERK!
YOU BETTER NOT BE THERE WHEN I GET OUT...
--OH GEEZ--
--HOW DID IT HAPPEN--
JOSH?
--HE MUST HAVE SLIPPED! IS HE BREATHING?

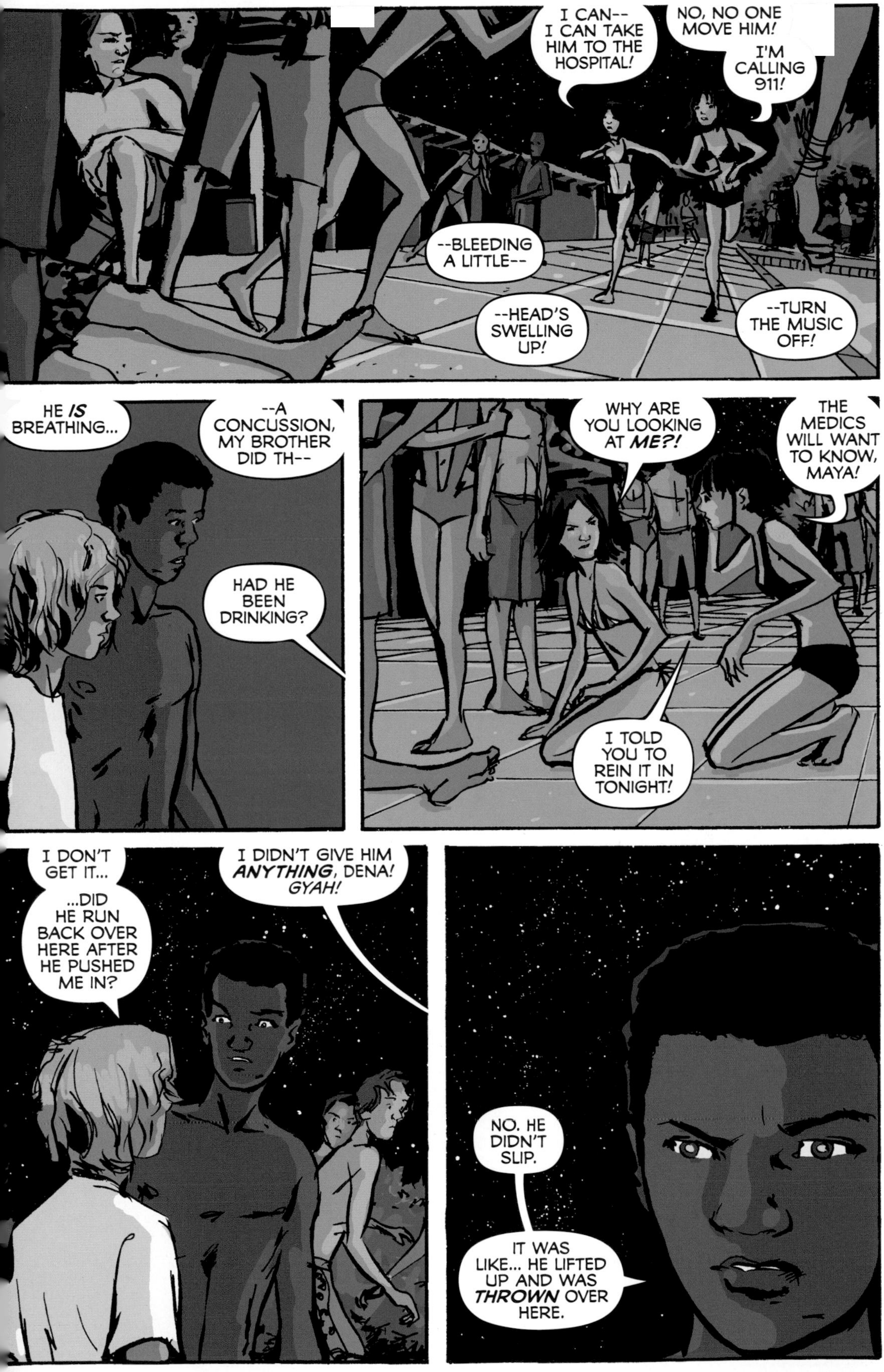
I CAN-- I CAN TAKE HIM TO THE HOSPITAL!
NO, NO ONE MOVE HIM!
I'M CALLING 911!
--BLEEDING A LITTLE--
--HEAD'S SWELLING UP!
--TURN THE MUSIC OFF!
HE *IS* BREATHING...
--A CONCUSSION, MY BROTHER DID TH--
HAD HE BEEN DRINKING?
WHY ARE YOU LOOKING AT *ME?!*
THE MEDICS WILL WANT TO KNOW, MAYA!
I TOLD YOU TO REIN IT IN TONIGHT!
I DON'T GET IT...
...DID HE RUN BACK OVER HERE AFTER HE PUSHED ME IN?
I DIDN'T GIVE HIM *ANYTHING*, DENA! *GYAH!*
NO. HE DIDN'T SLIP.
IT WAS LIKE... HE LIFTED UP AND WAS *THROWN* OVER HERE.

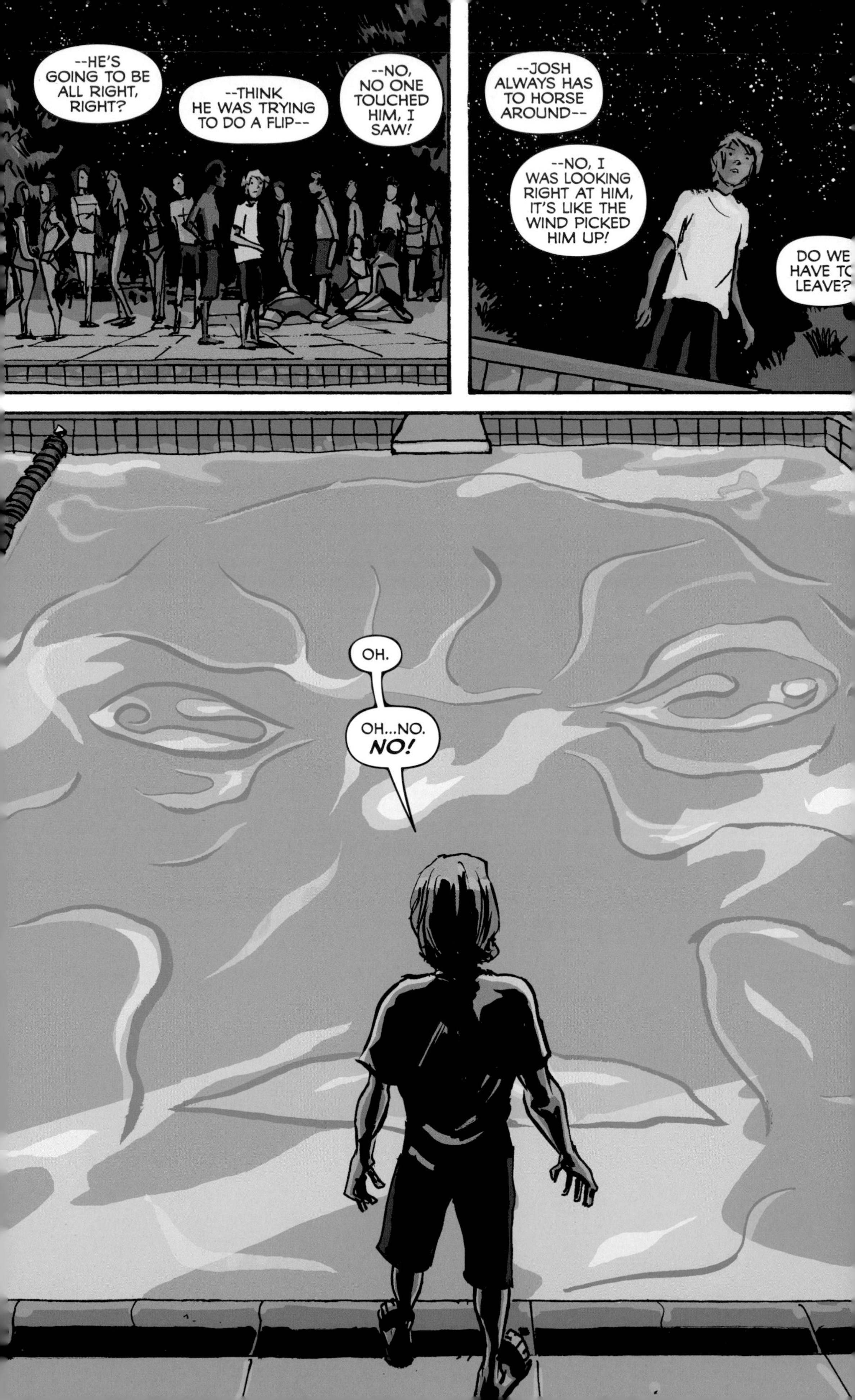
--HE'S GOING TO BE ALL RIGHT, RIGHT?
--THINK HE WAS TRYING TO DO A FLIP--
--NO, NO ONE TOUCHED HIM, I SAW!
--JOSH ALWAYS HAS TO HORSE AROUND--
--NO, I WAS LOOKING RIGHT AT HIM, IT'S LIKE THE WIND PICKED HIM UP!
DO WE HAVE TO LEAVE?
OH.
OH...NO. ***NO!***

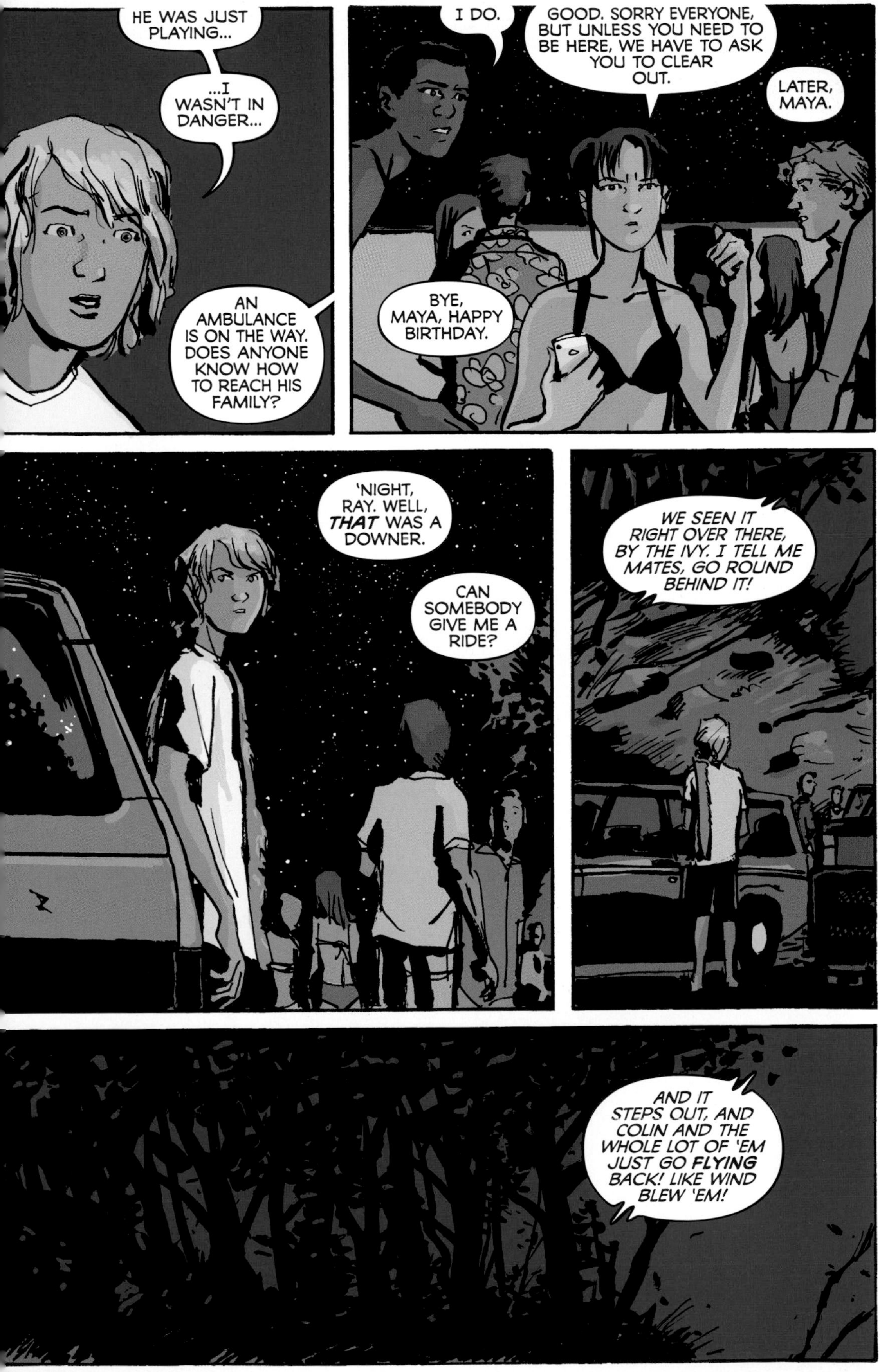
HE WAS JUST PLAYING...
...I WASN'T IN DANGER...
AN AMBULANCE IS ON THE WAY. DOES ANYONE KNOW HOW TO REACH HIS FAMILY?
I DO.
GOOD. SORRY EVERYONE, BUT UNLESS YOU NEED TO BE HERE, WE HAVE TO ASK YOU TO CLEAR OUT.
LATER, MAYA.
BYE, MAYA, HAPPY BIRTHDAY.
'NIGHT, RAY. WELL, *THAT* WAS A DOWNER.
CAN SOMEBODY GIVE ME A RIDE?
WE SEEN IT RIGHT OVER THERE, BY THE IVY. I TELL ME MATES, GO ROUND BEHIND IT!
AND IT STEPS OUT, AND COLIN AND THE WHOLE LOT OF 'EM JUST GO ***FLYING*** *BACK! LIKE WIND BLEW 'EM!*

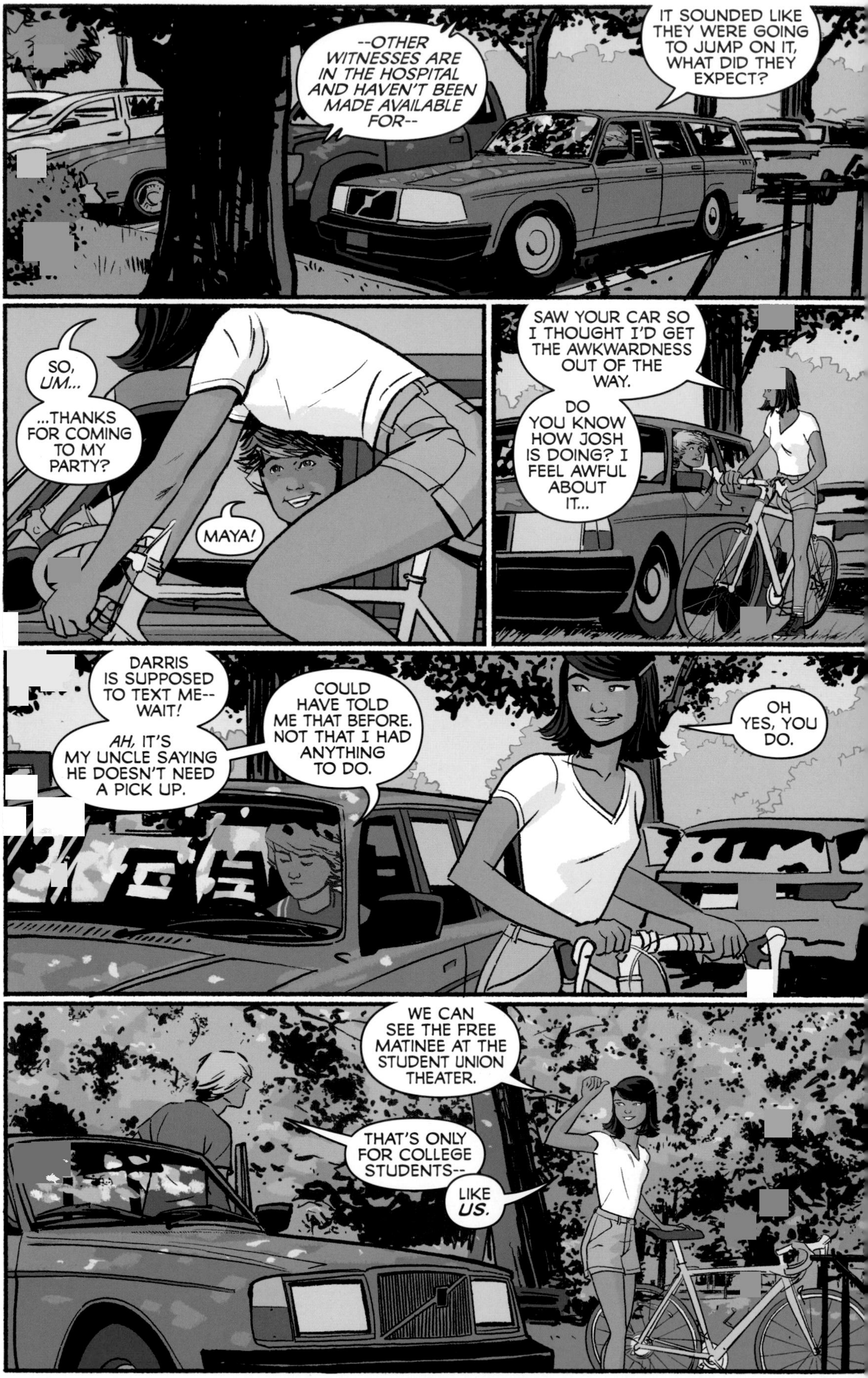
--*OTHER WITNESSES ARE IN THE HOSPITAL AND HAVEN'T BEEN MADE AVAILABLE FOR--*
IT SOUNDED LIKE THEY WERE GOING TO JUMP ON IT, WHAT DID THEY EXPECT?
SO, *UM...*
...THANKS FOR COMING TO MY PARTY?
MAYA!
SAW YOUR CAR SO I THOUGHT I'D GET THE AWKWARDNESS OUT OF THE WAY.
DO YOU KNOW HOW JOSH IS DOING? I FEEL AWFUL ABOUT IT...
DARRIS IS SUPPOSED TO TEXT ME-- WAIT!
AH, IT'S MY UNCLE SAYING HE DOESN'T NEED A PICK UP.
COULD HAVE TOLD ME THAT BEFORE. NOT THAT I HAD ANYTHING TO DO.
OH YES, YOU DO.
WE CAN SEE THE FREE MATINEE AT THE STUDENT UNION THEATER.
THAT'S ONLY FOR COLLEGE STUDENTS--
LIKE ***US.***

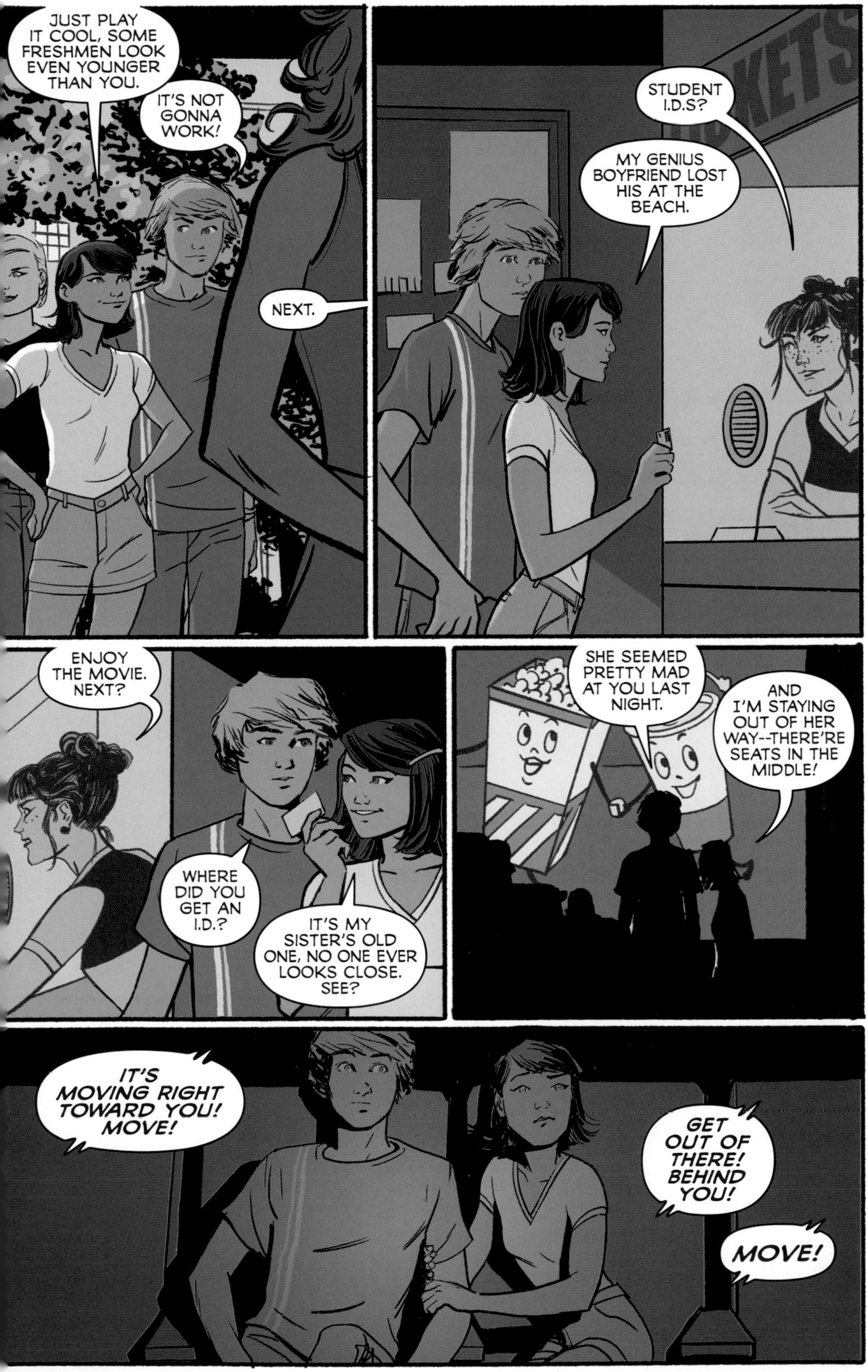
JUST PLAY IT COOL, SOME FRESHMEN LOOK EVEN YOUNGER THAN YOU.
IT'S NOT GONNA WORK!
NEXT.
STUDENT I.D.S?
MY GENIUS BOYFRIEND LOST HIS AT THE BEACH.
TICKETS
ENJOY THE MOVIE. NEXT?
WHERE DID YOU GET AN I.D.?
IT'S MY SISTER'S OLD ONE, NO ONE EVER LOOKS CLOSE. SEE?
SHE SEEMED PRETTY MAD AT YOU LAST NIGHT.
AND I'M STAYING OUT OF HER WAY--THERE'RE SEATS IN THE MIDDLE!
IT'S MOVING RIGHT TOWARD YOU! MOVE!
GET OUT OF THERE! BEHIND YOU!
MOVE!

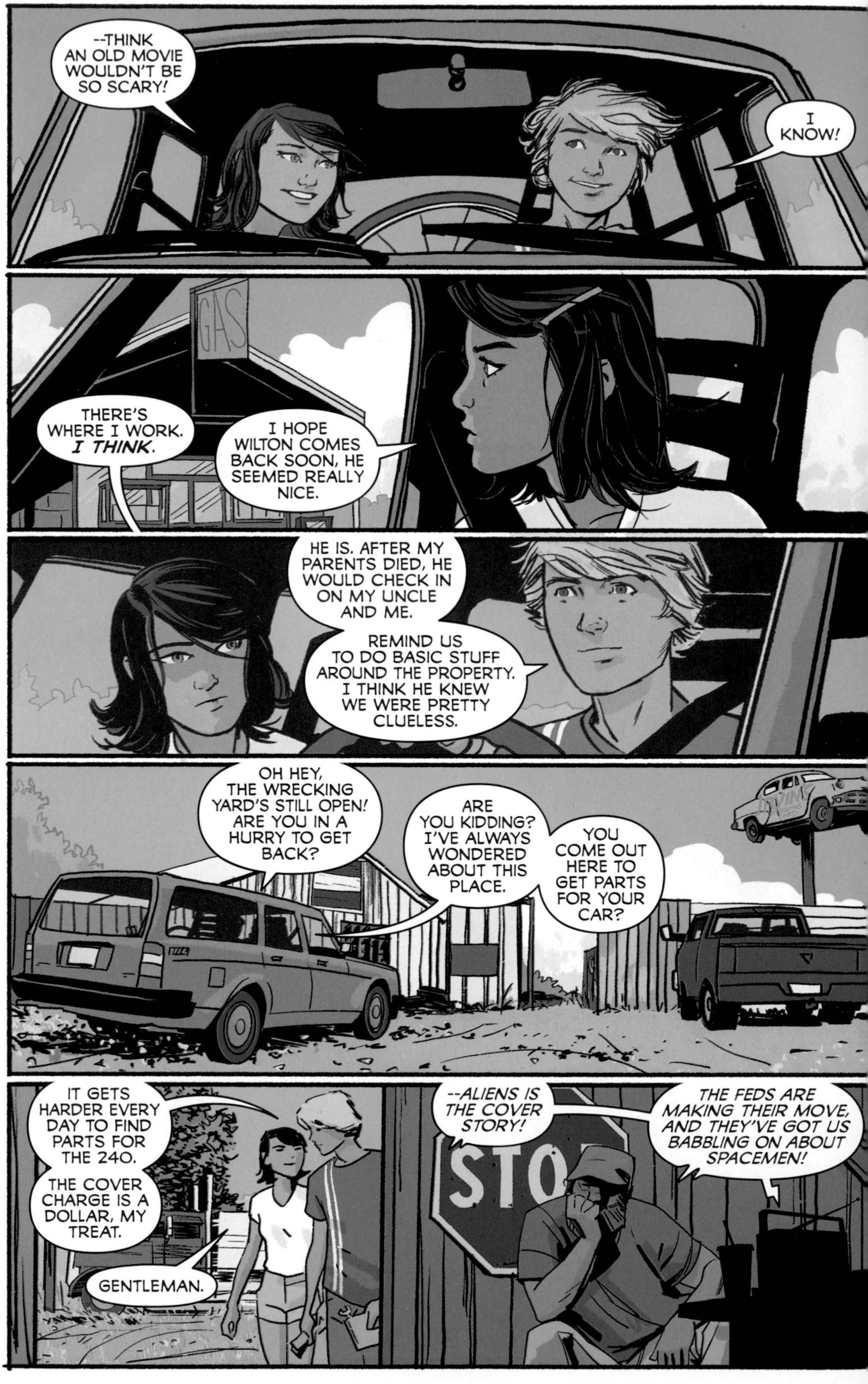
--THINK AN OLD MOVIE WOULDN'T BE SO SCARY!
I KNOW!
GAS
THERE'S WHERE I WORK. *I THINK*.
I HOPE WILTON COMES BACK SOON, HE SEEMED REALLY NICE.
HE IS. AFTER MY PARENTS DIED, HE WOULD CHECK IN ON MY UNCLE AND ME.
REMIND US TO DO BASIC STUFF AROUND THE PROPERTY. I THINK HE KNEW WE WERE PRETTY CLUELESS.
OH HEY, THE WRECKING YARD'S STILL OPEN! ARE YOU IN A HURRY TO GET BACK?
ARE YOU KIDDING? I'VE ALWAYS WONDERED ABOUT THIS PLACE.
YOU COME OUT HERE TO GET PARTS FOR YOUR CAR?
IT GETS HARDER EVERY DAY TO FIND PARTS FOR THE 240.
THE COVER CHARGE IS A DOLLAR, MY TREAT.
GENTLEMAN.
--ALIENS IS THE COVER STORY!
THE FEDS ARE MAKING THEIR MOVE, AND THEY'VE GOT US BABBLING ON ABOUT SPACEMEN!
STO

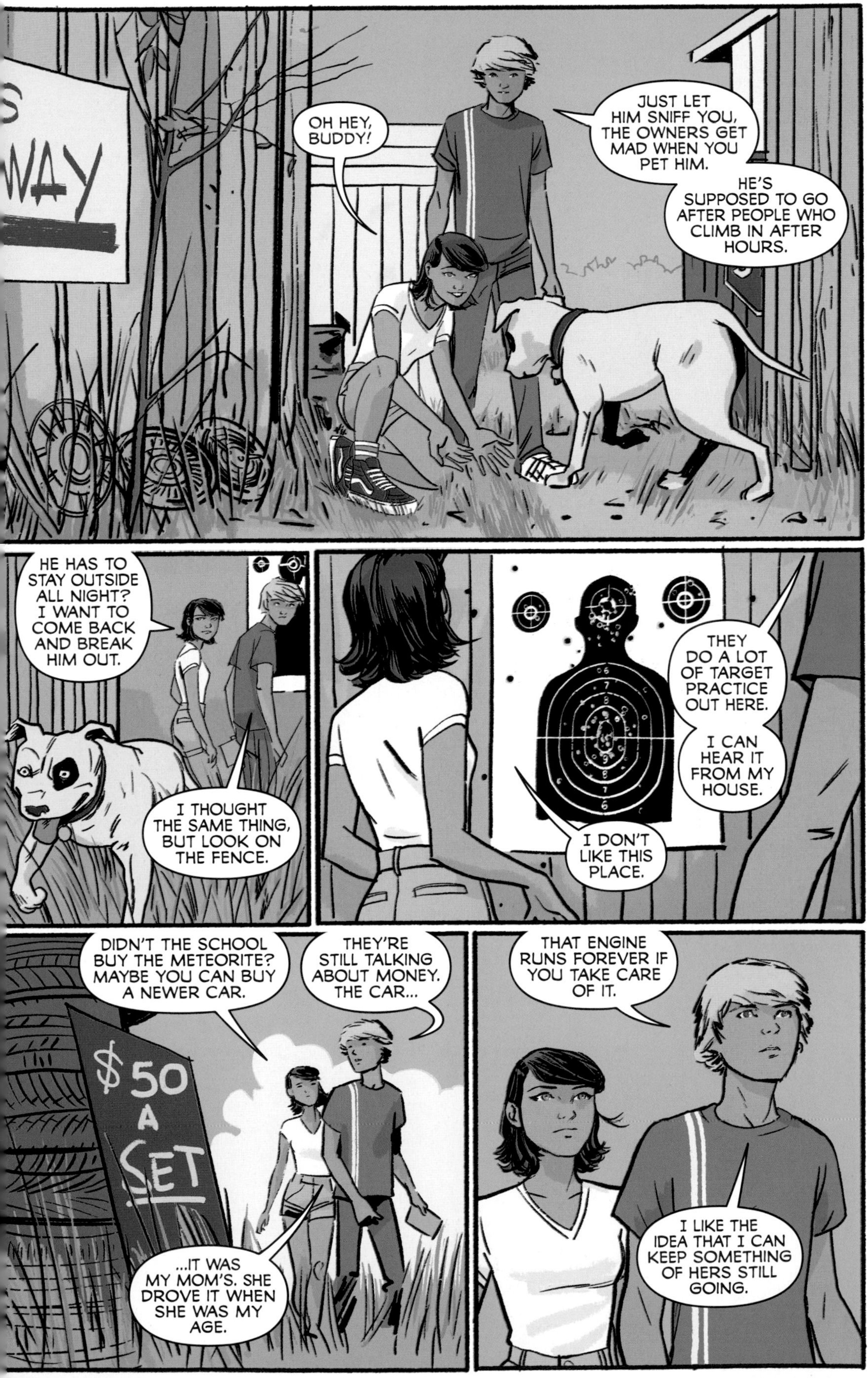
S
WAY
OH HEY, BUDDY!
JUST LET HIM SNIFF YOU, THE OWNERS GET MAD WHEN YOU PET HIM.
HE'S SUPPOSED TO GO AFTER PEOPLE WHO CLIMB IN AFTER HOURS.
HE HAS TO STAY OUTSIDE ALL NIGHT? I WANT TO COME BACK AND BREAK HIM OUT.
I THOUGHT THE SAME THING, BUT LOOK ON THE FENCE.
THEY DO A LOT OF TARGET PRACTICE OUT HERE.
I CAN HEAR IT FROM MY HOUSE.
I DON'T LIKE THIS PLACE.
DIDN'T THE SCHOOL BUY THE METEORITE? MAYBE YOU CAN BUY A NEWER CAR.
THEY'RE STILL TALKING ABOUT MONEY. THE CAR...
$50 A SET
...IT WAS MY MOM'S. SHE DROVE IT WHEN SHE WAS MY AGE.
THAT ENGINE RUNS FOREVER IF YOU TAKE CARE OF IT.
I LIKE THE IDEA THAT I CAN KEEP SOMETHING OF HERS STILL GOING.

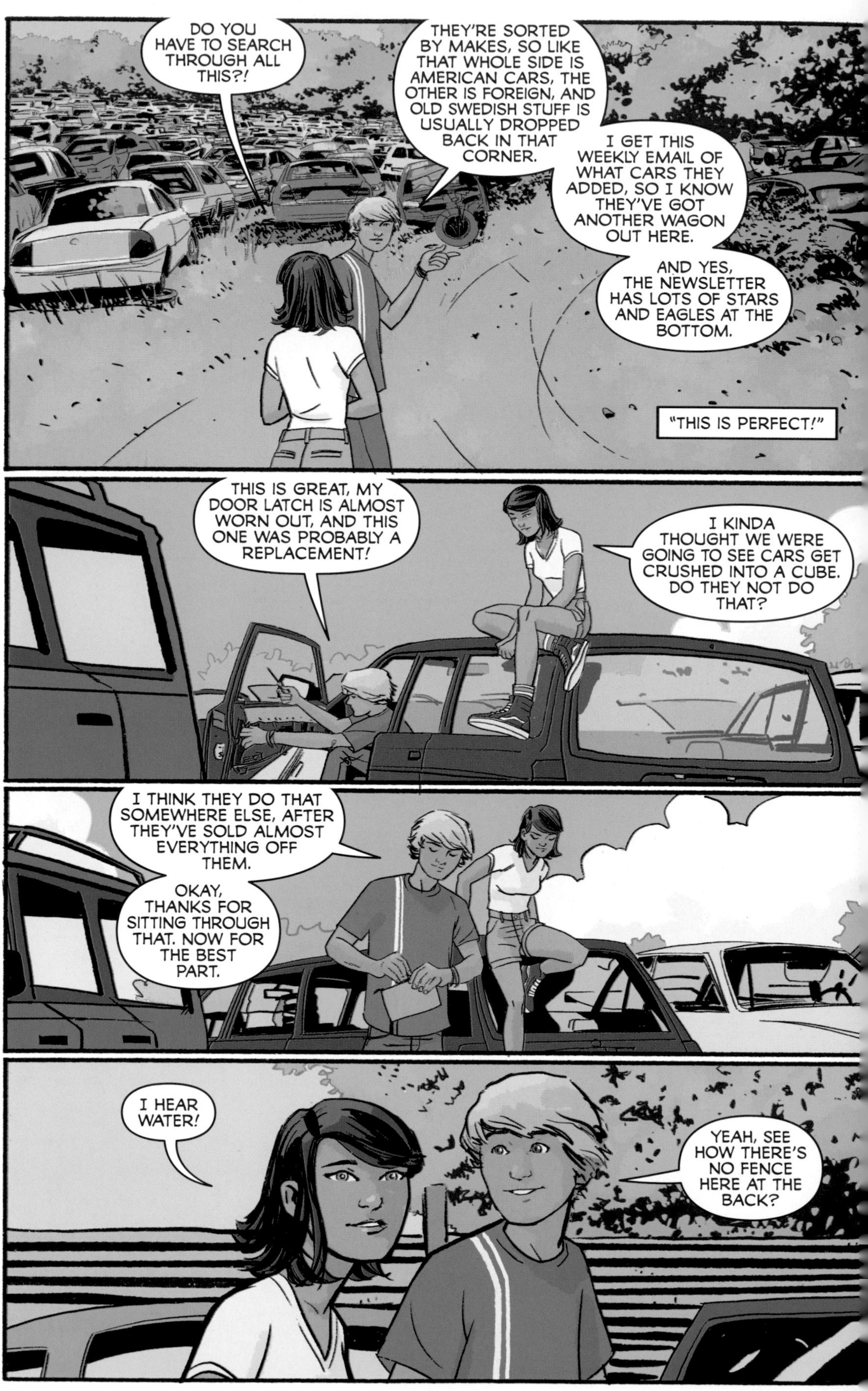
DO YOU HAVE TO SEARCH THROUGH ALL THIS?!
THEY'RE SORTED BY MAKES, SO LIKE THAT WHOLE SIDE IS AMERICAN CARS, THE OTHER IS FOREIGN, AND OLD SWEDISH STUFF IS USUALLY DROPPED BACK IN THAT CORNER.
I GET THIS WEEKLY EMAIL OF WHAT CARS THEY ADDED, SO I KNOW THEY'VE GOT ANOTHER WAGON OUT HERE.
AND YES, THE NEWSLETTER HAS LOTS OF STARS AND EAGLES AT THE BOTTOM.
"THIS IS PERFECT!"
THIS IS GREAT, MY DOOR LATCH IS ALMOST WORN OUT, AND THIS ONE WAS PROBABLY A REPLACEMENT!
I KINDA THOUGHT WE WERE GOING TO SEE CARS GET CRUSHED INTO A CUBE. DO THEY NOT DO THAT?
I THINK THEY DO THAT SOMEWHERE ELSE, AFTER THEY'VE SOLD ALMOST EVERYTHING OFF THEM.
OKAY, THANKS FOR SITTING THROUGH THAT. NOW FOR THE BEST PART.
I HEAR WATER!
YEAH, SEE HOW THERE'S NO FENCE HERE AT THE BACK?

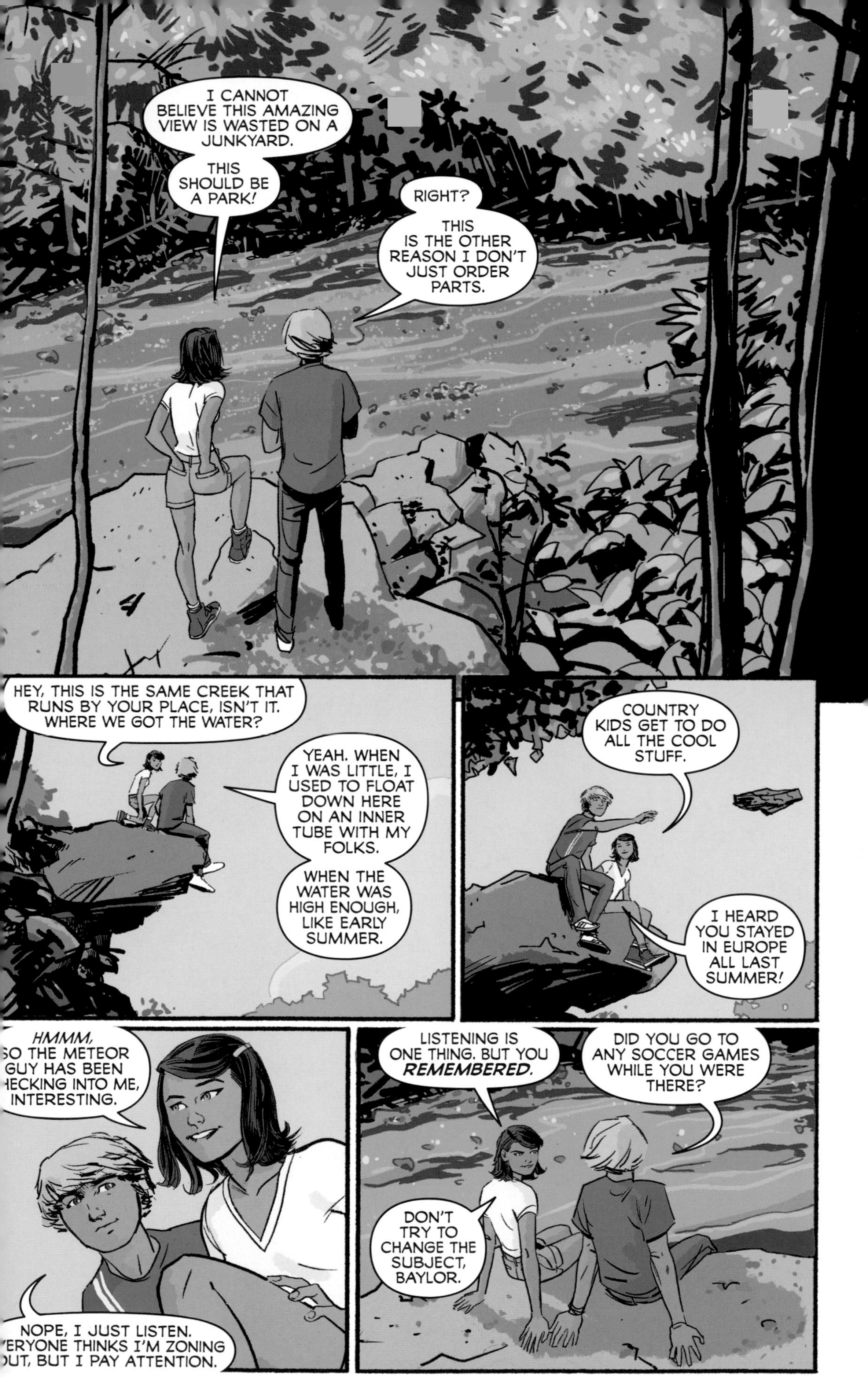
I CANNOT BELIEVE THIS AMAZING VIEW IS WASTED ON A JUNKYARD.
THIS SHOULD BE A PARK!
RIGHT?
THIS IS THE OTHER REASON I DON'T JUST ORDER PARTS.
HEY, THIS IS THE SAME CREEK THAT RUNS BY YOUR PLACE, ISN'T IT. WHERE WE GOT THE WATER?
YEAH. WHEN I WAS LITTLE, I USED TO FLOAT DOWN HERE ON AN INNER TUBE WITH MY FOLKS.
WHEN THE WATER WAS HIGH ENOUGH, LIKE EARLY SUMMER.
COUNTRY KIDS GET TO DO ALL THE COOL STUFF.
I HEARD YOU STAYED IN EUROPE ALL LAST SUMMER!
HMMM, O THE METEOR GUY HAS BEEN ECKING INTO ME, INTERESTING.
NOPE, I JUST LISTEN. ERYONE THINKS I'M ZONING UT, BUT I PAY ATTENTION.
LISTENING IS ONE THING. BUT YOU *REMEMBERED.*
DID YOU GO TO ANY SOCCER GAMES WHILE YOU WERE THERE?
DON'T TRY TO CHANGE THE SUBJECT, BAYLOR.

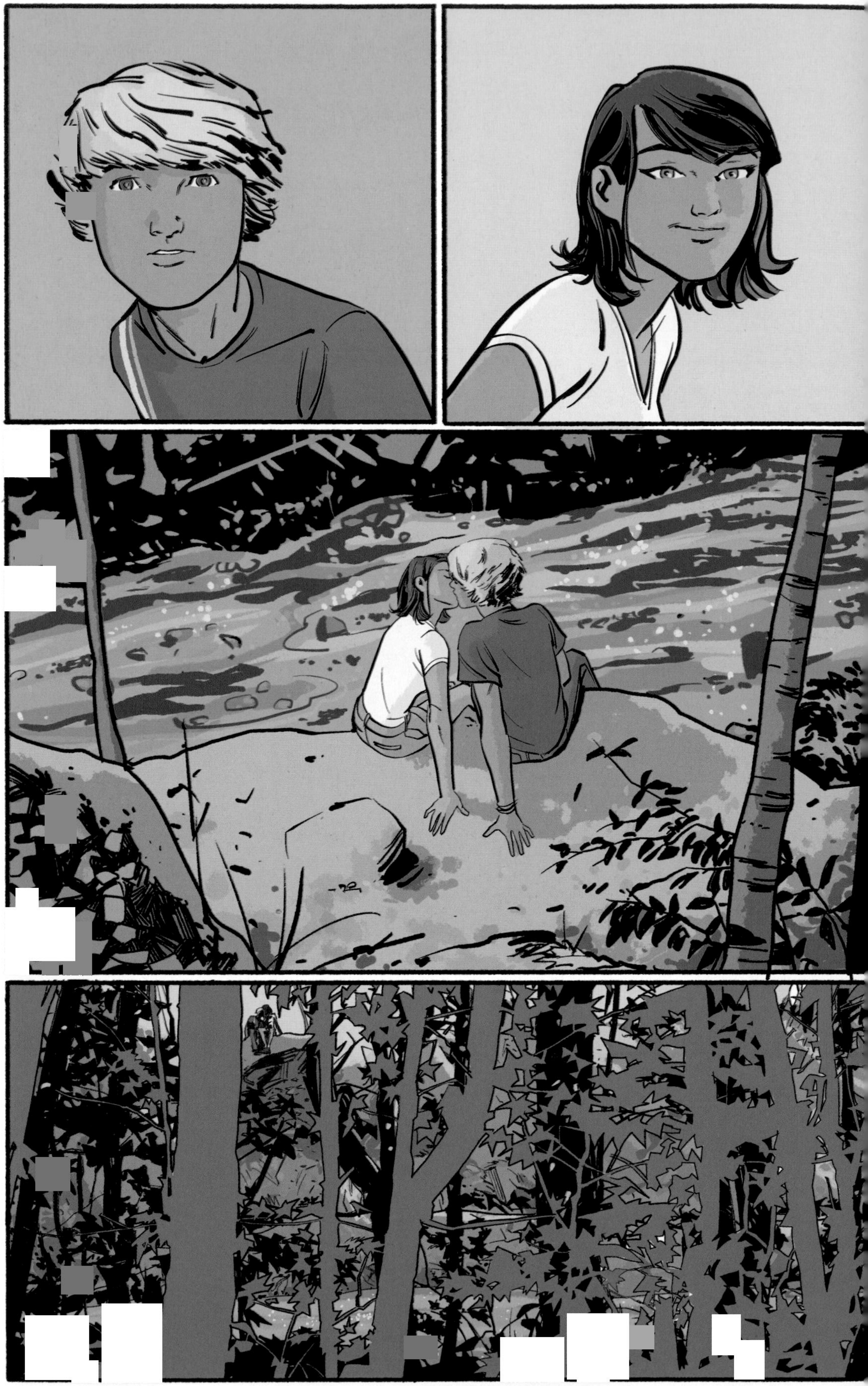

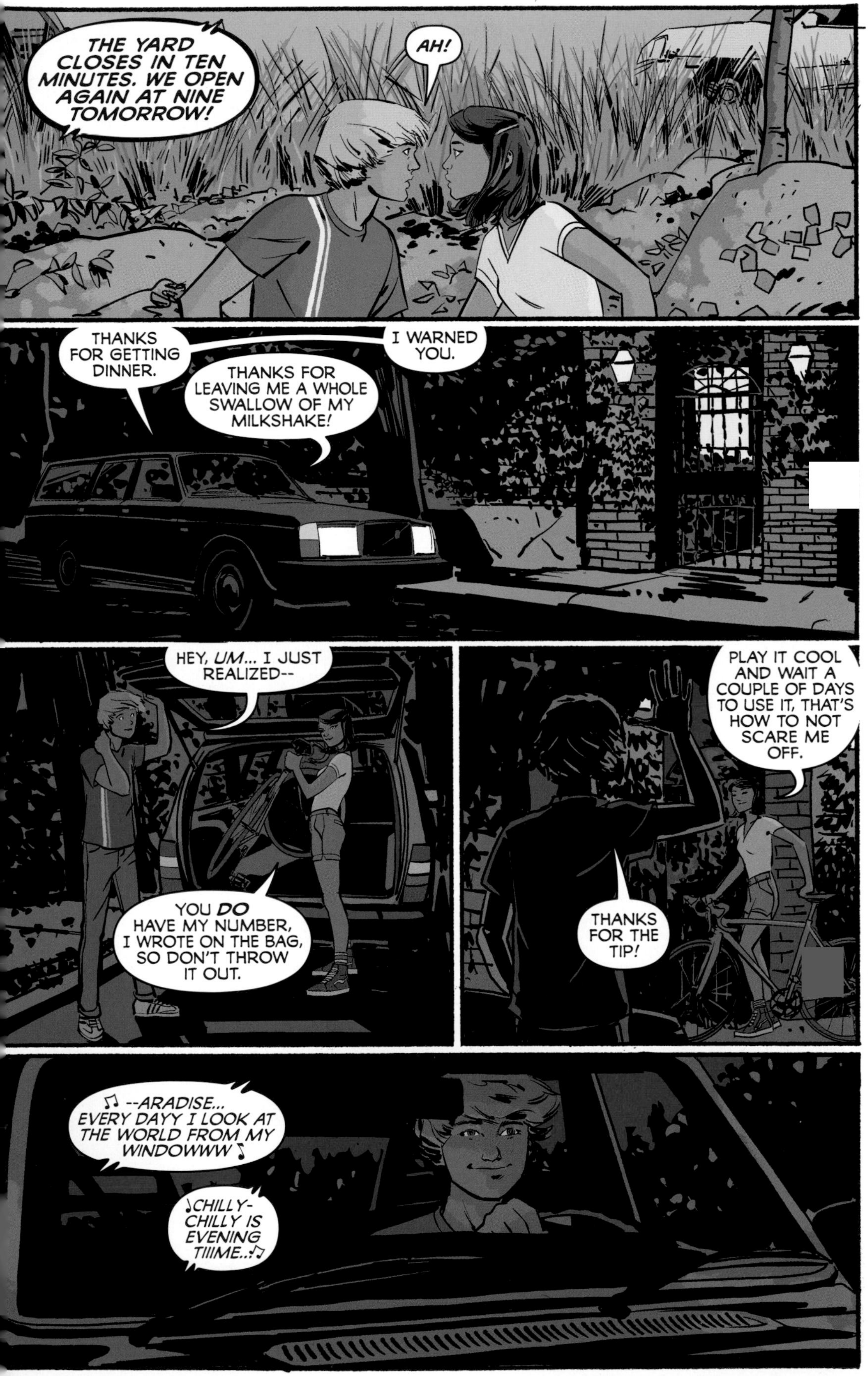
THE YARD CLOSES IN TEN MINUTES. WE OPEN AGAIN AT NINE TOMORROW!
AH!
THANKS FOR GETTING DINNER.
I WARNED YOU.
THANKS FOR LEAVING ME A WHOLE SWALLOW OF MY MILKSHAKE!
HEY, *UM*... I JUST REALIZED--
YOU ***DO*** HAVE MY NUMBER, I WROTE ON THE BAG, SO DON'T THROW IT OUT.
PLAY IT COOL AND WAIT A COUPLE OF DAYS TO USE IT, THAT'S HOW TO NOT SCARE ME OFF.
THANKS FOR THE TIP!
♫ --ARADISE... EVERY DAYY I LOOK AT THE WORLD FROM MY WINDOWWW ♪
♪ CHILLY-CHILLY IS EVENING TIIIME..♫

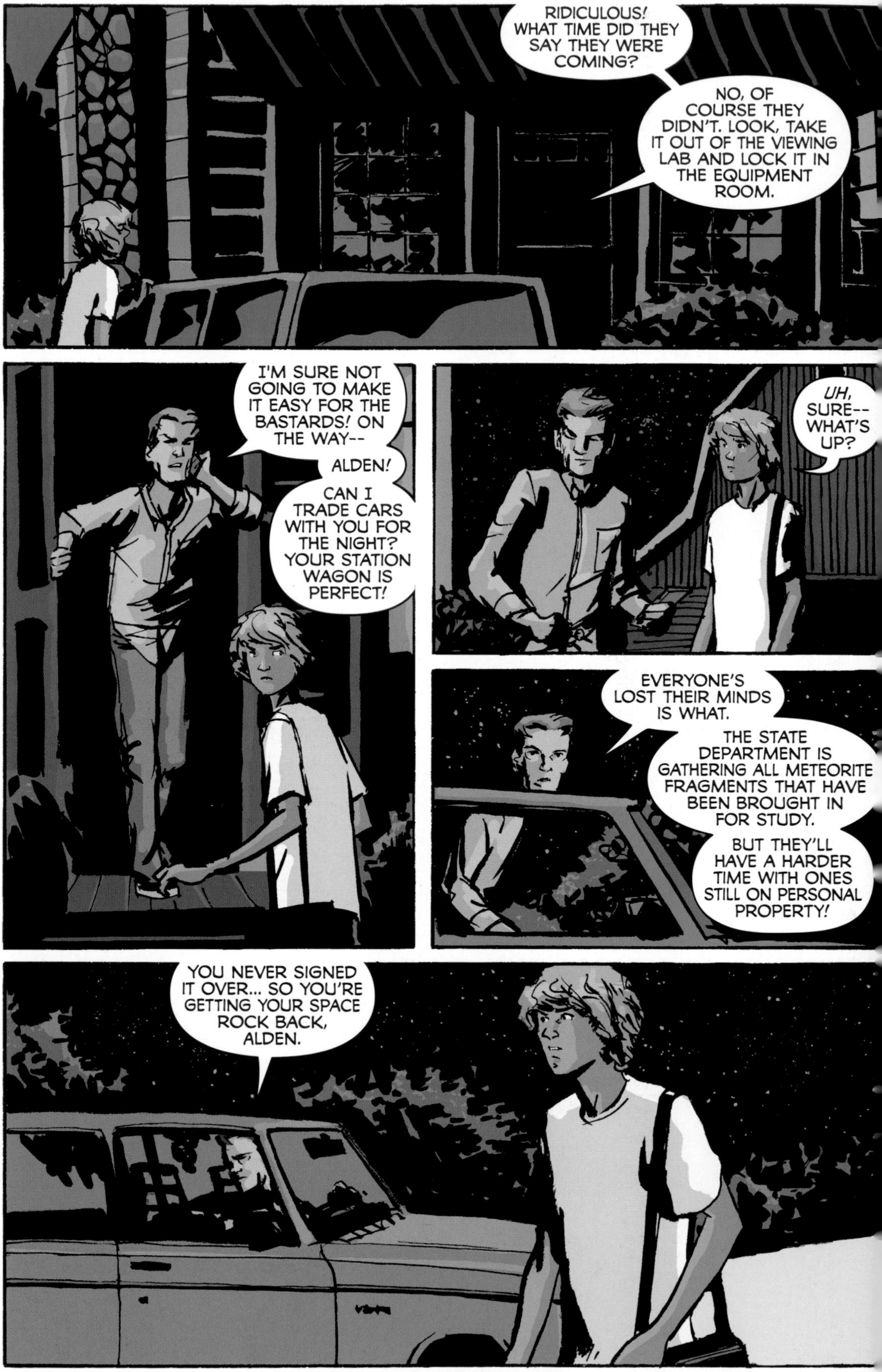
RIDICULOUS! WHAT TIME DID THEY SAY THEY WERE COMING?
NO, OF COURSE THEY DIDN'T. LOOK, TAKE IT OUT OF THE VIEWING LAB AND LOCK IT IN THE EQUIPMENT ROOM.
I'M SURE NOT GOING TO MAKE IT EASY FOR THE BASTARDS! ON THE WAY--
ALDEN!
CAN I TRADE CARS WITH YOU FOR THE NIGHT? YOUR STATION WAGON IS PERFECT!
UH, SURE-- WHAT'S UP?
EVERYONE'S LOST THEIR MINDS IS WHAT.
THE STATE DEPARTMENT IS GATHERING ALL METEORITE FRAGMENTS THAT HAVE BEEN BROUGHT IN FOR STUDY.
BUT THEY'LL HAVE A HARDER TIME WITH ONES STILL ON PERSONAL PROPERTY!
YOU NEVER SIGNED IT OVER... SO YOU'RE GETTING YOUR SPACE ROCK BACK, ALDEN.

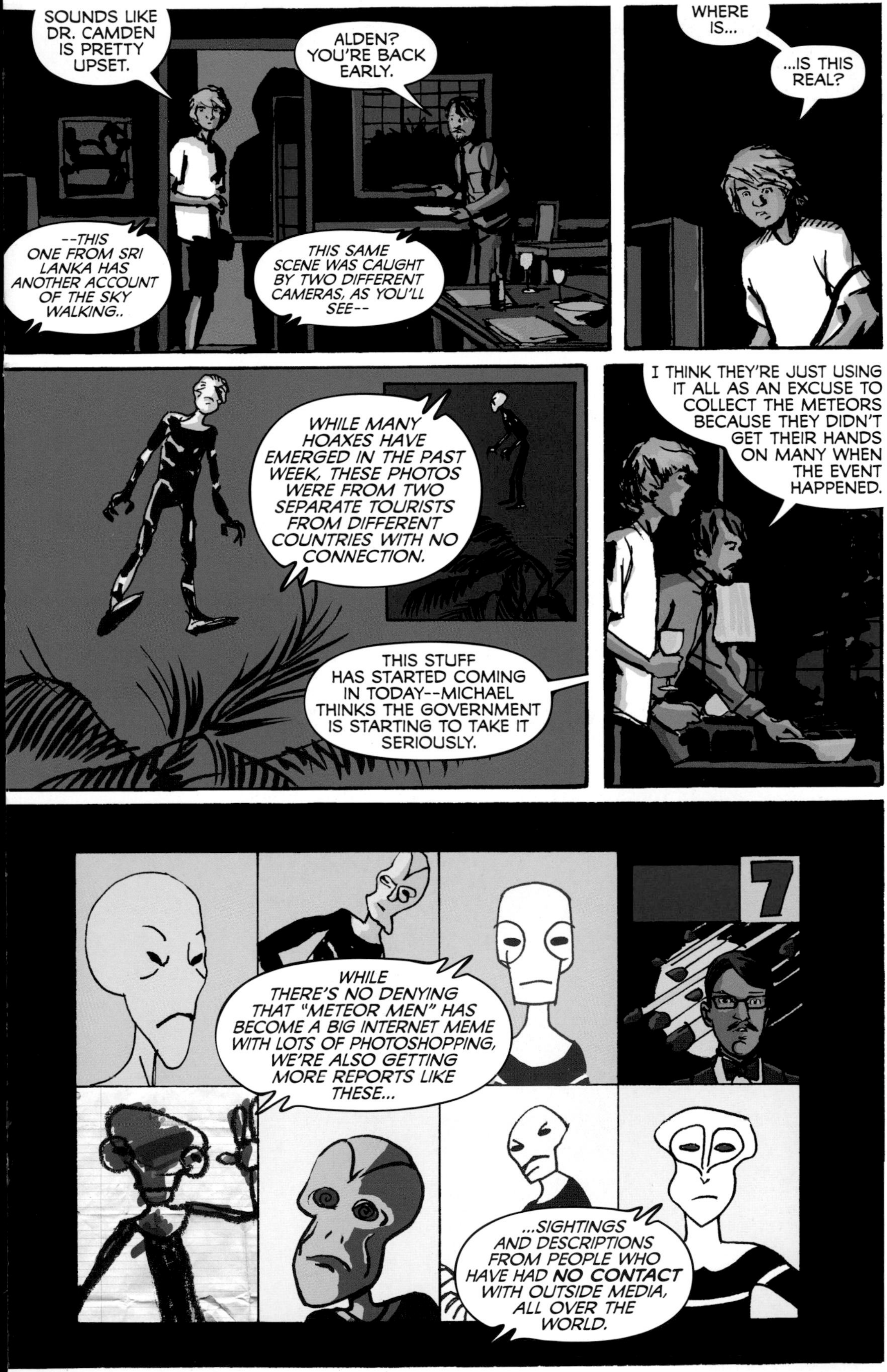
SOUNDS LIKE DR. CAMDEN IS PRETTY UPSET.
ALDEN? YOU'RE BACK EARLY.
--THIS ONE FROM SRI LANKA HAS ANOTHER ACCOUNT OF THE SKY WALKING..
THIS SAME SCENE WAS CAUGHT BY TWO DIFFERENT CAMERAS, AS YOU'LL SEE--
WHERE IS...
...IS THIS REAL?
WHILE MANY HOAXES HAVE EMERGED IN THE PAST WEEK, THESE PHOTOS WERE FROM TWO SEPARATE TOURISTS FROM DIFFERENT COUNTRIES WITH NO CONNECTION.
THIS STUFF HAS STARTED COMING IN TODAY--MICHAEL THINKS THE GOVERNMENT IS STARTING TO TAKE IT SERIOUSLY.
I THINK THEY'RE JUST USING IT ALL AS AN EXCUSE TO COLLECT THE METEORS BECAUSE THEY DIDN'T GET THEIR HANDS ON MANY WHEN THE EVENT HAPPENED.
7
WHILE THERE'S NO DENYING THAT "METEOR MEN" HAS BECOME A BIG INTERNET MEME WITH LOTS OF PHOTOSHOPPING, WE'RE ALSO GETTING MORE REPORTS LIKE THESE...
...SIGHTINGS AND DESCRIPTIONS FROM PEOPLE WHO HAVE HAD **NO CONTACT** WITH OUTSIDE MEDIA, ALL OVER THE WORLD.

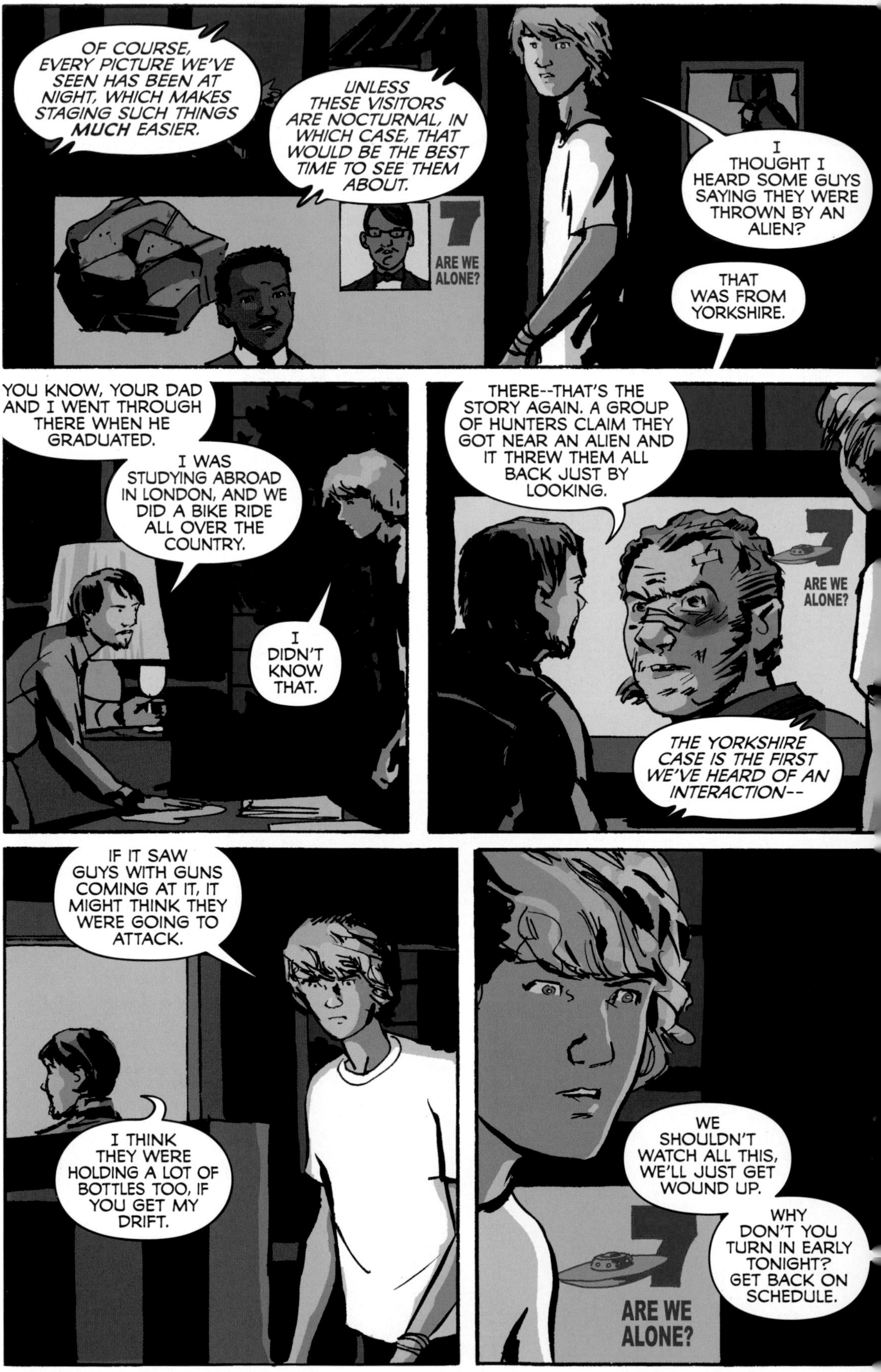
OF COURSE, EVERY PICTURE WE'VE SEEN HAS BEEN AT NIGHT, WHICH MAKES STAGING SUCH THINGS MUCH EASIER.
UNLESS THESE VISITORS ARE NOCTURNAL, IN WHICH CASE, THAT WOULD BE THE BEST TIME TO SEE THEM ABOUT.
7 ARE WE ALONE?
I THOUGHT I HEARD SOME GUYS SAYING THEY WERE THROWN BY AN ALIEN?
THAT WAS FROM YORKSHIRE.
YOU KNOW, YOUR DAD AND I WENT THROUGH THERE WHEN HE GRADUATED.
I WAS STUDYING ABROAD IN LONDON, AND WE DID A BIKE RIDE ALL OVER THE COUNTRY.
I DIDN'T KNOW THAT.
THERE--THAT'S THE STORY AGAIN. A GROUP OF HUNTERS CLAIM THEY GOT NEAR AN ALIEN AND IT THREW THEM ALL BACK JUST BY LOOKING.
7 ARE WE ALONE?
THE YORKSHIRE CASE IS THE FIRST WE'VE HEARD OF AN INTERACTION--
IF IT SAW GUYS WITH GUNS COMING AT IT, IT MIGHT THINK THEY WERE GOING TO ATTACK.
I THINK THEY WERE HOLDING A LOT OF BOTTLES TOO, IF YOU GET MY DRIFT.
WE SHOULDN'T WATCH ALL THIS, WE'LL JUST GET WOUND UP.
WHY DON'T YOU TURN IN EARLY TONIGHT? GET BACK ON SCHEDULE.
7 ARE WE ALONE?

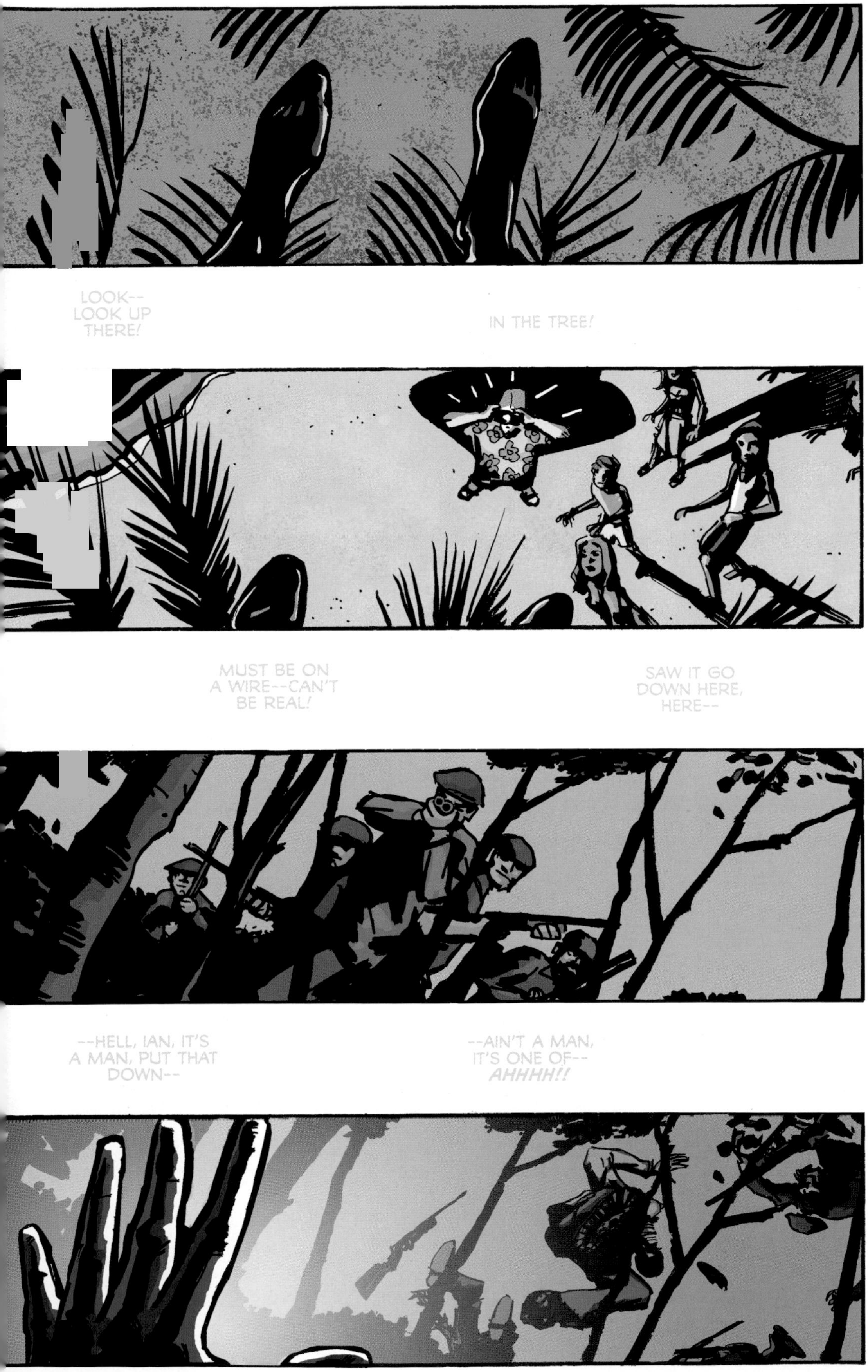
LOOK--
LOOK UP
THERE!
IN THE TREE!
MUST BE ON
A WIRE--CAN'T
BE REAL!
SAW IT GO
DOWN HERE,
HERE--
--HELL, IAN, IT'S
A MAN, PUT THAT
DOWN--
--AIN'T A MAN,
IT'S ONE OF--
AHHHH!!

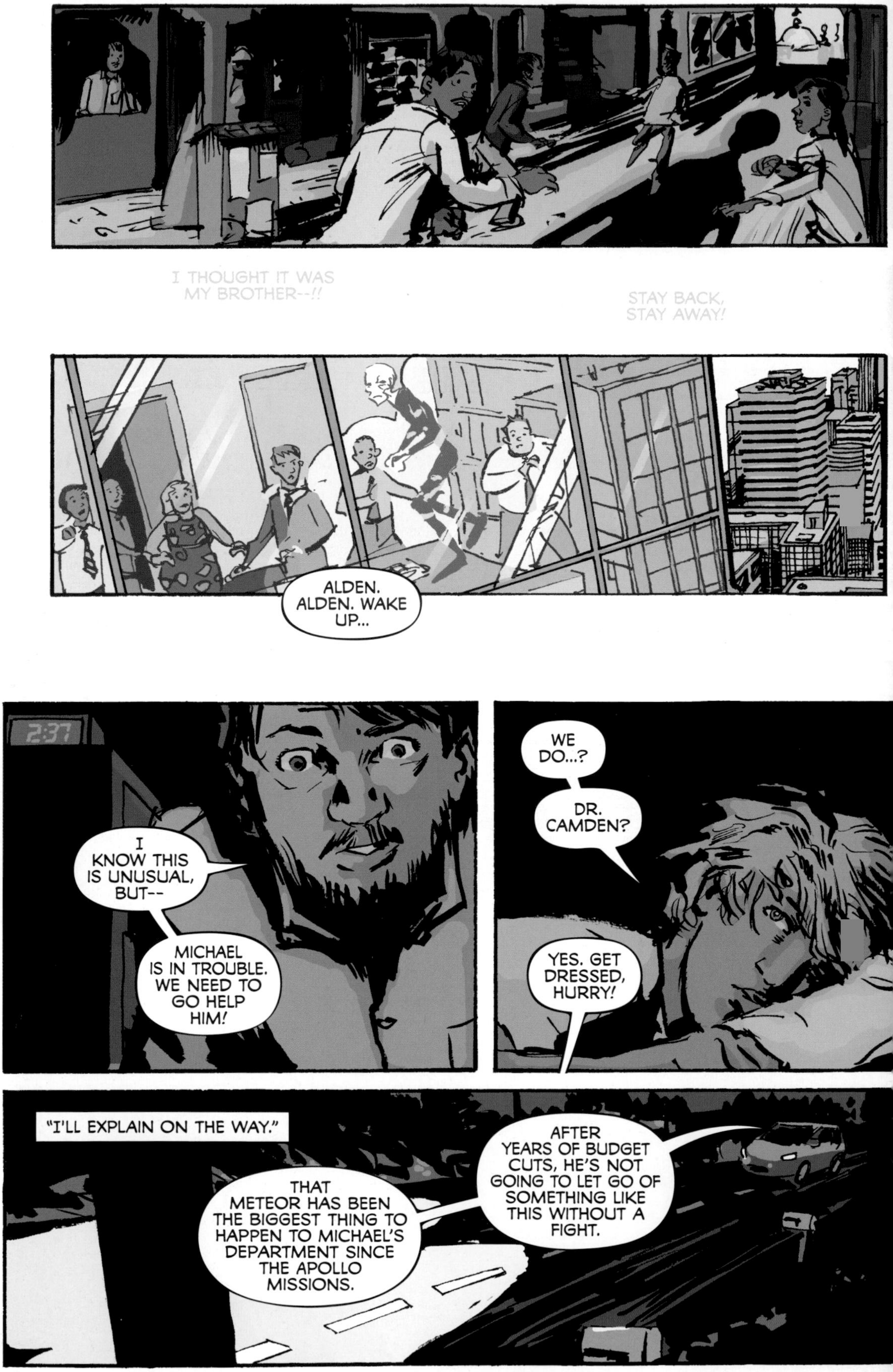
I THOUGHT IT WAS MY BROTHER--!!
STAY BACK, STAY AWAY!
ALDEN. ALDEN. WAKE UP...
2:37
I KNOW THIS IS UNUSUAL, BUT--
MICHAEL IS IN TROUBLE. WE NEED TO GO HELP HIM!
WE DO...?
DR. CAMDEN?
YES. GET DRESSED, HURRY!
"I'LL EXPLAIN ON THE WAY."
THAT METEOR HAS BEEN THE BIGGEST THING TO HAPPEN TO MICHAEL'S DEPARTMENT SINCE THE APOLLO MISSIONS.
AFTER YEARS OF BUDGET CUTS, HE'S NOT GOING TO LET GO OF SOMETHING LIKE THIS WITHOUT A FIGHT.

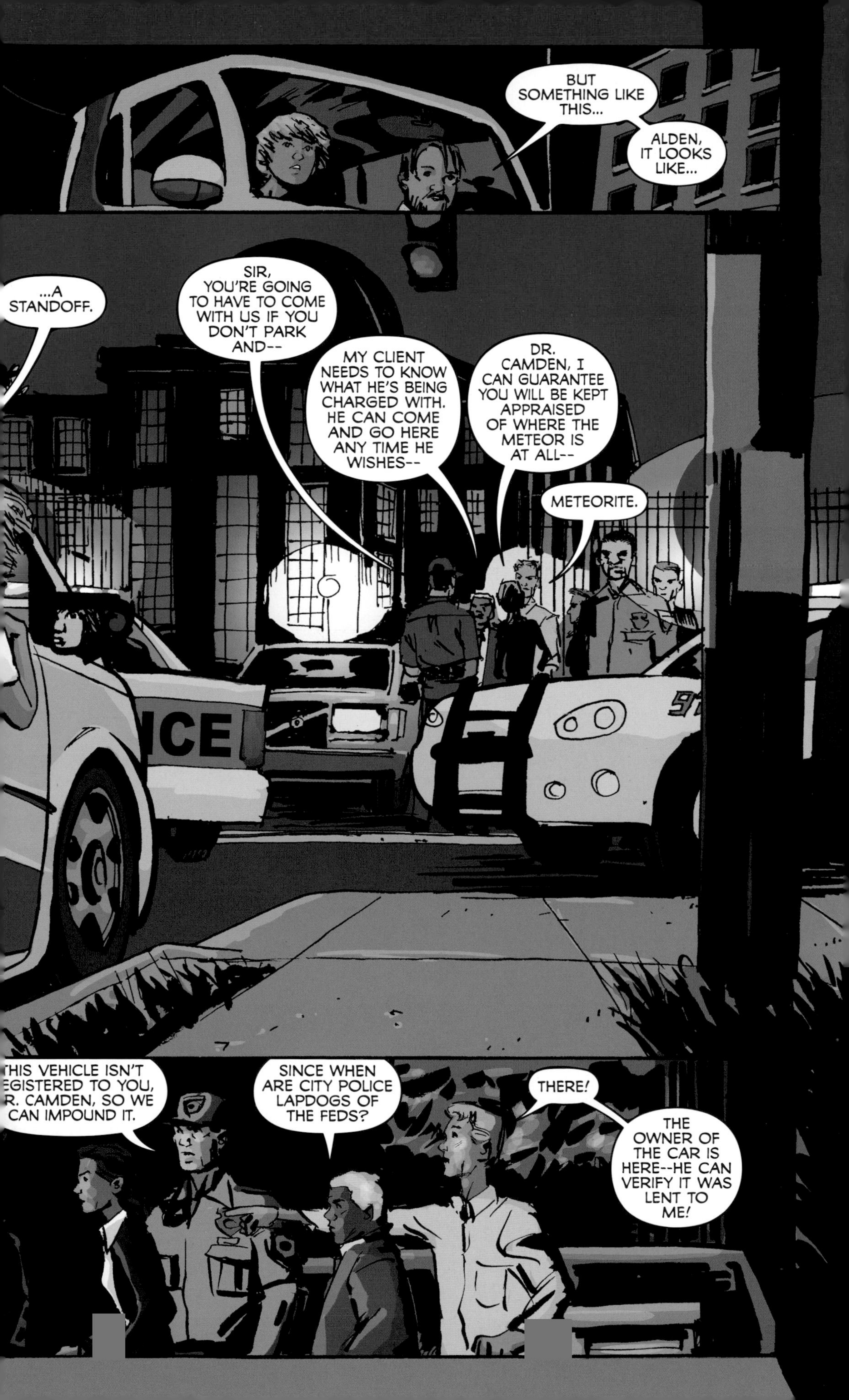
BUT SOMETHING LIKE THIS...
ALDEN, IT LOOKS LIKE...
...A STANDOFF.
SIR, YOU'RE GOING TO HAVE TO COME WITH US IF YOU DON'T PARK AND--
MY CLIENT NEEDS TO KNOW WHAT HE'S BEING CHARGED WITH. HE CAN COME AND GO HERE ANY TIME HE WISHES--
DR. CAMDEN, I CAN GUARANTEE YOU WILL BE KEPT APPRAISED OF WHERE THE METEOR IS AT ALL--
METEORITE.
THIS VEHICLE ISN'T EGISTERED TO YOU, R. CAMDEN, SO WE CAN IMPOUND IT.
SINCE WHEN ARE CITY POLICE LAPDOGS OF THE FEDS?
THERE!
THE OWNER OF THE CAR IS HERE--HE CAN VERIFY IT WAS LENT TO ME!

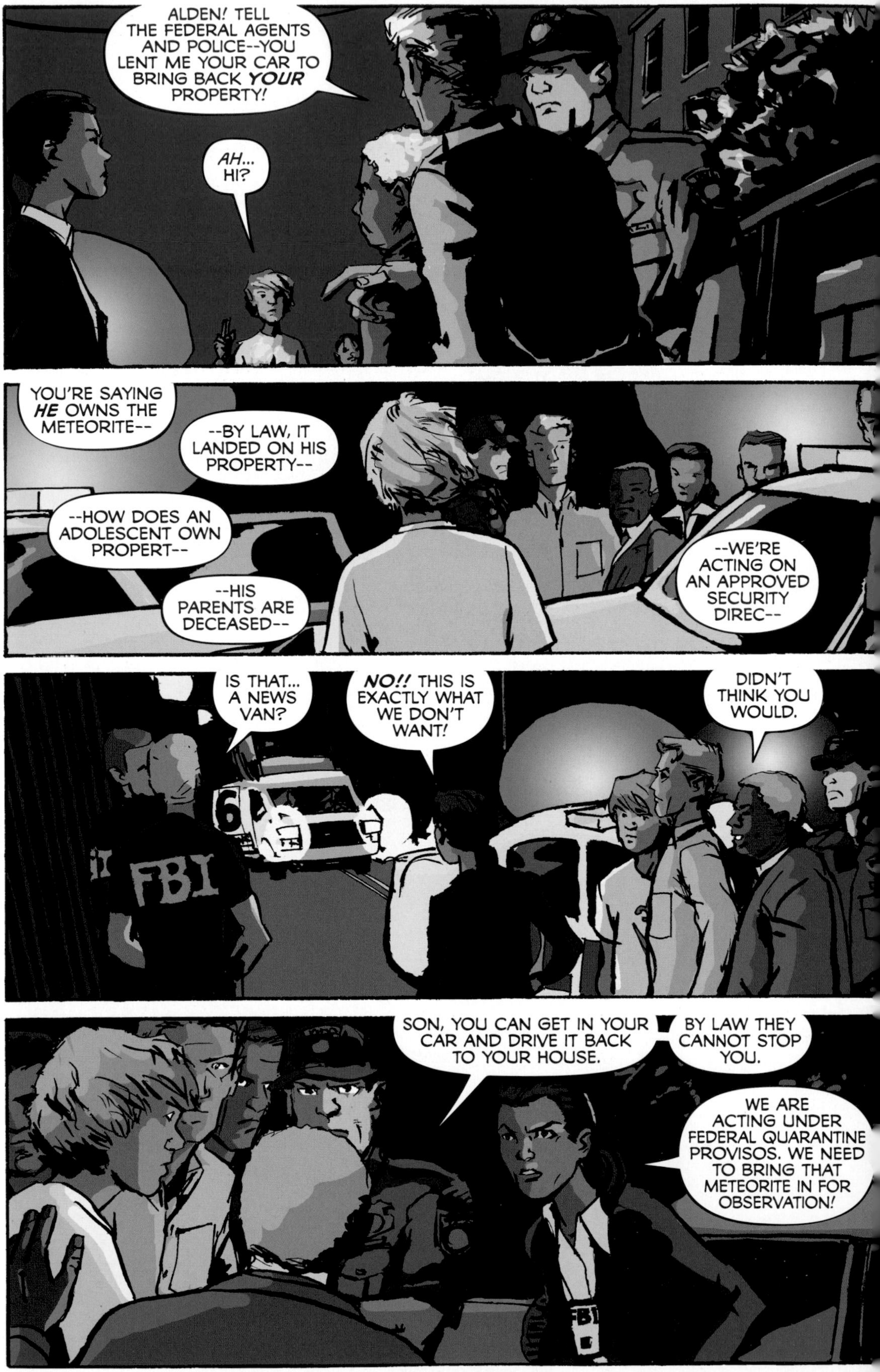
ALDEN! TELL THE FEDERAL AGENTS AND POLICE--YOU LENT ME YOUR CAR TO BRING BACK *YOUR* PROPERTY!
AH... HI?
YOU'RE SAYING *HE* OWNS THE METEORITE--
--BY LAW, IT LANDED ON HIS PROPERTY--
--HOW DOES AN ADOLESCENT OWN PROPERT--
--HIS PARENTS ARE DECEASED--
--WE'RE ACTING ON AN APPROVED SECURITY DIREC--
IS THAT... A NEWS VAN?
NO!! THIS IS EXACTLY WHAT WE DON'T WANT!
DIDN'T THINK YOU WOULD.
6
FBI
SON, YOU CAN GET IN YOUR CAR AND DRIVE IT BACK TO YOUR HOUSE.
BY LAW THEY CANNOT STOP YOU.
WE ARE ACTING UNDER FEDERAL QUARANTINE PROVISOS. WE NEED TO BRING THAT METEORITE IN FOR OBSERVATION!

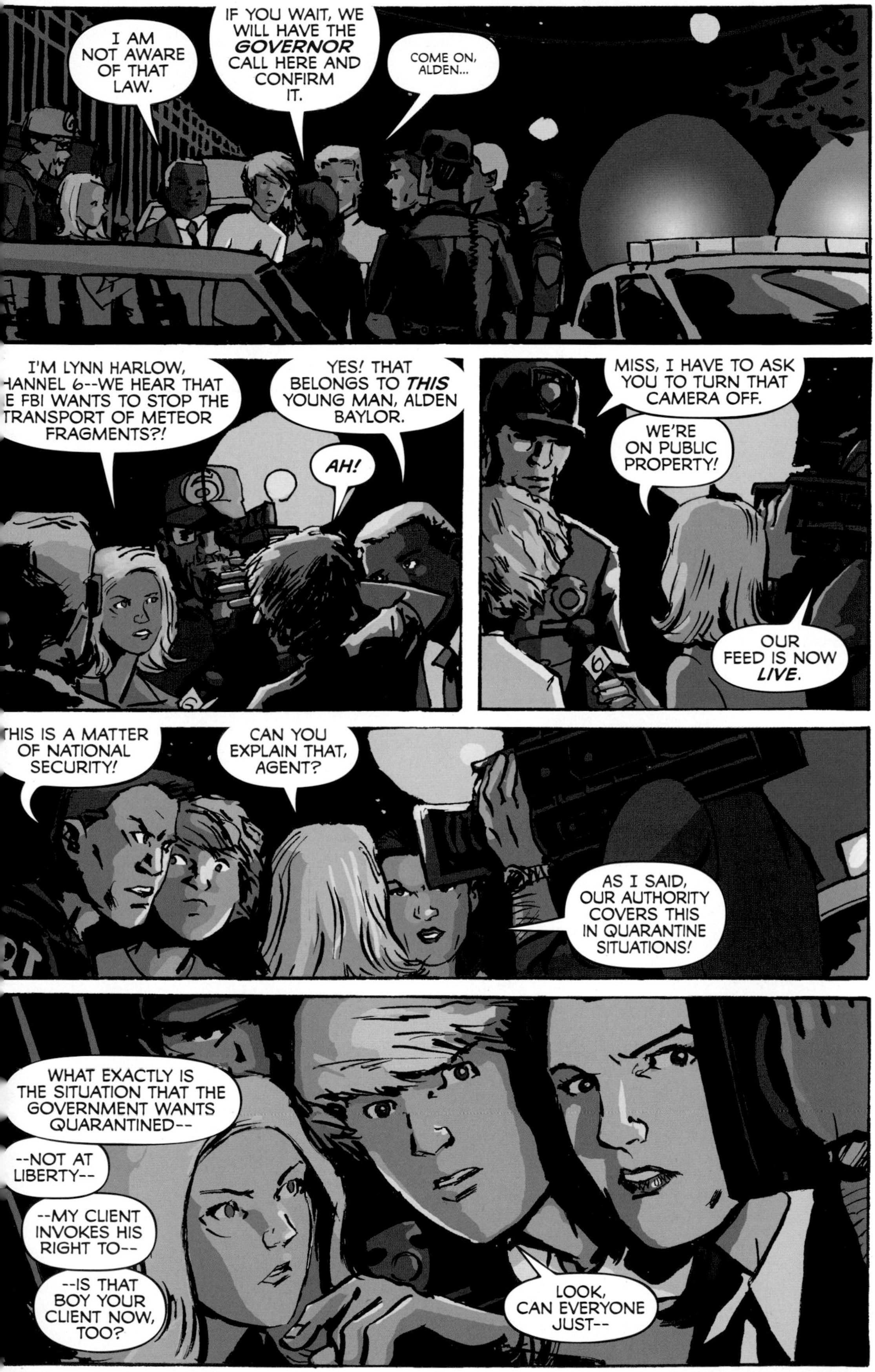
I AM NOT AWARE OF THAT LAW.
IF YOU WAIT, WE WILL HAVE THE ***GOVERNOR*** CALL HERE AND CONFIRM IT.
COME ON, ALDEN...
I'M LYNN HARLOW, HANNEL 6--WE HEAR THAT E FBI WANTS TO STOP THE TRANSPORT OF METEOR FRAGMENTS?!
YES! THAT BELONGS TO ***THIS*** YOUNG MAN, ALDEN BAYLOR.
AH!
MISS, I HAVE TO ASK YOU TO TURN THAT CAMERA OFF.
WE'RE ON PUBLIC PROPERTY!
OUR FEED IS NOW ***LIVE***.
HIS IS A MATTER OF NATIONAL SECURITY!
CAN YOU EXPLAIN THAT, AGENT?
AS I SAID, OUR AUTHORITY COVERS THIS IN QUARANTINE SITUATIONS!
WHAT EXACTLY IS THE SITUATION THAT THE GOVERNMENT WANTS QUARANTINED--
--NOT AT LIBERTY--
--MY CLIENT INVOKES HIS RIGHT TO--
--IS THAT BOY YOUR CLIENT NOW, TOO?
LOOK, CAN EVERYONE JUST--

KEEP YOUR HANDS TO YOURSELF!
HEY!
WHAT-- WHAT ARE YOU DOING!
HE'S DONE NOTHING WRONG!
EVERYONE NEEDS TO STEP BACK *NOW*--
TAKE THAT CAMERA OUT OF HERE OR YOU WILL BE--
AH--
POLICE
A STORM?
I'M INVOKING FEDERAL AUTHORITY, IF YOU DON'T ALL MOVE AWAY--
LOOK! LOOK UP THERE!
JASON, ARE YOU RECORDING?!
THERE'S NO WAY--
THERE *IS* ONE... *HERE!*

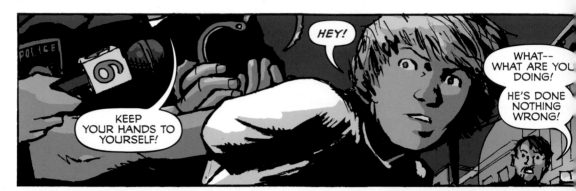

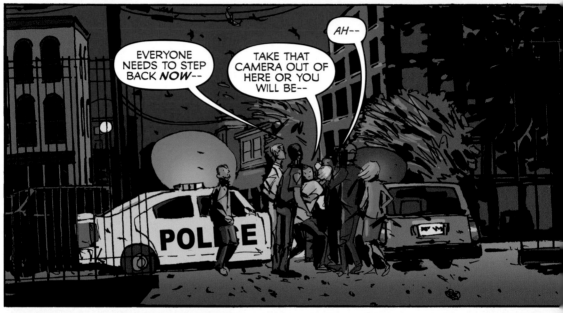

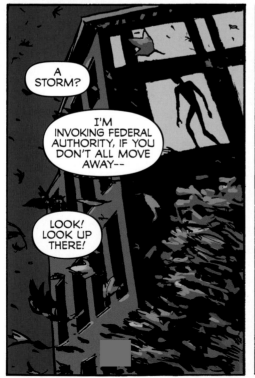

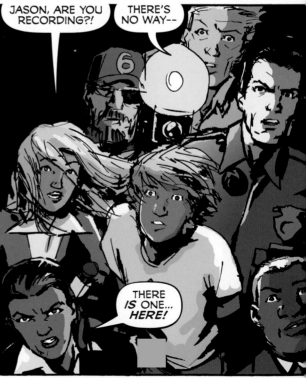

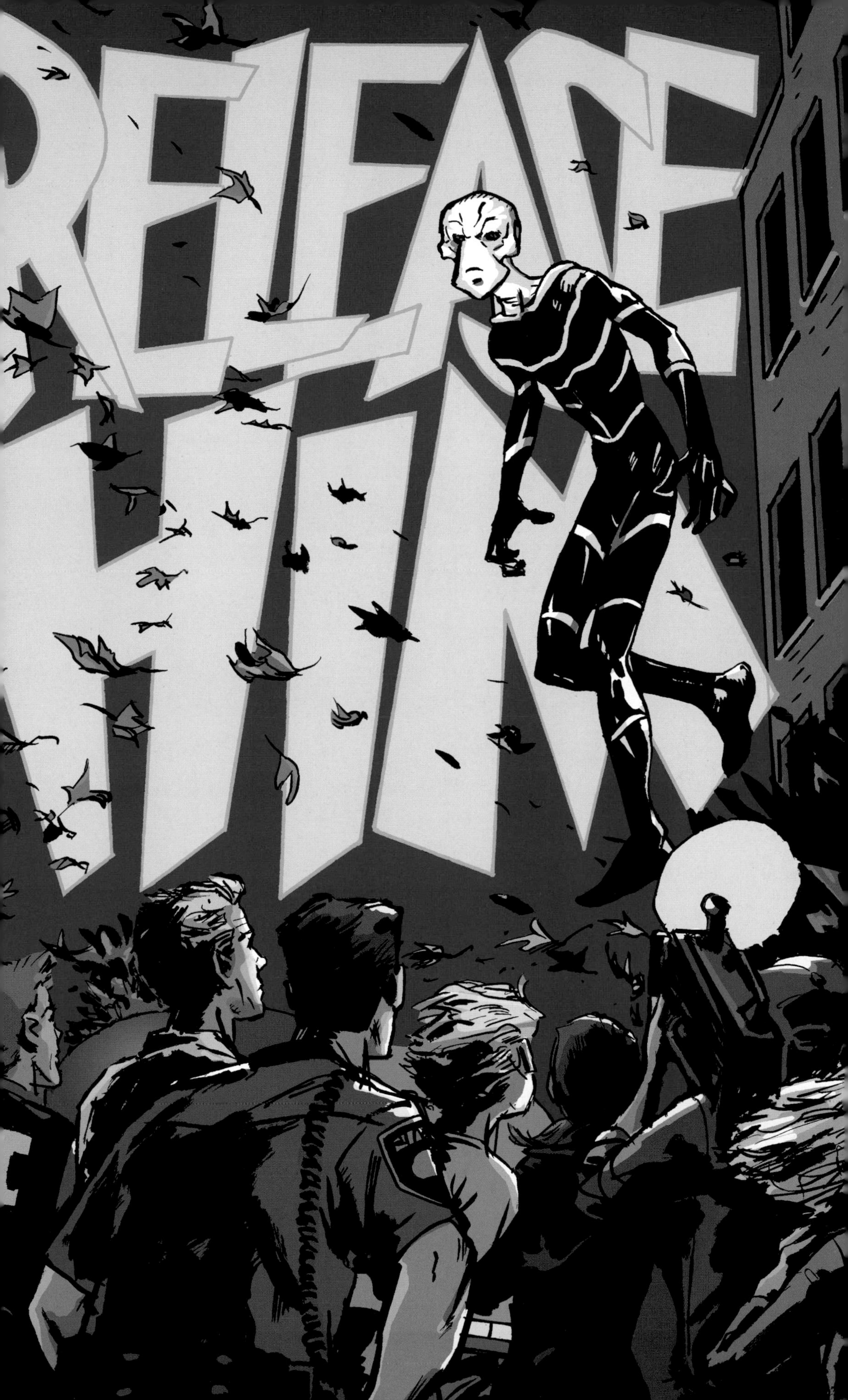
RELEASE HIM

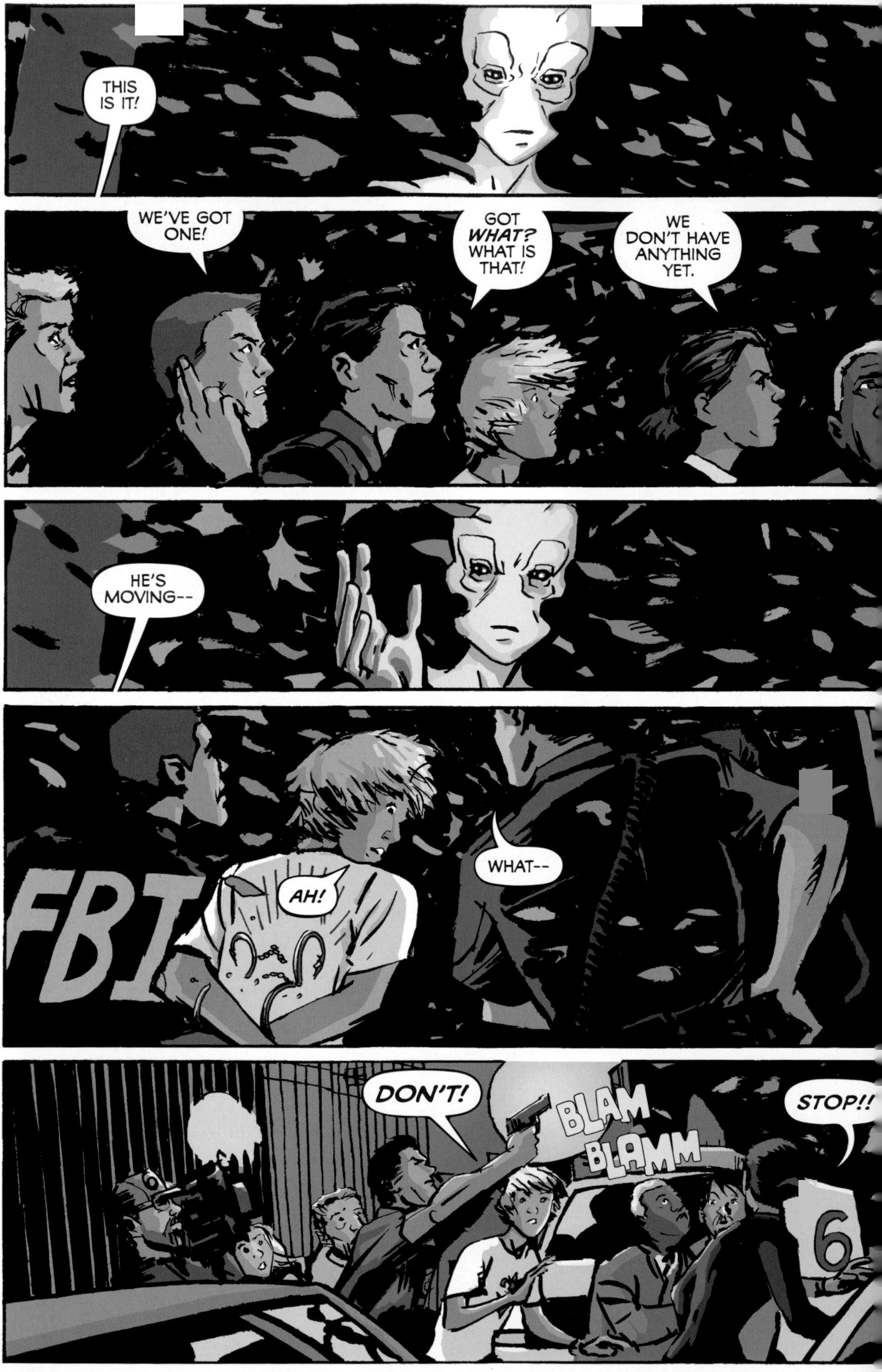
THIS IS IT!
WE'VE GOT ONE!
GOT *WHAT?* WHAT IS THAT!
WE DON'T HAVE ANYTHING YET.
HE'S MOVING--
FBI
AH!
WHAT--
DON'T!
BLAM
BLAMM
STOP!!
6

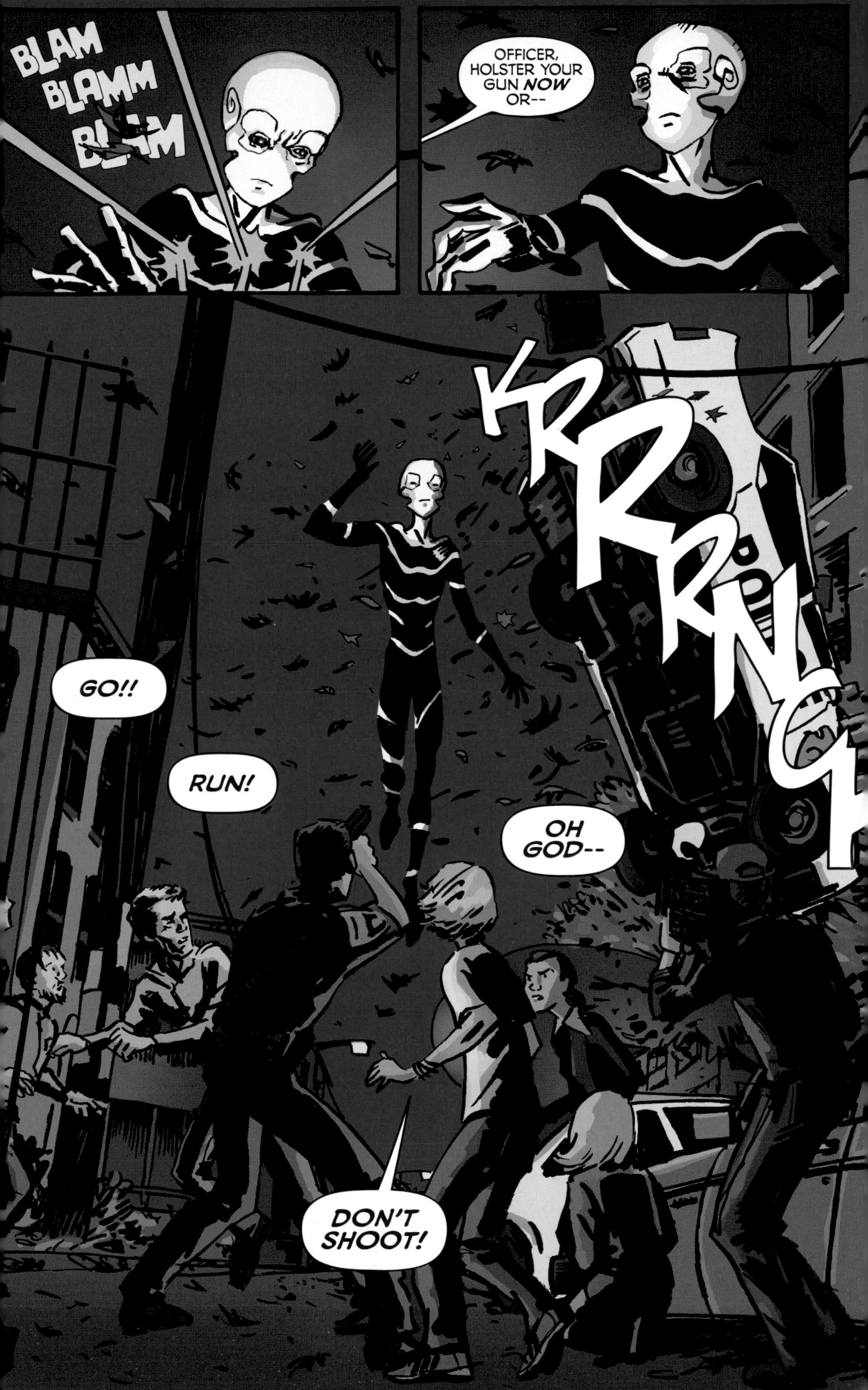
BLAM
BLAMM
BLAM
OFFICER, HOLSTER YOUR GUN *NOW* OR--
KRRRNCH
GO!!
RUN!
OH GOD--
DON'T SHOOT!

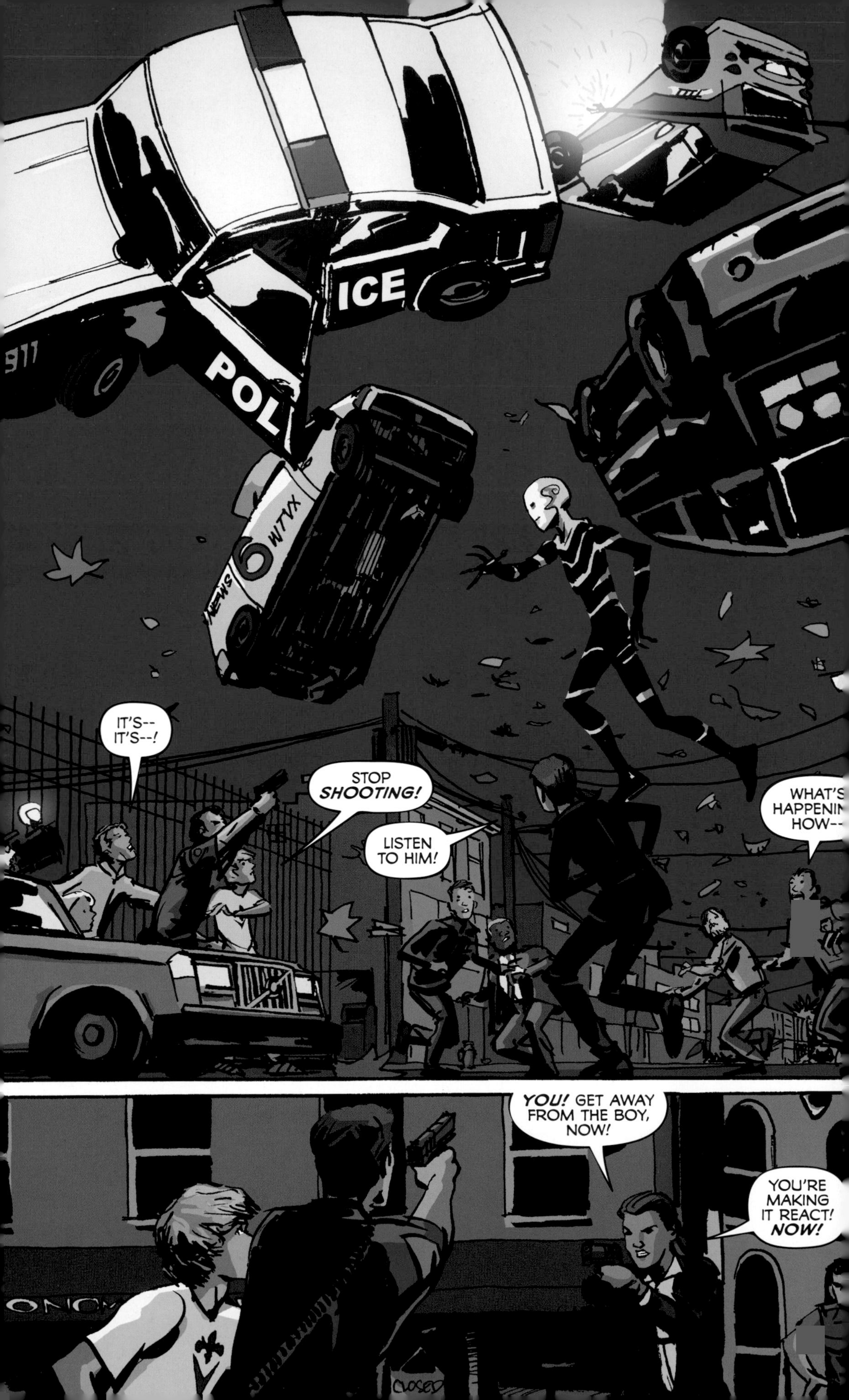
ICE
POL
911
WTVX
NEWS 6
IT'S-- IT'S--!
STOP SHOOTING!
LISTEN TO HIM!
WHAT'S HAPPENIN HOW--
YOU! GET AWAY FROM THE BOY, NOW!
YOU'RE MAKING IT REACT! NOW!
CLOSED

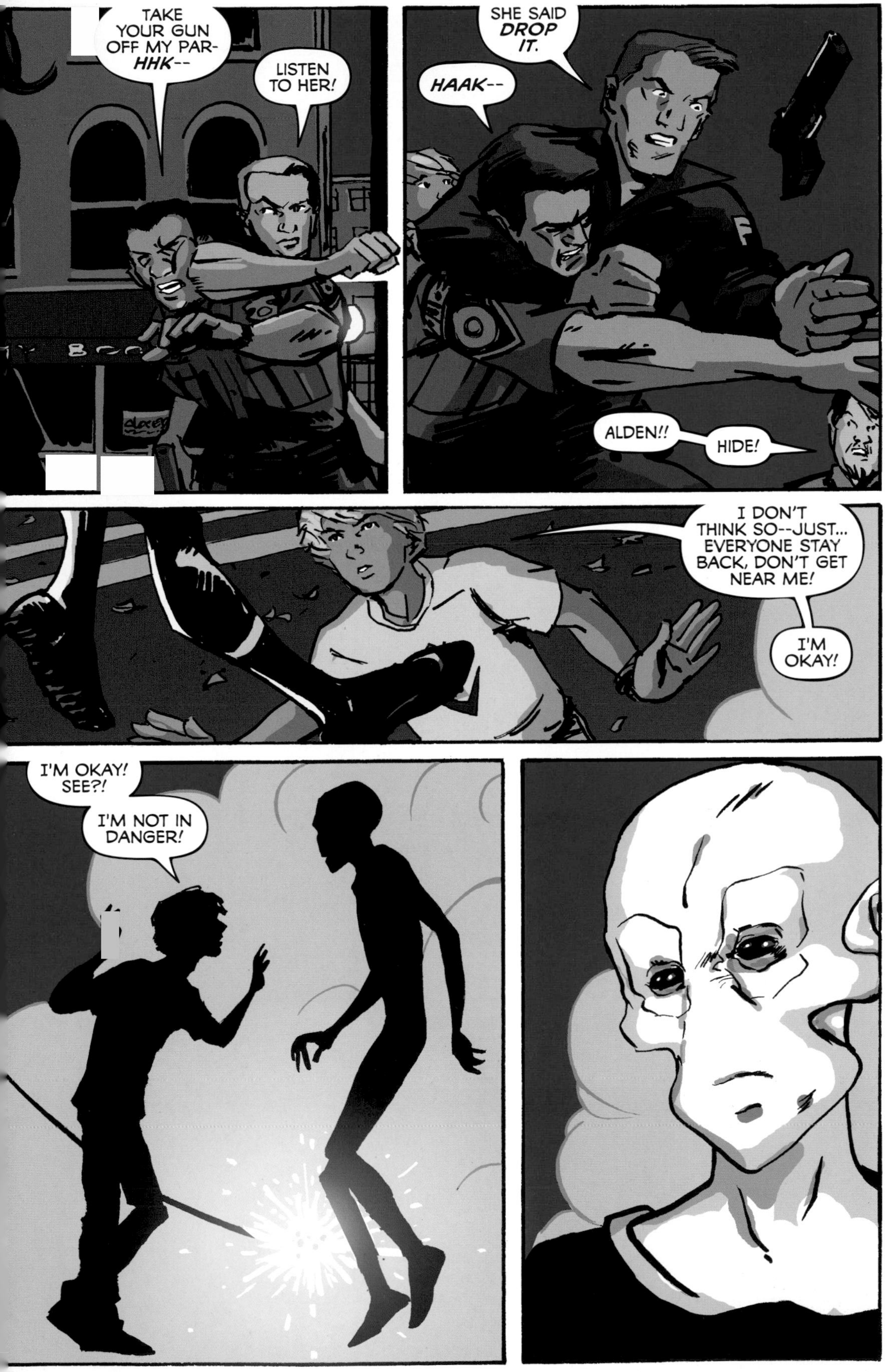
TAKE YOUR GUN OFF MY PAR-HHK--
LISTEN TO HER!
SHE SAID DROP IT.
HAAK--
ALDEN!!
HIDE!
I DON'T THINK SO--JUST... EVERYONE STAY BACK, DON'T GET NEAR ME!
I'M OKAY!
I'M OKAY! SEE?!
I'M NOT IN DANGER!

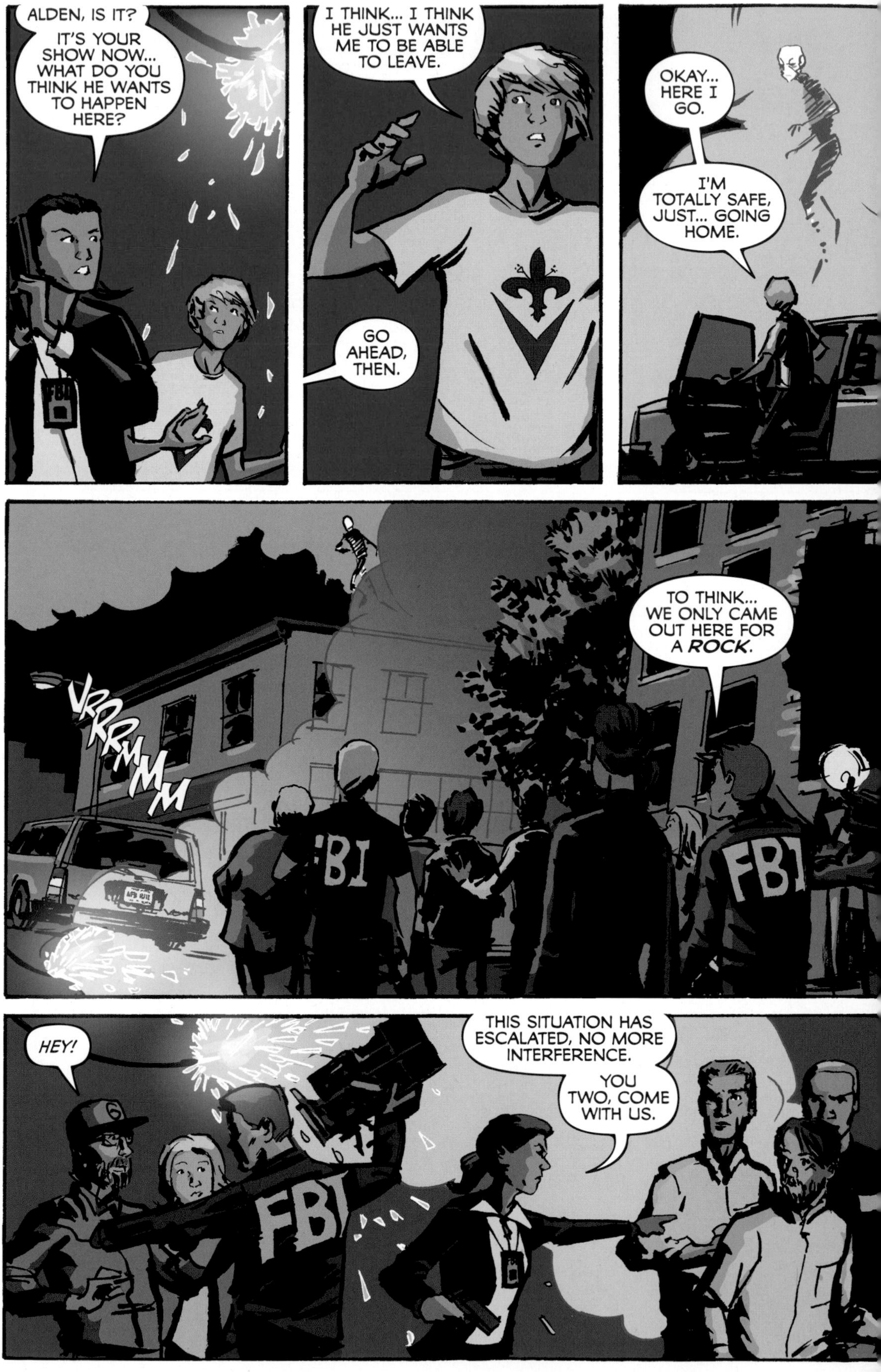
ALDEN, IS IT?
IT'S YOUR SHOW NOW... WHAT DO YOU THINK HE WANTS TO HAPPEN HERE?
I THINK... I THINK HE JUST WANTS ME TO BE ABLE TO LEAVE.
GO AHEAD, THEN.
OKAY... HERE I GO.
I'M TOTALLY SAFE, JUST... GOING HOME.
VRRRMMMM
TO THINK... WE ONLY CAME OUT HERE FOR A *ROCK*.
FBI
FBI
HEY!
THIS SITUATION HAS ESCALATED, NO MORE INTERFERENCE.
YOU TWO, COME WITH US.
FBI

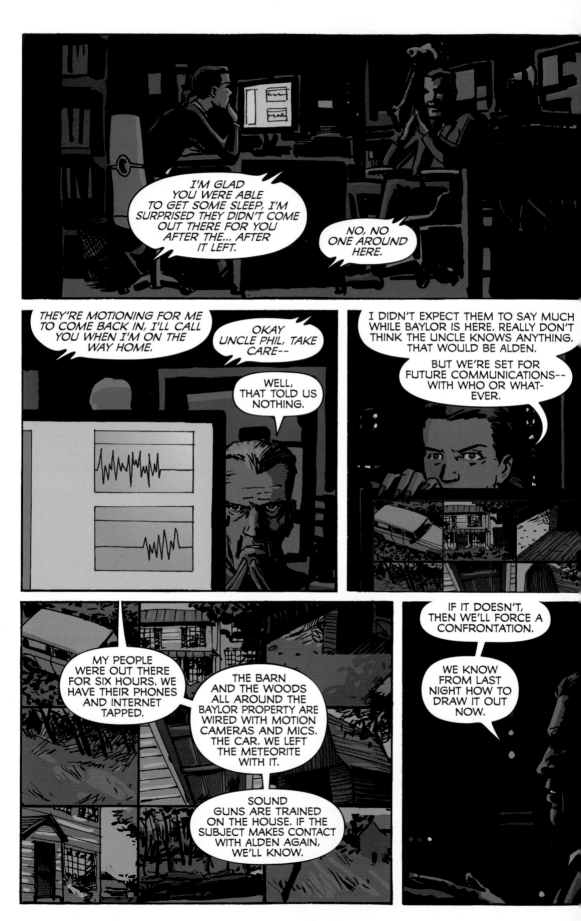

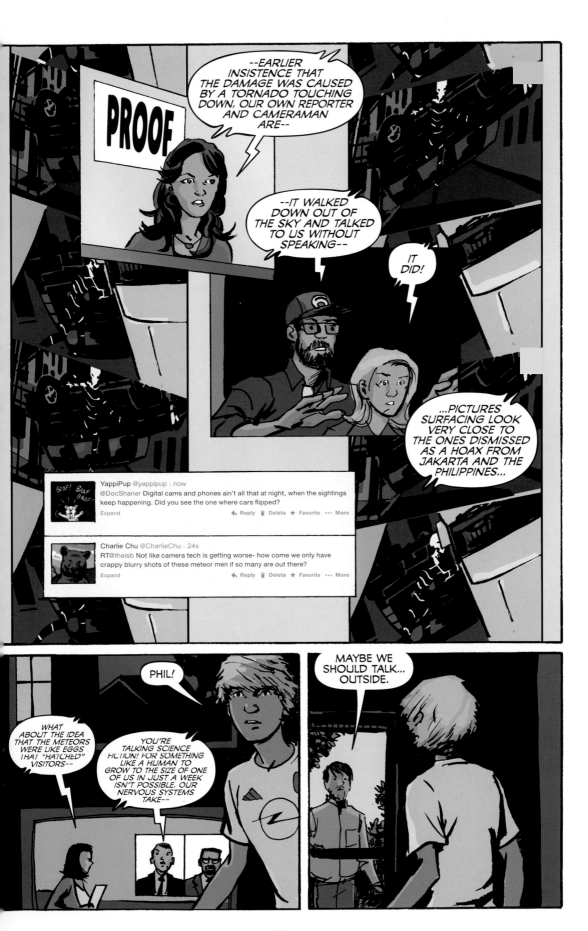

89

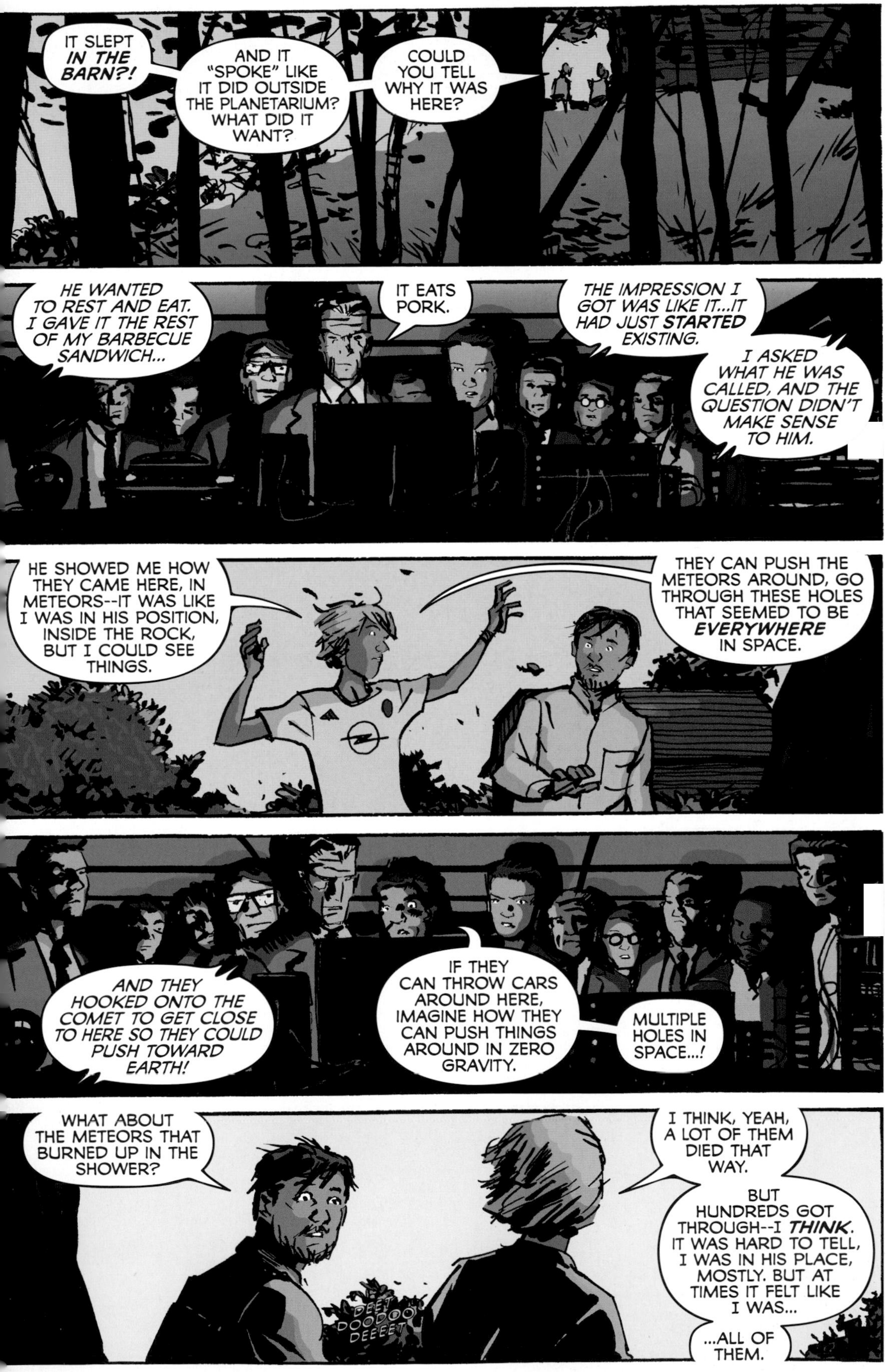
IT SLEPT *IN THE BARN?!*
AND IT "SPOKE" LIKE IT DID OUTSIDE THE PLANETARIUM? WHAT DID IT WANT?
COULD YOU TELL WHY IT WAS HERE?
HE WANTED TO REST AND EAT. I GAVE IT THE REST OF MY BARBECUE SANDWICH...
IT EATS PORK.
*THE IMPRESSION I GOT WAS LIKE IT...IT HAD JUST **STARTED** EXISTING.*
I ASKED WHAT HE WAS CALLED, AND THE QUESTION DIDN'T MAKE SENSE TO HIM.
HE SHOWED ME HOW THEY CAME HERE, IN METEORS--IT WAS LIKE I WAS IN HIS POSITION, INSIDE THE ROCK, BUT I COULD SEE THINGS.
THEY CAN PUSH THE METEORS AROUND, GO THROUGH THESE HOLES THAT SEEMED TO BE ***EVERYWHERE*** IN SPACE.
AND THEY HOOKED ONTO THE COMET TO GET CLOSE TO HERE SO THEY COULD PUSH TOWARD EARTH!
IF THEY CAN THROW CARS AROUND HERE, IMAGINE HOW THEY CAN PUSH THINGS AROUND IN ZERO GRAVITY.
MULTIPLE HOLES IN SPACE...!
WHAT ABOUT THE METEORS THAT BURNED UP IN THE SHOWER?
I THINK, YEAH, A LOT OF THEM DIED THAT WAY.
BUT HUNDREDS GOT THROUGH--I ***THINK***. IT WAS HARD TO TELL, I WAS IN HIS PLACE, MOSTLY. BUT AT TIMES IT FELT LIKE I WAS...
...ALL OF THEM.
DEET DOODOO DEEEET

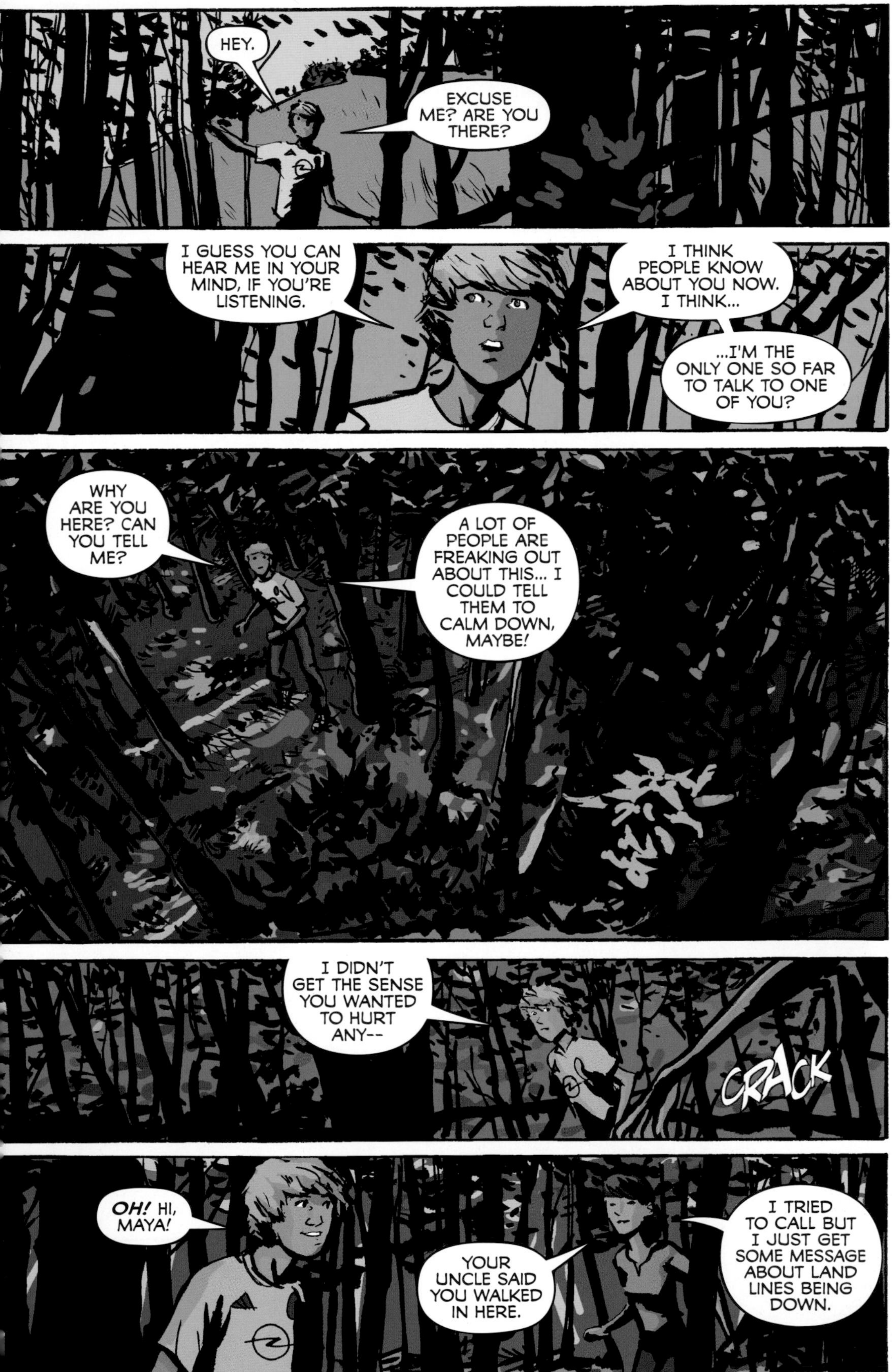
HEY.
EXCUSE ME? ARE YOU THERE?
I GUESS YOU CAN HEAR ME IN YOUR MIND, IF YOU'RE LISTENING.
I THINK PEOPLE KNOW ABOUT YOU NOW. I THINK...
...I'M THE ONLY ONE SO FAR TO TALK TO ONE OF YOU?
WHY ARE YOU HERE? CAN YOU TELL ME?
A LOT OF PEOPLE ARE FREAKING OUT ABOUT THIS... I COULD TELL THEM TO CALM DOWN, MAYBE!
I DIDN'T GET THE SENSE YOU WANTED TO HURT ANY--
CRACK
OH! HI, MAYA!
YOUR UNCLE SAID YOU WALKED IN HERE.
I TRIED TO CALL BUT I JUST GET SOME MESSAGE ABOUT LAND LINES BEING DOWN.

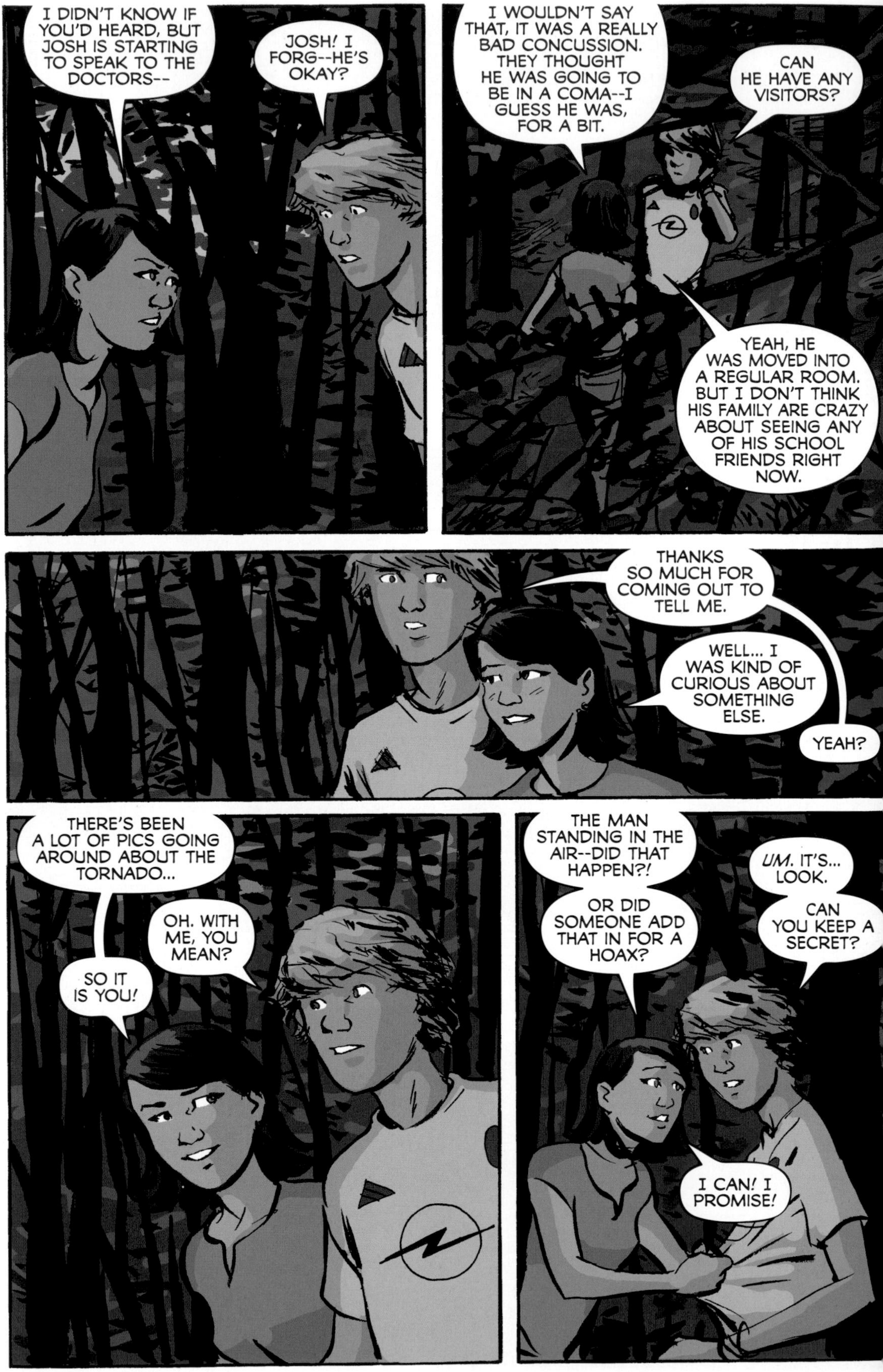
I DIDN'T KNOW IF YOU'D HEARD, BUT JOSH IS STARTING TO SPEAK TO THE DOCTORS--
JOSH! I FORG--HE'S OKAY?
I WOULDN'T SAY THAT, IT WAS A REALLY BAD CONCUSSION. THEY THOUGHT HE WAS GOING TO BE IN A COMA--I GUESS HE WAS, FOR A BIT.
CAN HE HAVE ANY VISITORS?
YEAH, HE WAS MOVED INTO A REGULAR ROOM. BUT I DON'T THINK HIS FAMILY ARE CRAZY ABOUT SEEING ANY OF HIS SCHOOL FRIENDS RIGHT NOW.
THANKS SO MUCH FOR COMING OUT TO TELL ME.
WELL... I WAS KIND OF CURIOUS ABOUT SOMETHING ELSE.
YEAH?
THERE'S BEEN A LOT OF PICS GOING AROUND ABOUT THE TORNADO...
OH. WITH ME, YOU MEAN?
SO IT IS YOU!
THE MAN STANDING IN THE AIR--DID THAT HAPPEN?!
OR DID SOMEONE ADD THAT IN FOR A HOAX?
UM. IT'S... LOOK.
CAN YOU KEEP A SECRET?
I CAN! I PROMISE!

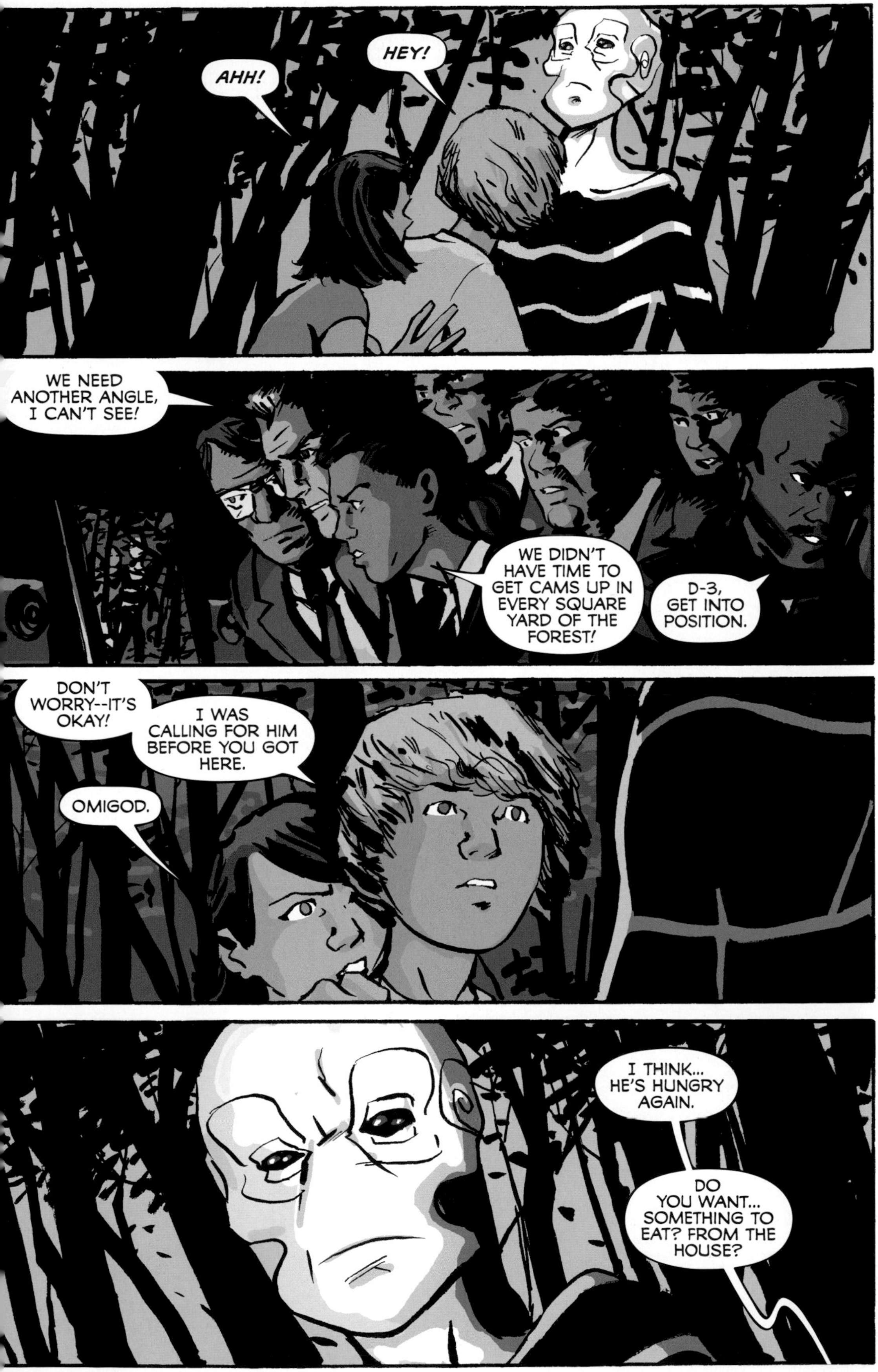
AHH!
HEY!
WE NEED ANOTHER ANGLE, I CAN'T SEE!
WE DIDN'T HAVE TIME TO GET CAMS UP IN EVERY SQUARE YARD OF THE FOREST!
D-3, GET INTO POSITION.
DON'T WORRY--IT'S OKAY!
I WAS CALLING FOR HIM BEFORE YOU GOT HERE.
OMIGOD.
I THINK... HE'S HUNGRY AGAIN.
DO YOU WANT... SOMETHING TO EAT? FROM THE HOUSE?

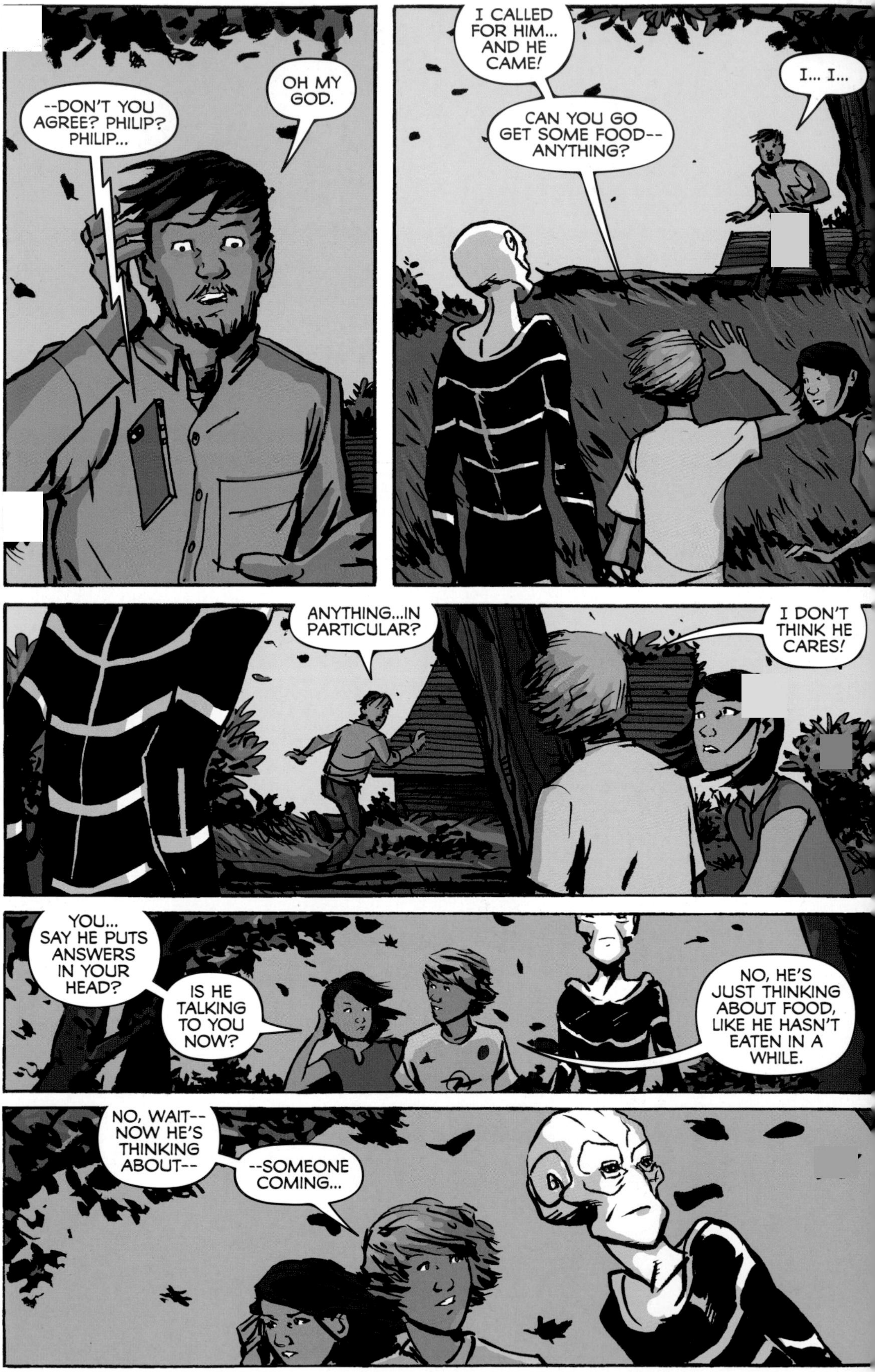
--DON'T YOU AGREE? PHILIP? PHILIP...
OH MY GOD.
I CALLED FOR HIM... AND HE CAME!
CAN YOU GO GET SOME FOOD-- ANYTHING?
I... I...
ANYTHING...IN PARTICULAR?
I DON'T THINK HE CARES!
YOU... SAY HE PUTS ANSWERS IN YOUR HEAD?
IS HE TALKING TO YOU NOW?
NO, HE'S JUST THINKING ABOUT FOOD, LIKE HE HASN'T EATEN IN A WHILE.
NO, WAIT-- NOW HE'S THINKING ABOUT--
--SOMEONE COMING...

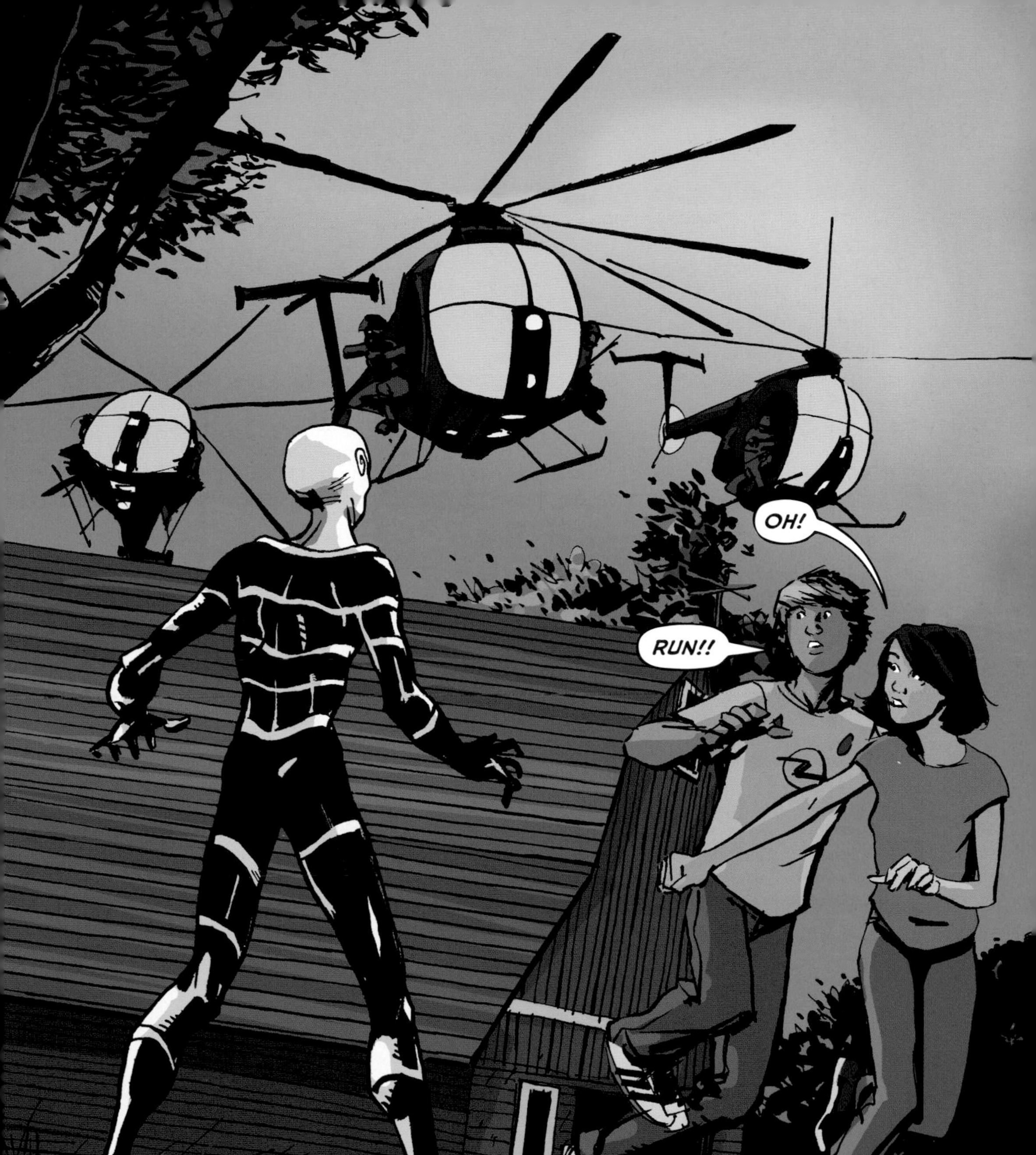
OH!
RUN!!
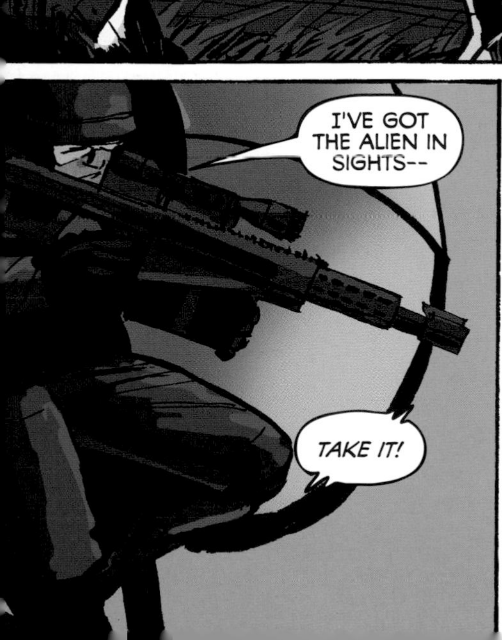
I'VE GOT THE ALIEN IN SIGHTS--
TAKE IT!
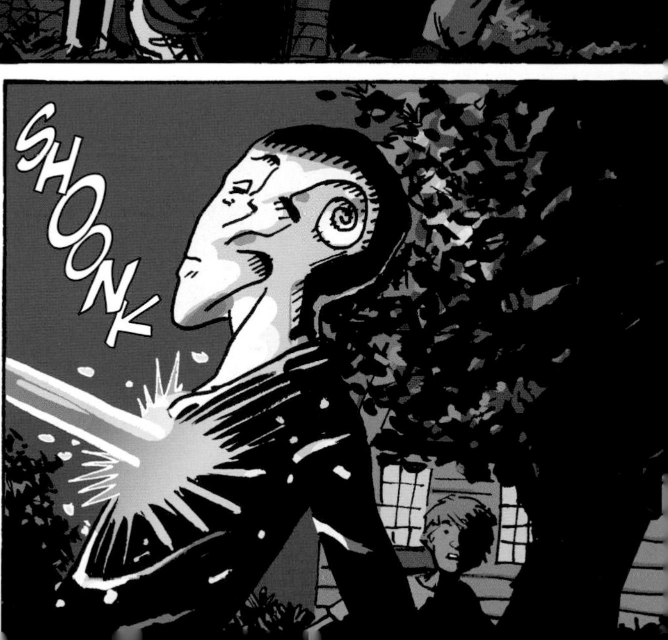
SHOONK

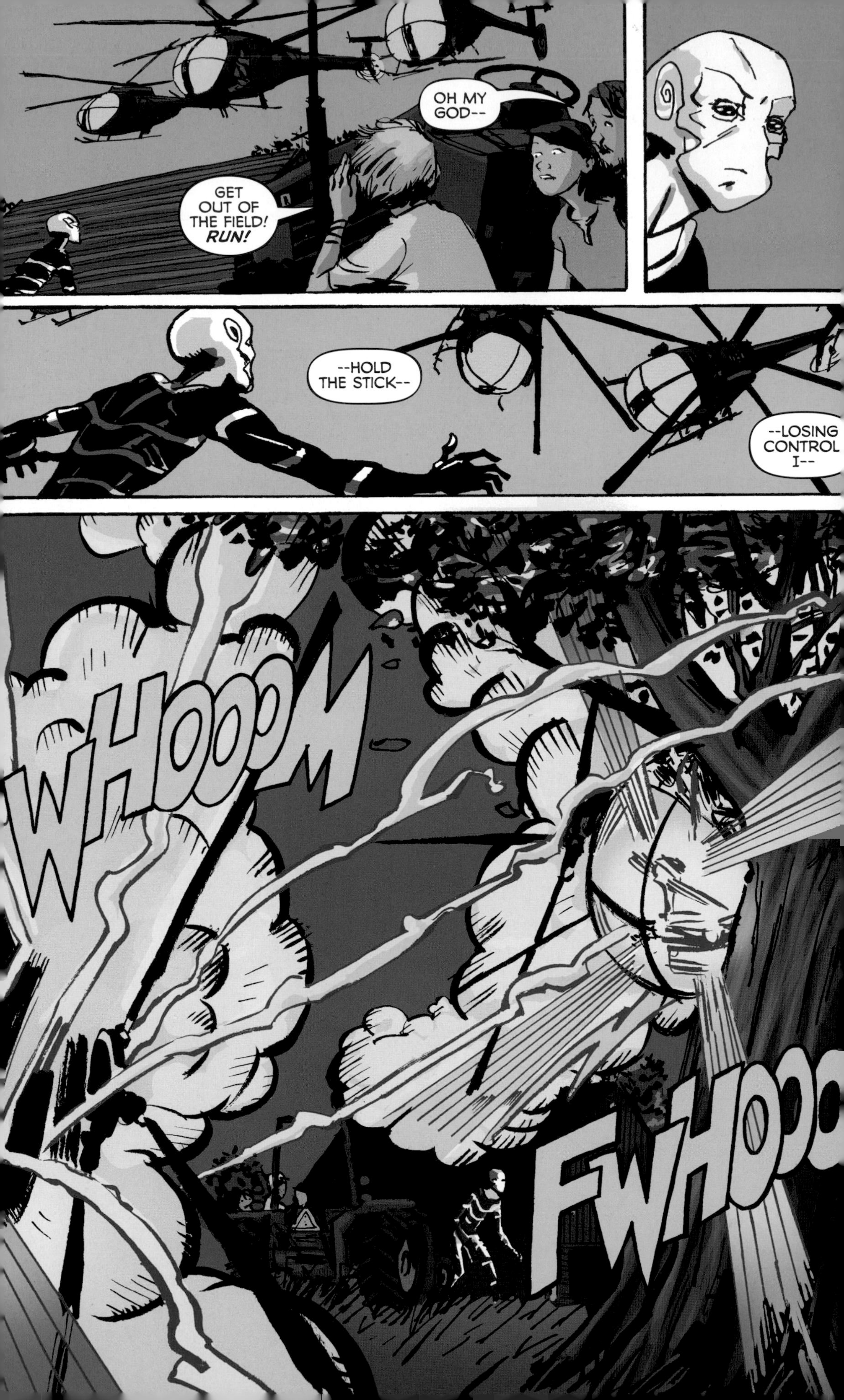
OH MY GOD--
GET OUT OF THE FIELD! *RUN!*
--HOLD THE STICK--
--LOSING CONTROL I--
WHOOOM
FWHOO

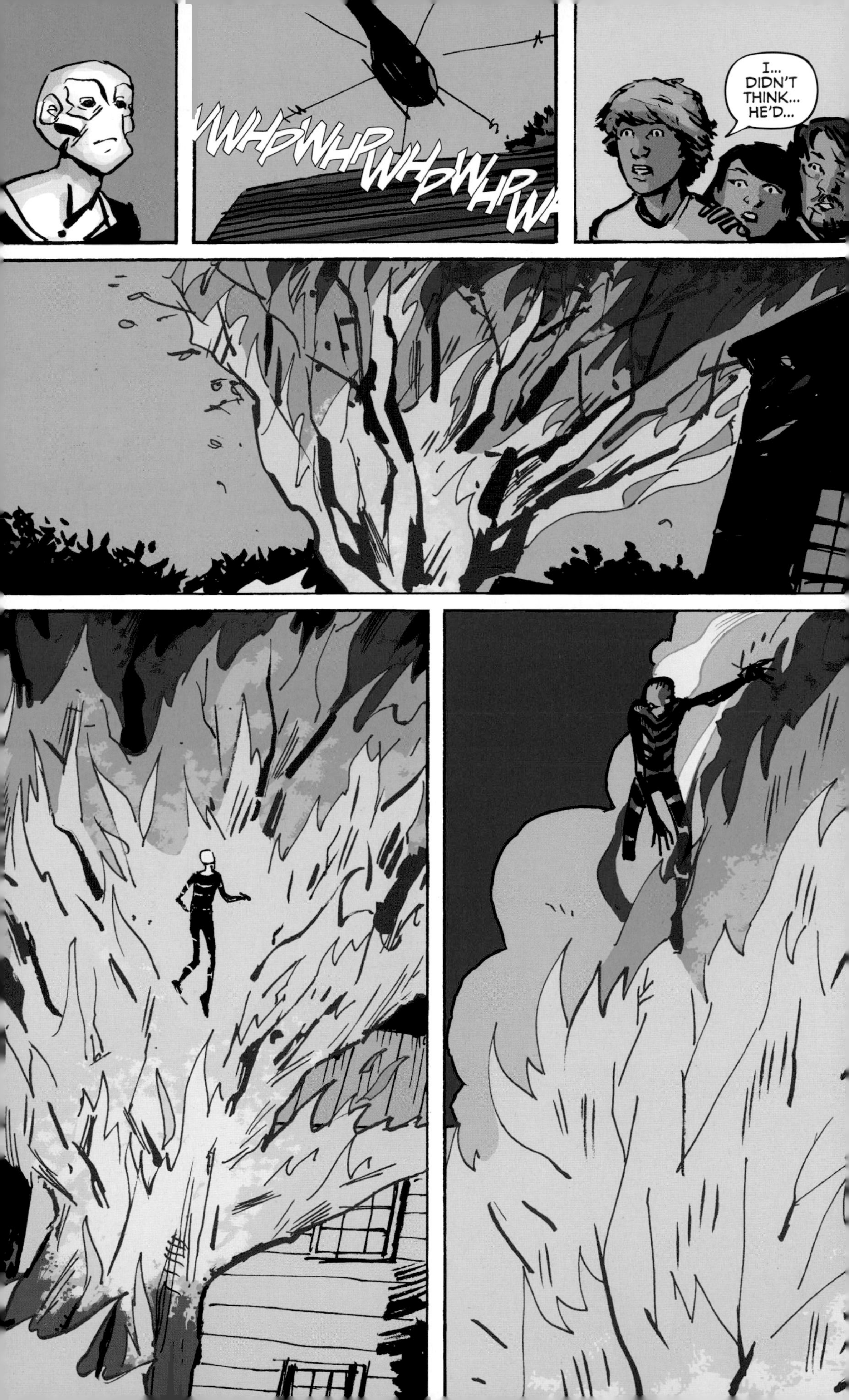
WHPWHPWHPWHPWA
I... DIDN'T THINK... HE'D...

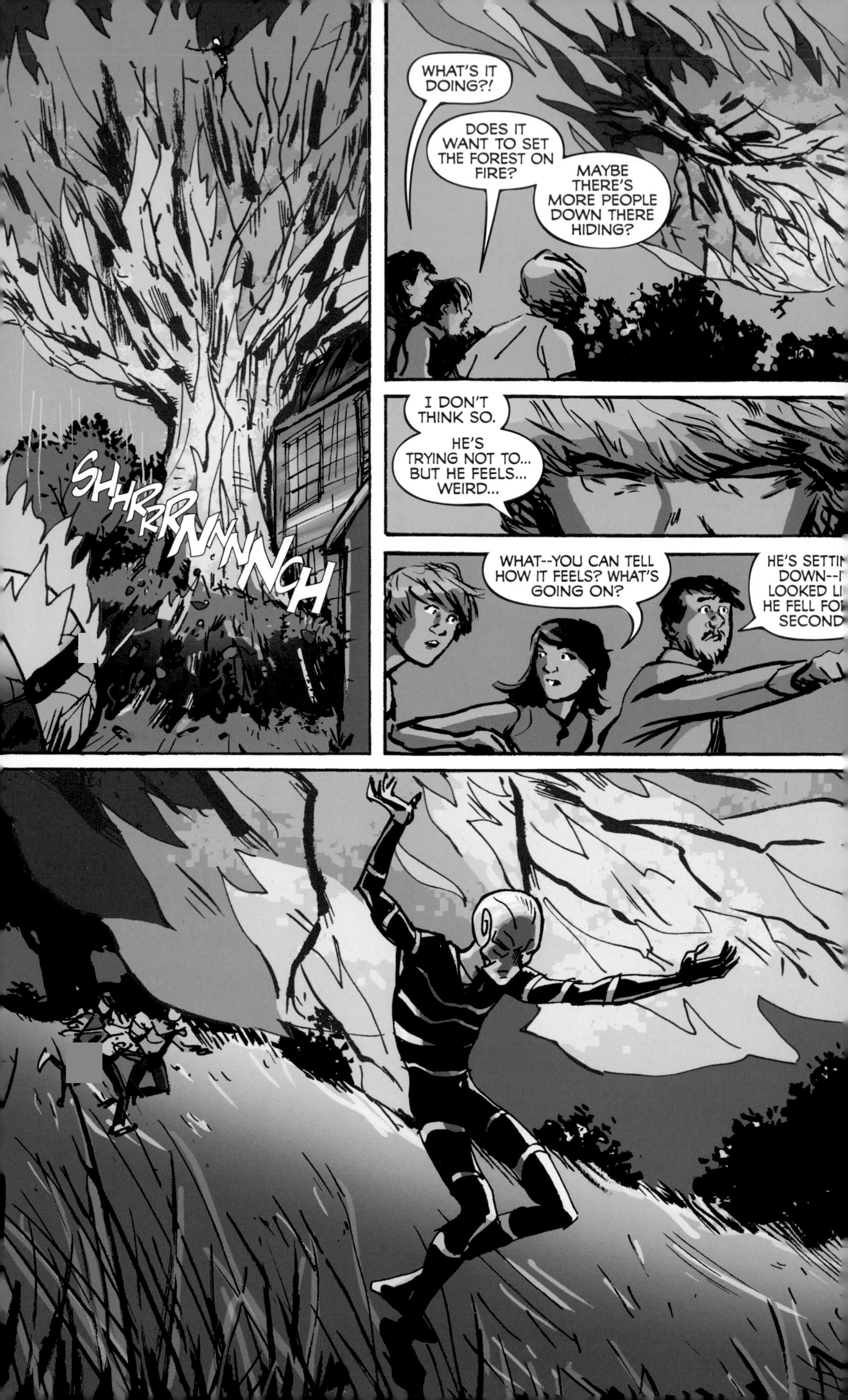
SHHRRRNNNNCH
WHAT'S IT DOING?!
DOES IT WANT TO SET THE FOREST ON FIRE?
MAYBE THERE'S MORE PEOPLE DOWN THERE HIDING?
I DON'T THINK SO.
HE'S TRYING NOT TO... BUT HE FEELS... WEIRD...
WHAT--YOU CAN TELL HOW IT FEELS? WHAT'S GOING ON?
HE'S SETTIN DOWN--I LOOKED LI HE FELL FOR SECOND

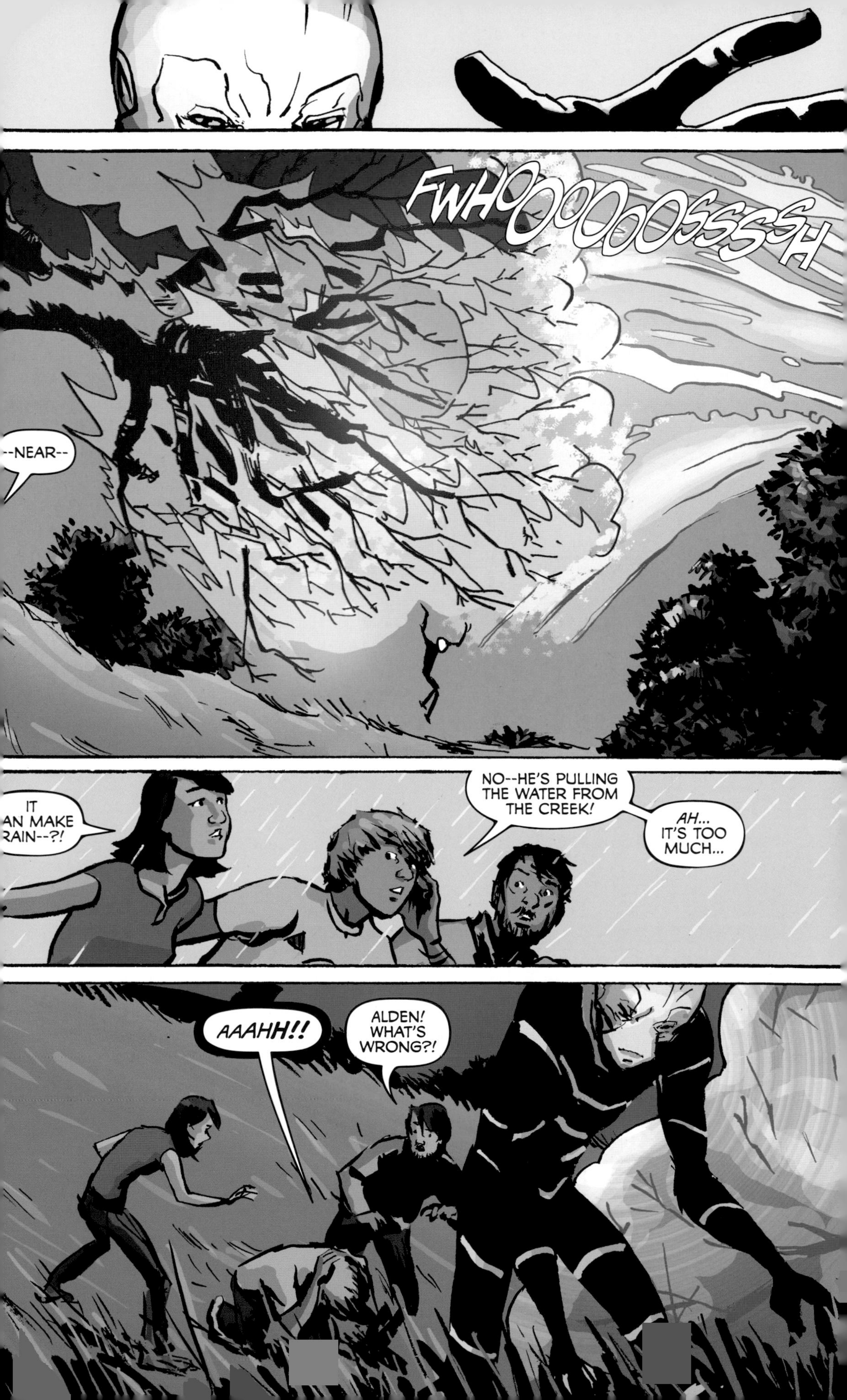
FWHOOOOOOOSSSSSH
--NEAR--
IT
AN MAKE
RAIN--?!
NO--HE'S PULLING
THE WATER FROM
THE CREEK!
AH...
IT'S TOO
MUCH...
AAAHH!!
ALDEN!
WHAT'S
WRONG?!

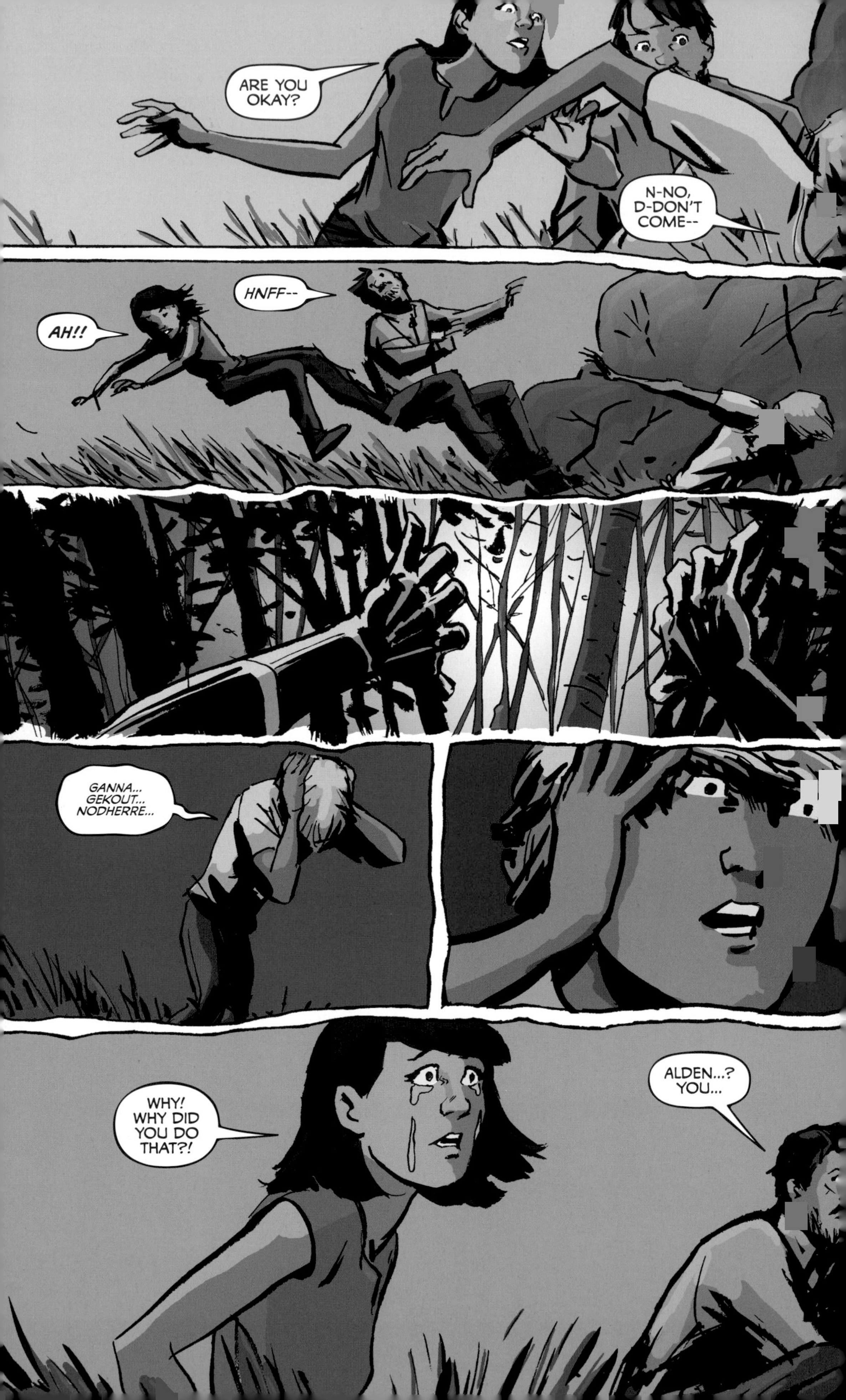
ARE YOU OKAY?
N-NO, D-DON'T COME--
AH!!
HNFF--
GANNA... GEKOUT... NODHERRE...
WHY! WHY DID YOU DO THAT?!
ALDEN...? YOU...

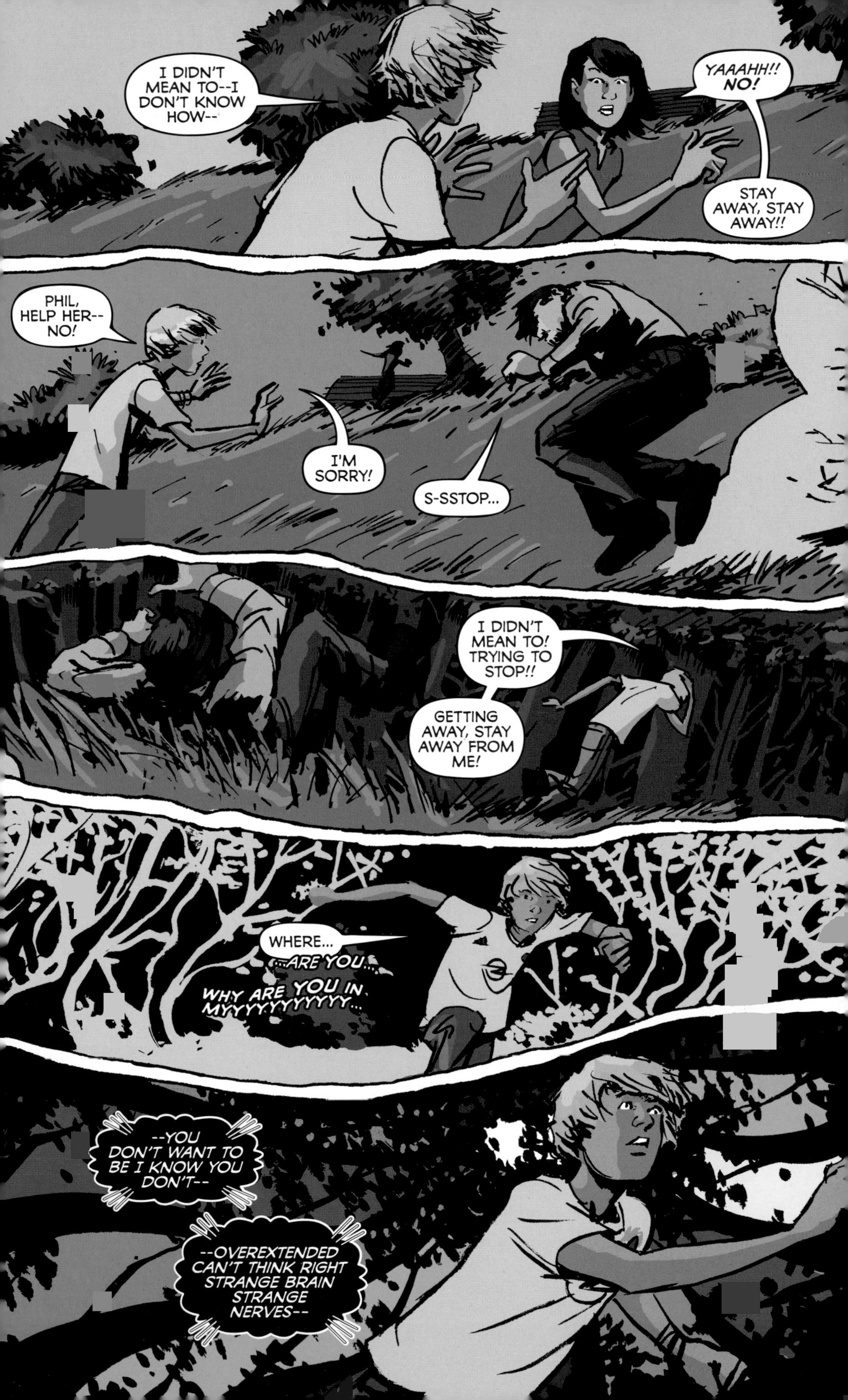
I DIDN'T MEAN TO--I DON'T KNOW HOW--
YAAAHH!! NO!
STAY AWAY, STAY AWAY!!
PHIL, HELP HER-- NO!
I'M SORRY!
S-SSTOP...
I DIDN'T MEAN TO! TRYING TO STOP!!
GETTING AWAY, STAY AWAY FROM ME!
WHERE...
...ARE YOU...
WHY ARE YOU IN MYYYYYYYYYY...
--YOU DON'T WANT TO BE I KNOW YOU DON'T--
--OVEREXTENDED CAN'T THINK RIGHT STRANGE BRAIN STRANGE NERVES--

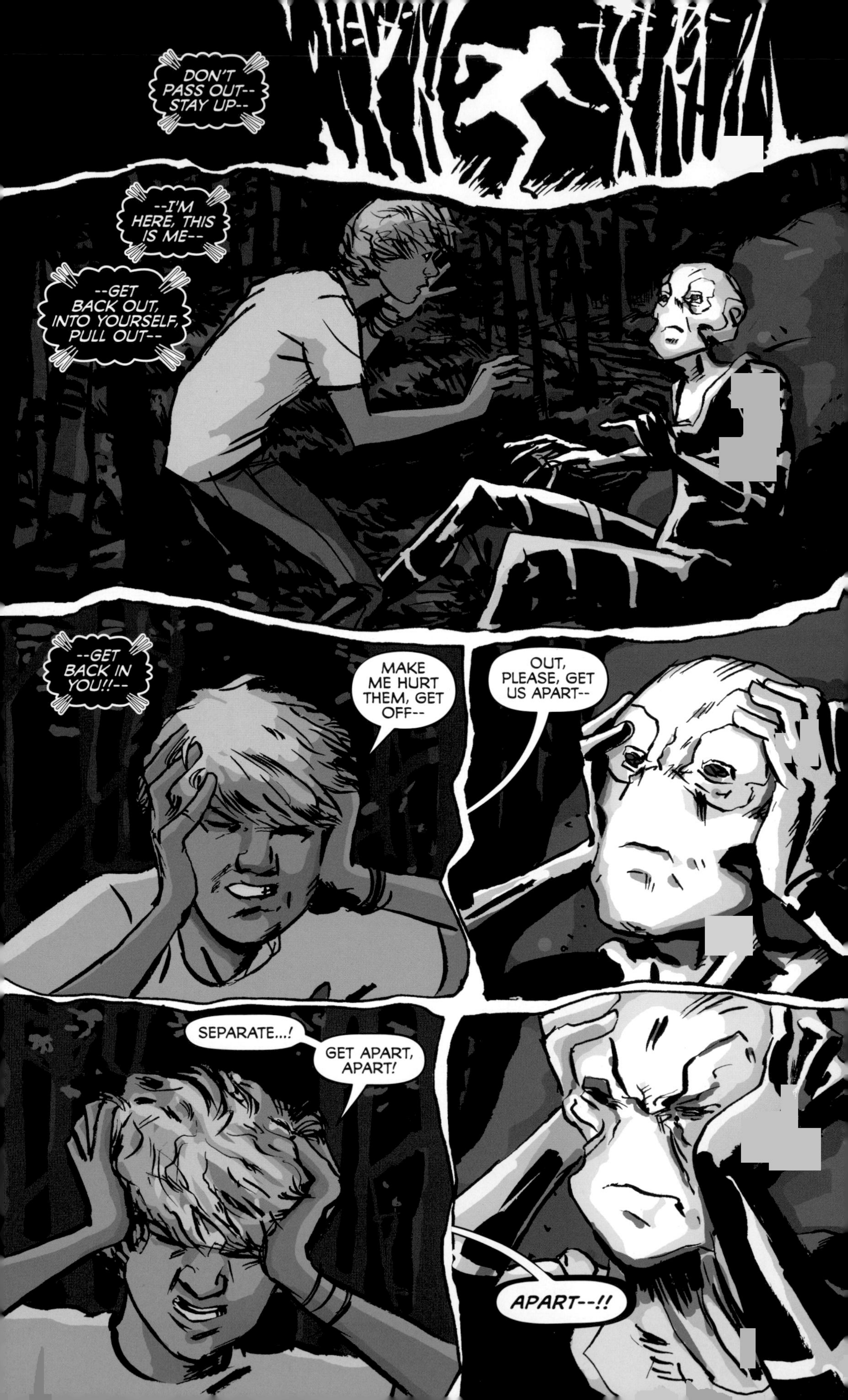

DON'T PASS OUT-- STAY UP--
--I'M HERE, THIS IS ME--
--GET BACK OUT, INTO YOURSELF, PULL OUT--
--GET BACK IN YOU!!--
MAKE ME HURT THEM, GET OFF--
OUT, PLEASE, GET US APART--
SEPARATE...!
GET APART, APART!
APART--!!

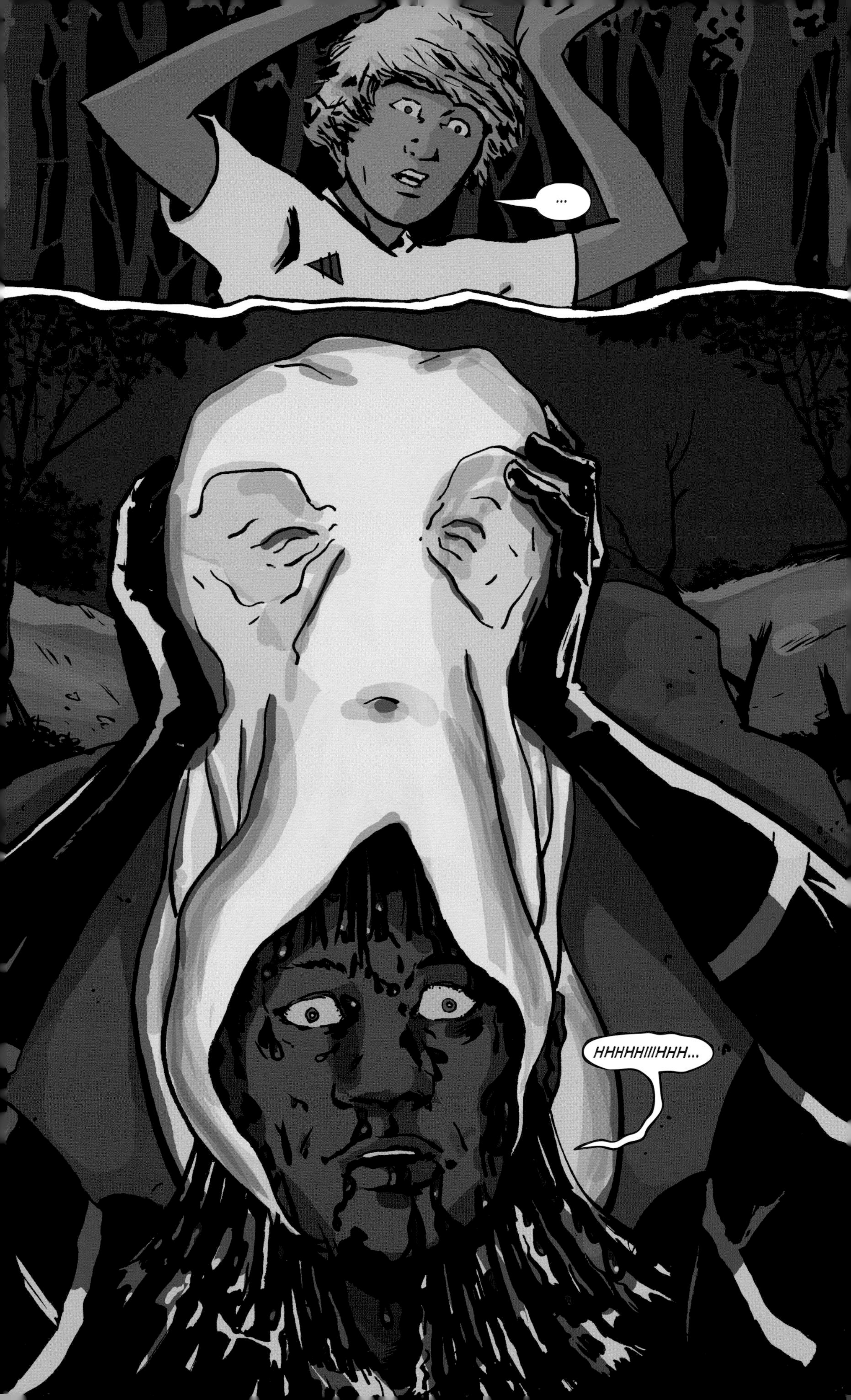
...
HHHHHIIIHHH...

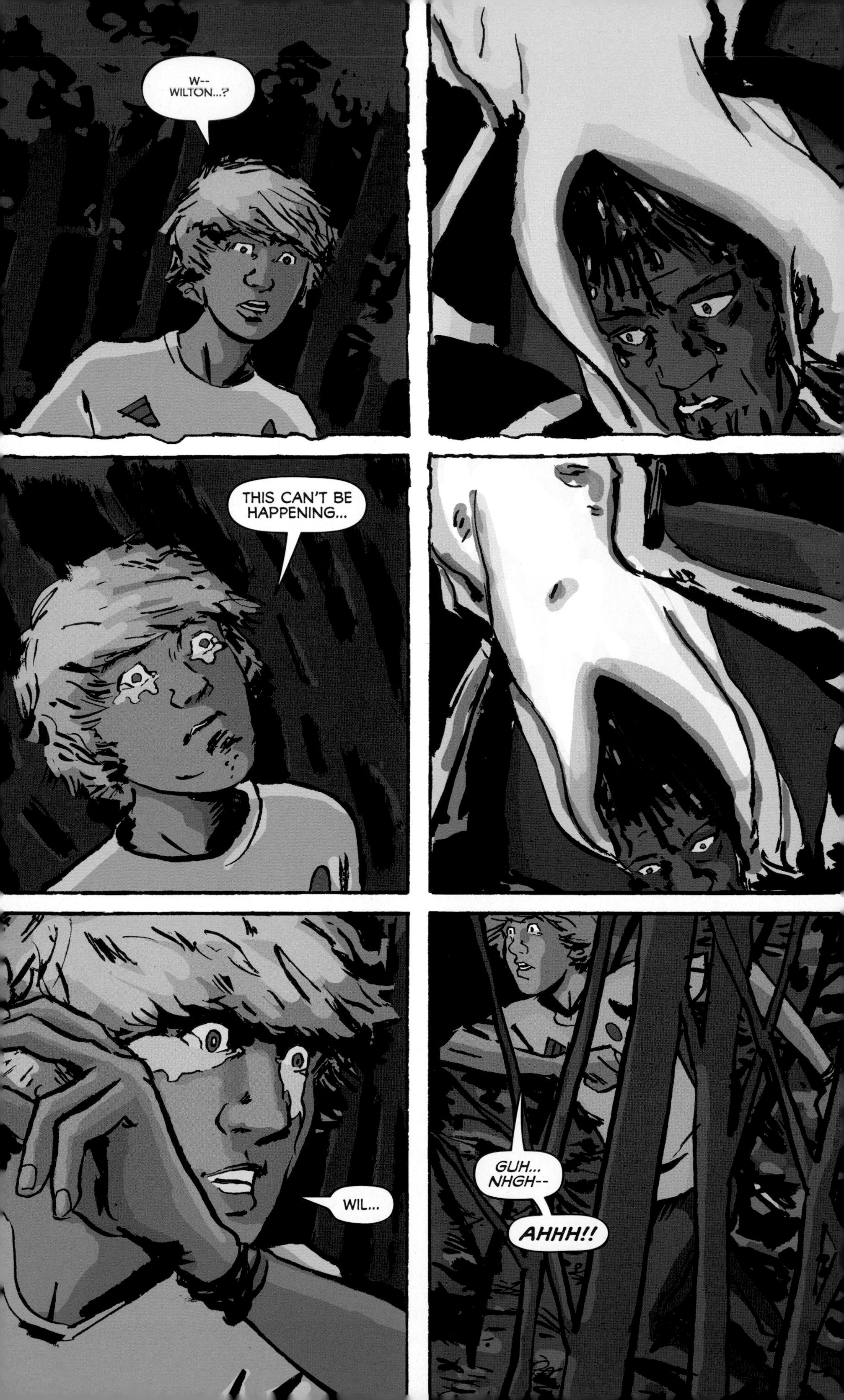
W--
WILTON...?
THIS CAN'T BE
HAPPENING...
WIL...
GUH...
NHGH--
AHHH!!

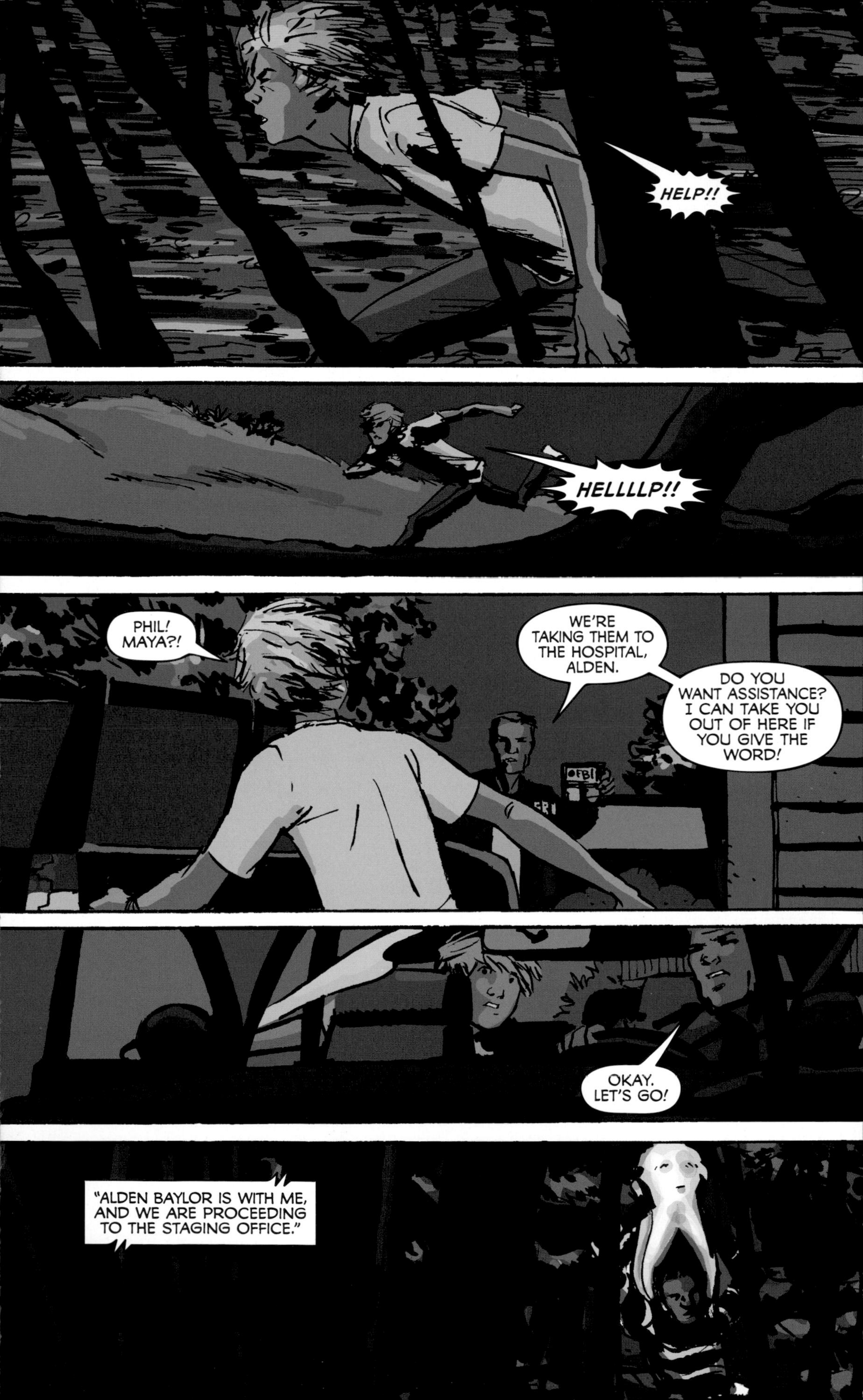
HELP!!
HELLLLP!!
PHIL! MAYA?!
WE'RE TAKING THEM TO THE HOSPITAL, ALDEN.
DO YOU WANT ASSISTANCE? I CAN TAKE YOU OUT OF HERE IF YOU GIVE THE WORD!
FBI
OKAY. LET'S GO!
"ALDEN BAYLOR IS WITH ME, AND WE ARE PROCEEDING TO THE STAGING OFFICE."

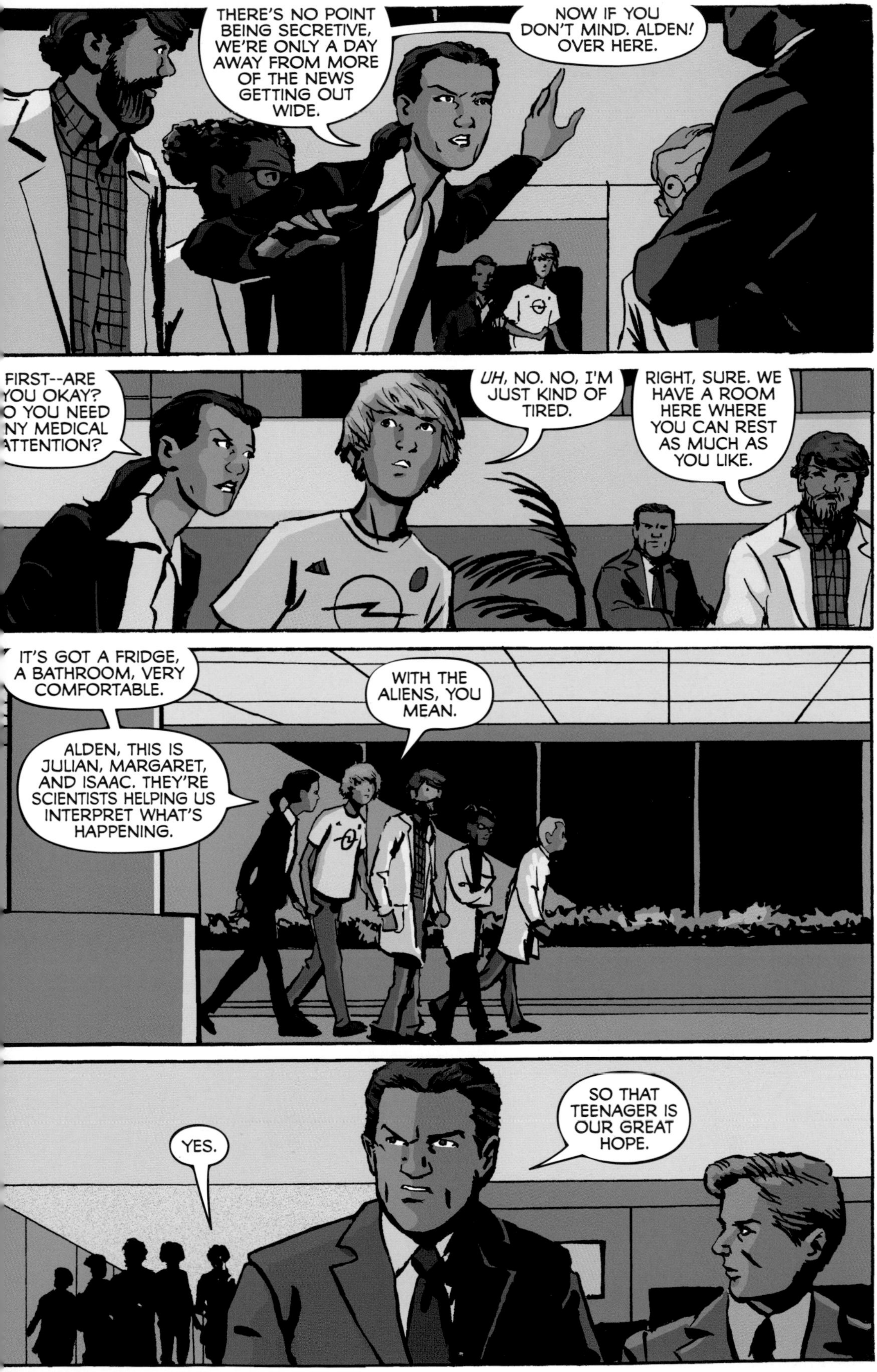
THERE'S NO POINT BEING SECRETIVE, WE'RE ONLY A DAY AWAY FROM MORE OF THE NEWS GETTING OUT WIDE.
NOW IF YOU DON'T MIND. ALDEN! OVER HERE.
FIRST--ARE YOU OKAY? O YOU NEED NY MEDICAL ATTENTION?
UH, NO. NO, I'M JUST KIND OF TIRED.
RIGHT, SURE. WE HAVE A ROOM HERE WHERE YOU CAN REST AS MUCH AS YOU LIKE.
IT'S GOT A FRIDGE, A BATHROOM, VERY COMFORTABLE.
ALDEN, THIS IS JULIAN, MARGARET, AND ISAAC. THEY'RE SCIENTISTS HELPING US INTERPRET WHAT'S HAPPENING.
WITH THE ALIENS, YOU MEAN.
YES.
SO THAT TEENAGER IS OUR GREAT HOPE.

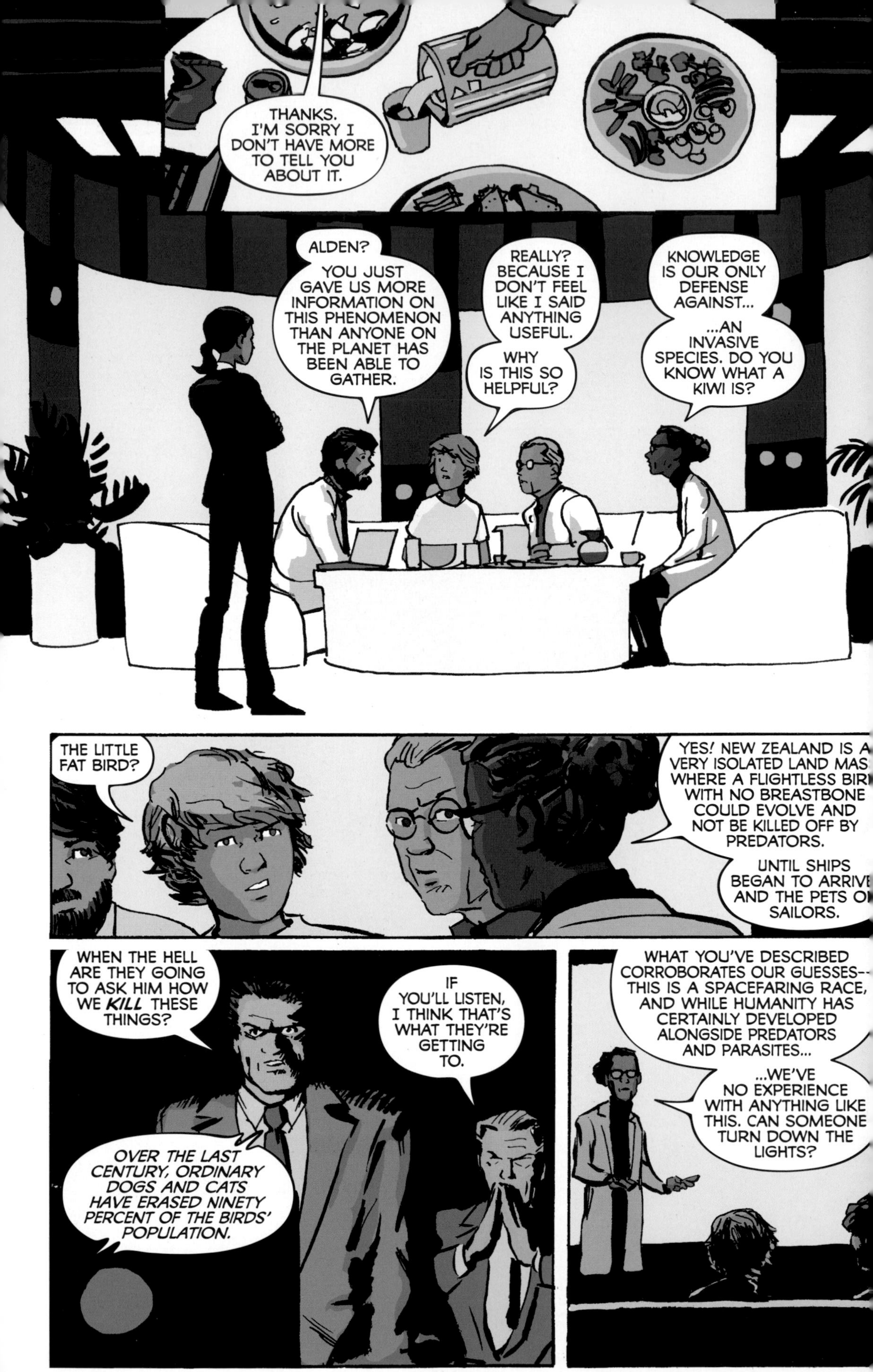

THANKS. I'M SORRY I DON'T HAVE MORE TO TELL YOU ABOUT IT.
ALDEN?
YOU JUST GAVE US MORE INFORMATION ON THIS PHENOMENON THAN ANYONE ON THE PLANET HAS BEEN ABLE TO GATHER.
REALLY? BECAUSE I DON'T FEEL LIKE I SAID ANYTHING USEFUL.
WHY IS THIS SO HELPFUL?
KNOWLEDGE IS OUR ONLY DEFENSE AGAINST...
...AN INVASIVE SPECIES. DO YOU KNOW WHAT A KIWI IS?
THE LITTLE FAT BIRD?
YES! NEW ZEALAND IS A VERY ISOLATED LAND MAS WHERE A FLIGHTLESS BIR WITH NO BREASTBONE COULD EVOLVE AND NOT BE KILLED OFF BY PREDATORS.
UNTIL SHIPS BEGAN TO ARRIVE AND THE PETS O SAILORS.
WHEN THE HELL ARE THEY GOING TO ASK HIM HOW WE *KILL* THESE THINGS?
IF YOU'LL LISTEN, I THINK THAT'S WHAT THEY'RE GETTING TO.
OVER THE LAST CENTURY, ORDINARY DOGS AND CATS HAVE ERASED NINETY PERCENT OF THE BIRDS' POPULATION.
WHAT YOU'VE DESCRIBED CORROBORATES OUR GUESSES-- THIS IS A SPACEFARING RACE, AND WHILE HUMANITY HAS CERTAINLY DEVELOPED ALONGSIDE PREDATORS AND PARASITES...
...WE'VE NO EXPERIENCE WITH ANYTHING LIKE THIS. CAN SOMEONE TURN DOWN THE LIGHTS?

SEVERAL COUNTRIES WHERE THE BEINGS LANDED ARE SHARING DATA AND TRYING TO KEEP THIS UNDER WRAPS TO PREVENT MASS HYSTERIA.

THAT SHOULD HAPPEN ABOUT, OH, TOMORROW.

WHEN THE FIRST IMAGES CAME IN, EVERYONE ASSUMED AS YOU DID, THAT THEY WERE BIPEDALS, WEARING A PROTECTIVE SUIT.

NOW WE KNOW THE RIDGED BLACK COVERING IS A MEMBRANE THAT THE CEPHALUS EXUDES TO COVER AND PROTECT THE HOST BODY.

IT SEEMS TO ATTACH TO THE MOST COMPLEX ANIMALS IT CAN FIND, OF A SIMILAR PROPORTION.

IT'S NOT A PERFECT, CONSISTENT PROCESS-- IT'S LIFE, AFTER ALL. WE'VE EVIDENCE OF OTHER JOININGS THAT HAVE HAPPENED IN AREAS WHERE THERE WEREN'T HUMAN HOSTS. MANY OF THESE DIED WITHIN DAYS.

AS HAVE HUMANS. BUT THE ONES WHO'VE SURVIVED...

THEY'RE UNSTOPPABLE.

ANY BEINGS THAT CAN SURVIVE IN THE ABSOLUTE ZERO OF SPACE, BEING HAMMERED WITH RADIATION, HAVE TO BE EXTREMELY TOUGH.

WHEN HE SHARED THE MEMORY WITH ME, THEY SEEMED TO BE ASLEEP WHILE IN SPACE.

BUT STILL MAKING CHOICES.

I THINK THEY'RE DORMANT, THEN.

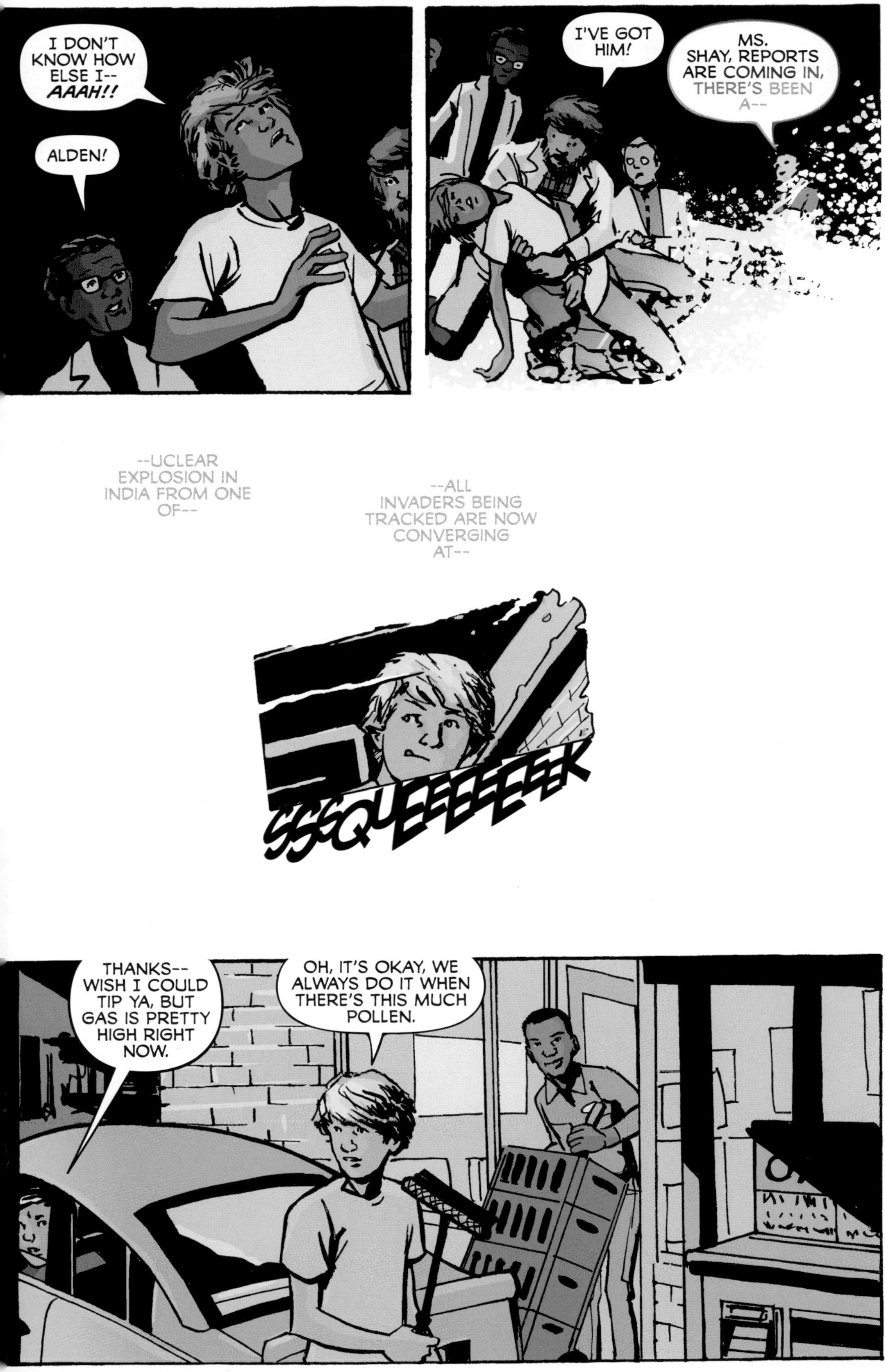
I DON'T KNOW HOW ELSE I-- AAAH!!
ALDEN!
I'VE GOT HIM!
MS. SHAY, REPORTS ARE COMING IN, THERE'S BEEN A--
--UCLEAR EXPLOSION IN INDIA FROM ONE OF--
--ALL INVADERS BEING TRACKED ARE NOW CONVERGING AT--
SSSQUEEEEEEEEK
THANKS-- WISH I COULD TIP YA, BUT GAS IS PRETTY HIGH RIGHT NOW.
OH, IT'S OKAY, WE ALWAYS DO IT WHEN THERE'S THIS MUCH POLLEN.

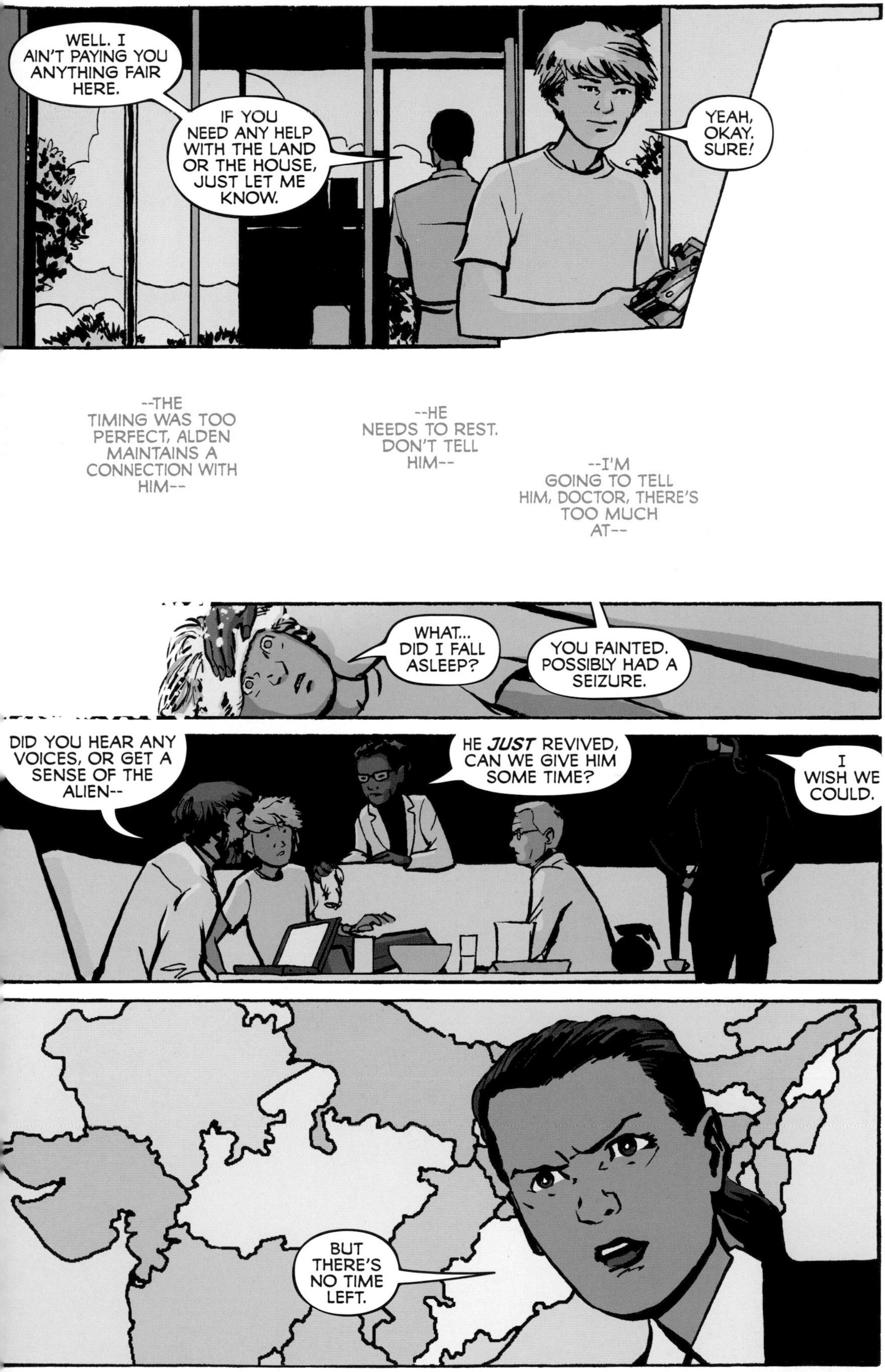
WELL. I AIN'T PAYING YOU ANYTHING FAIR HERE.
IF YOU NEED ANY HELP WITH THE LAND OR THE HOUSE, JUST LET ME KNOW.
YEAH, OKAY. SURE!
--THE TIMING WAS TOO PERFECT, ALDEN MAINTAINS A CONNECTION WITH HIM--
--HE NEEDS TO REST. DON'T TELL HIM--
--I'M GOING TO TELL HIM, DOCTOR, THERE'S TOO MUCH AT--
WHAT... DID I FALL ASLEEP?
YOU FAINTED. POSSIBLY HAD A SEIZURE.
DID YOU HEAR ANY VOICES, OR GET A SENSE OF THE ALIEN--
HE *JUST* REVIVED, CAN WE GIVE HIM SOME TIME?
I WISH WE COULD.
BUT THERE'S NO TIME LEFT.

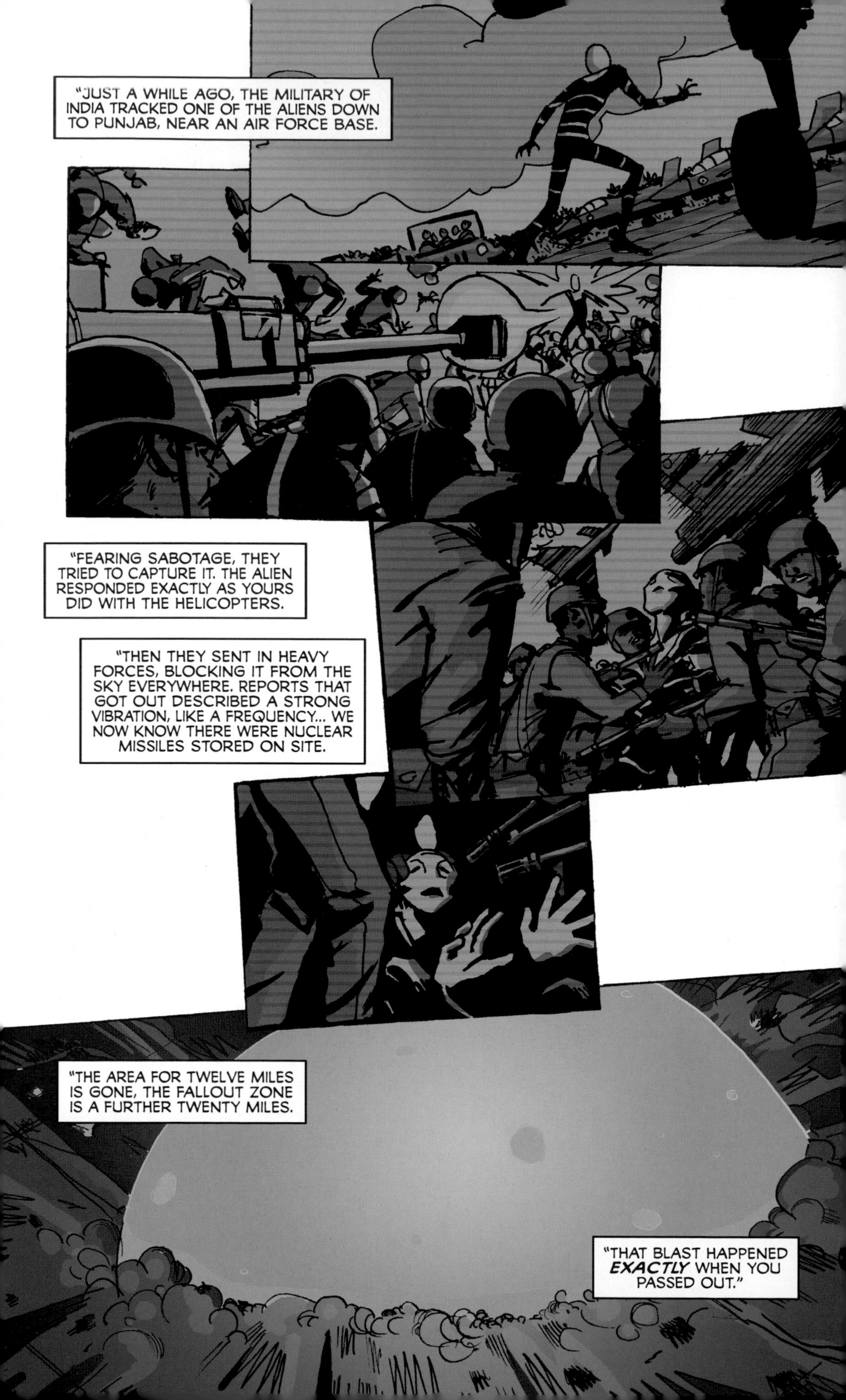
"JUST A WHILE AGO, THE MILITARY OF INDIA TRACKED ONE OF THE ALIENS DOWN TO PUNJAB, NEAR AN AIR FORCE BASE.
"FEARING SABOTAGE, THEY TRIED TO CAPTURE IT. THE ALIEN RESPONDED EXACTLY AS YOURS DID WITH THE HELICOPTERS.
"THEN THEY SENT IN HEAVY FORCES, BLOCKING IT FROM THE SKY EVERYWHERE. REPORTS THAT GOT OUT DESCRIBED A STRONG VIBRATION, LIKE A FREQUENCY... WE NOW KNOW THERE WERE NUCLEAR MISSILES STORED ON SITE.
"THE AREA FOR TWELVE MILES IS GONE, THE FALLOUT ZONE IS A FURTHER TWENTY MILES.
"THAT BLAST HAPPENED *EXACTLY* WHEN YOU PASSED OUT."

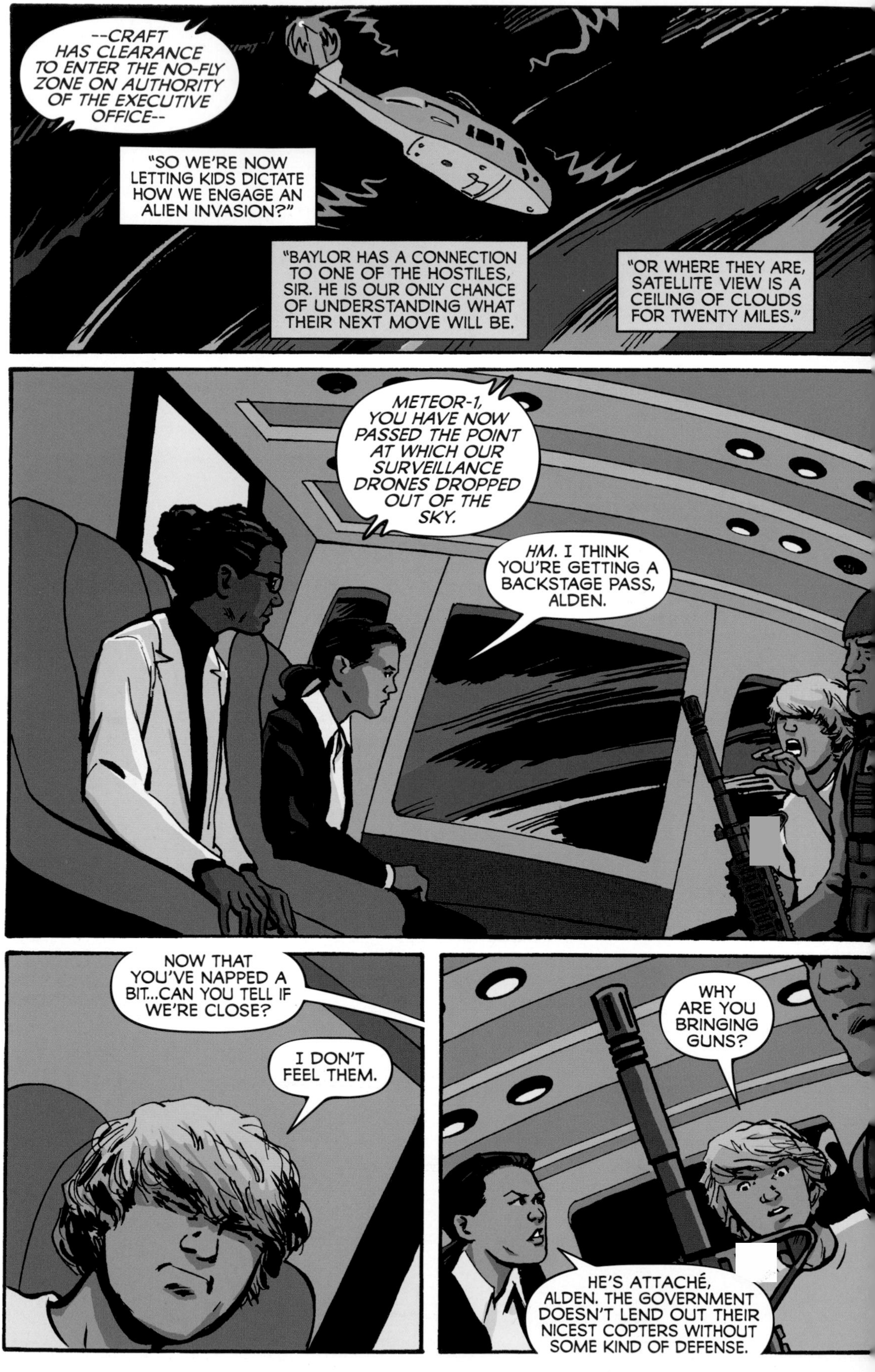
--CRAFT HAS CLEARANCE TO ENTER THE NO-FLY ZONE ON AUTHORITY OF THE EXECUTIVE OFFICE--
"SO WE'RE NOW LETTING KIDS DICTATE HOW WE ENGAGE AN ALIEN INVASION?"
"BAYLOR HAS A CONNECTION TO ONE OF THE HOSTILES, SIR. HE IS OUR ONLY CHANCE OF UNDERSTANDING WHAT THEIR NEXT MOVE WILL BE.
"OR WHERE THEY ARE, SATELLITE VIEW IS A CEILING OF CLOUDS FOR TWENTY MILES."
METEOR-1, YOU HAVE NOW PASSED THE POINT AT WHICH OUR SURVEILLANCE DRONES DROPPED OUT OF THE SKY.
HM. I THINK YOU'RE GETTING A BACKSTAGE PASS, ALDEN.
NOW THAT YOU'VE NAPPED A BIT...CAN YOU TELL IF WE'RE CLOSE?
I DON'T FEEL THEM.
WHY ARE YOU BRINGING GUNS?
HE'S ATTACHÉ, ALDEN. THE GOVERNMENT DOESN'T LEND OUT THEIR NICEST COPTERS WITHOUT SOME KIND OF DEFENSE.

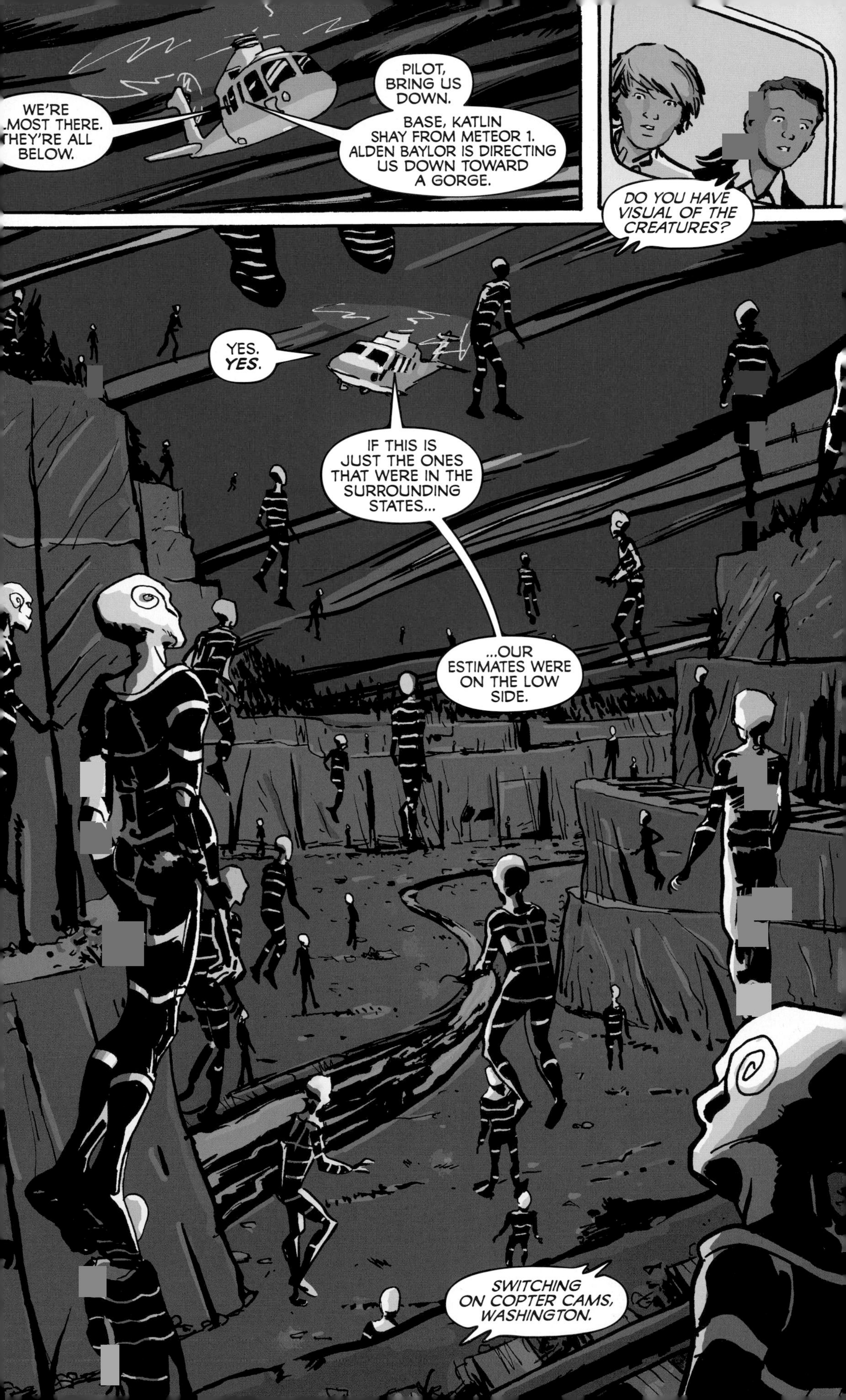
WE'RE .MOST THERE. HEY'RE ALL BELOW.
PILOT, BRING US DOWN.
BASE, KATLIN SHAY FROM METEOR 1. ALDEN BAYLOR IS DIRECTING US DOWN TOWARD A GORGE.
DO YOU HAVE VISUAL OF THE CREATURES?
YES. *YES*.
IF THIS IS JUST THE ONES THAT WERE IN THE SURROUNDING STATES...
...OUR ESTIMATES WERE ON THE LOW SIDE.
SWITCHING ON COPTER CAMS, WASHINGTON.

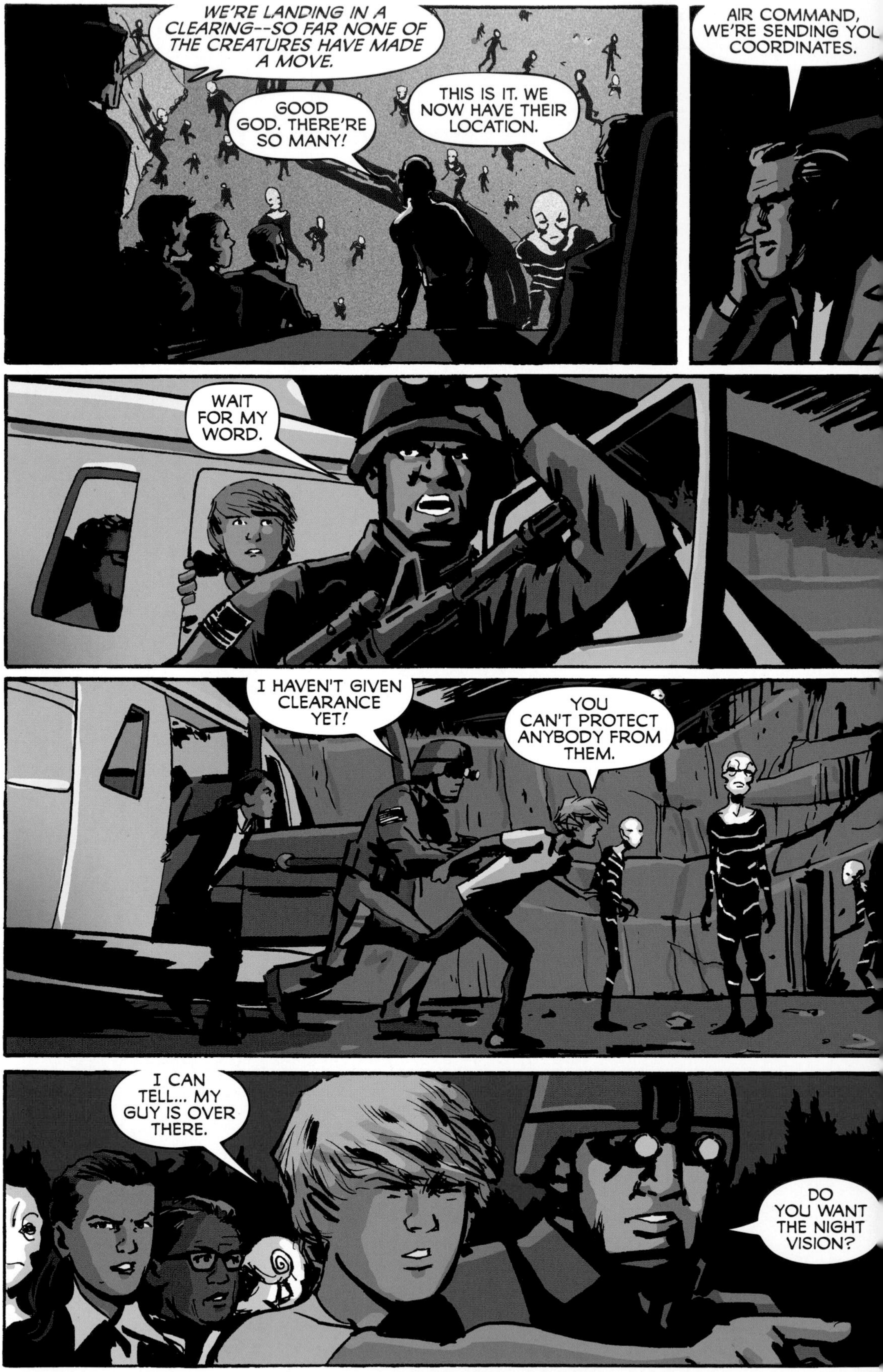
WE'RE LANDING IN A CLEARING--SO FAR NONE OF THE CREATURES HAVE MADE A MOVE.
GOOD GOD. THERE'RE SO MANY!
THIS IS IT. WE NOW HAVE THEIR LOCATION.
AIR COMMAND, WE'RE SENDING YOU COORDINATES.
WAIT FOR MY WORD.
I HAVEN'T GIVEN CLEARANCE YET!
YOU CAN'T PROTECT ANYBODY FROM THEM.
I CAN TELL... MY GUY IS OVER THERE.
DO YOU WANT THE NIGHT VISION?

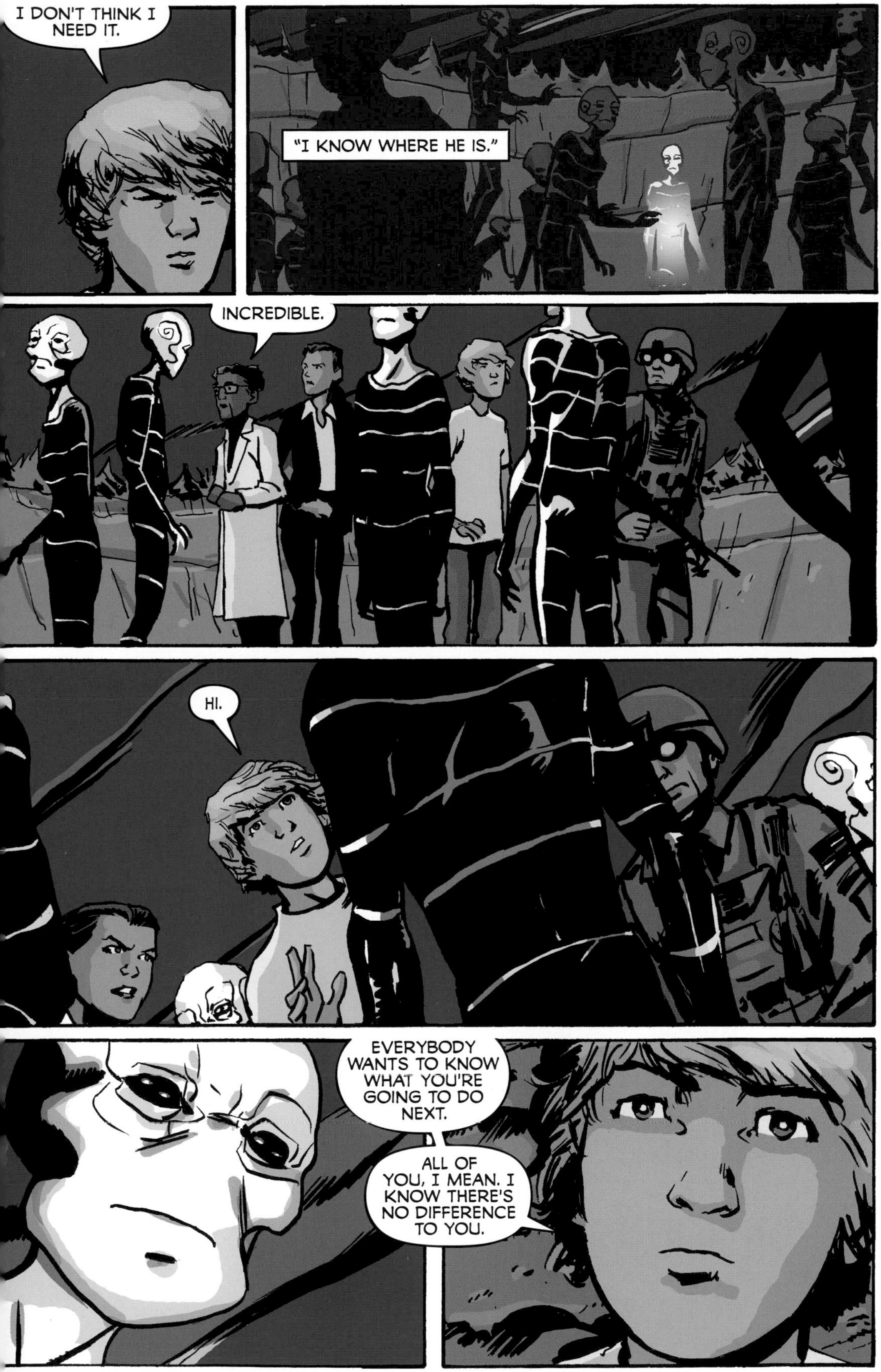
I DON'T THINK I NEED IT.
"I KNOW WHERE HE IS."
INCREDIBLE.
HI.
EVERYBODY WANTS TO KNOW WHAT YOU'RE GOING TO DO NEXT.
ALL OF YOU, I MEAN. I KNOW THERE'S NO DIFFERENCE TO YOU.

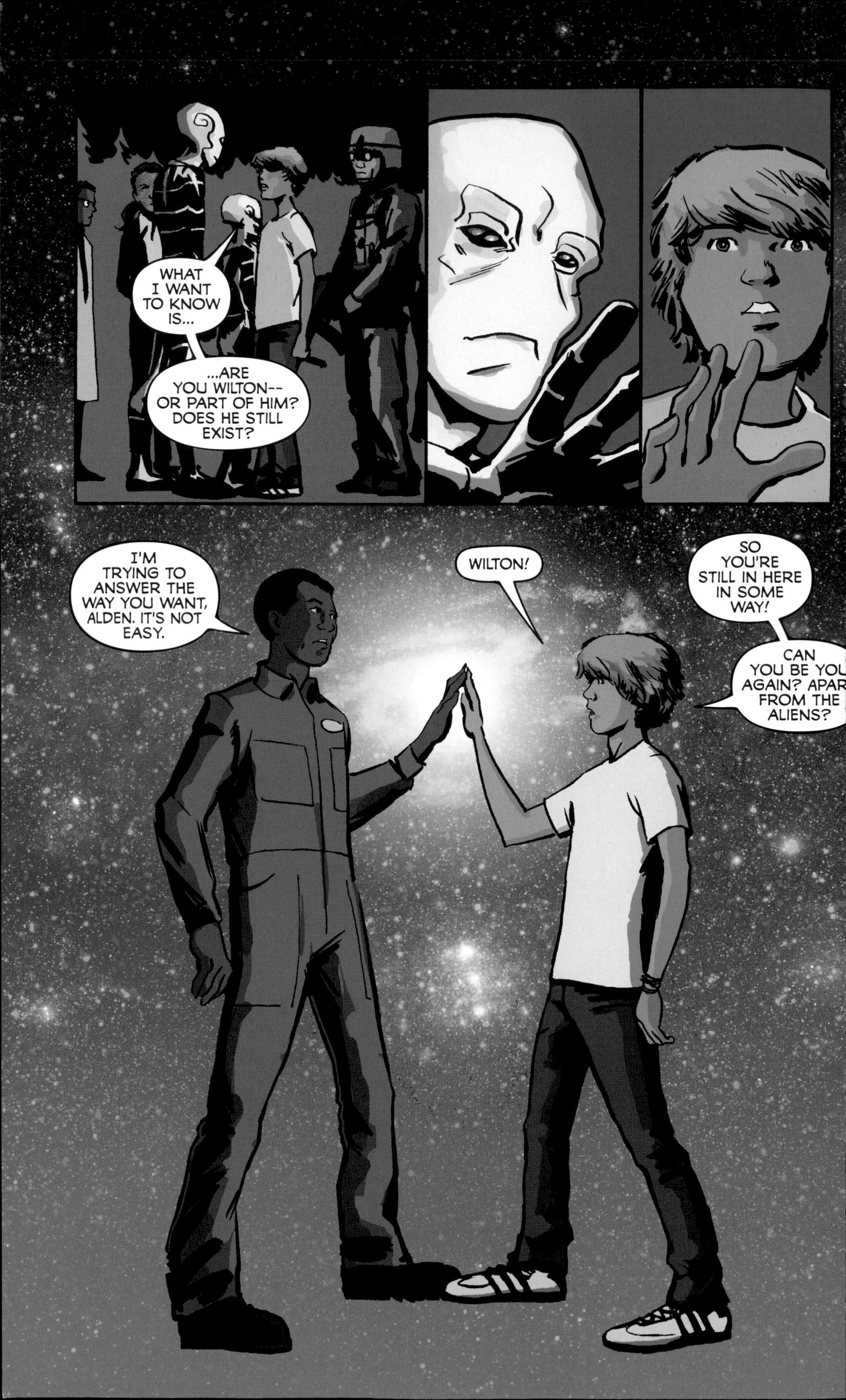
WHAT I WANT TO KNOW IS...
...ARE YOU WILTON-- OR PART OF HIM? DOES HE STILL EXIST?
I'M TRYING TO ANSWER THE WAY YOU WANT, ALDEN. IT'S NOT EASY.
WILTON!
SO YOU'RE STILL IN HERE IN SOME WAY!
CAN YOU BE YOU AGAIN? APAR FROM THE ALIENS?

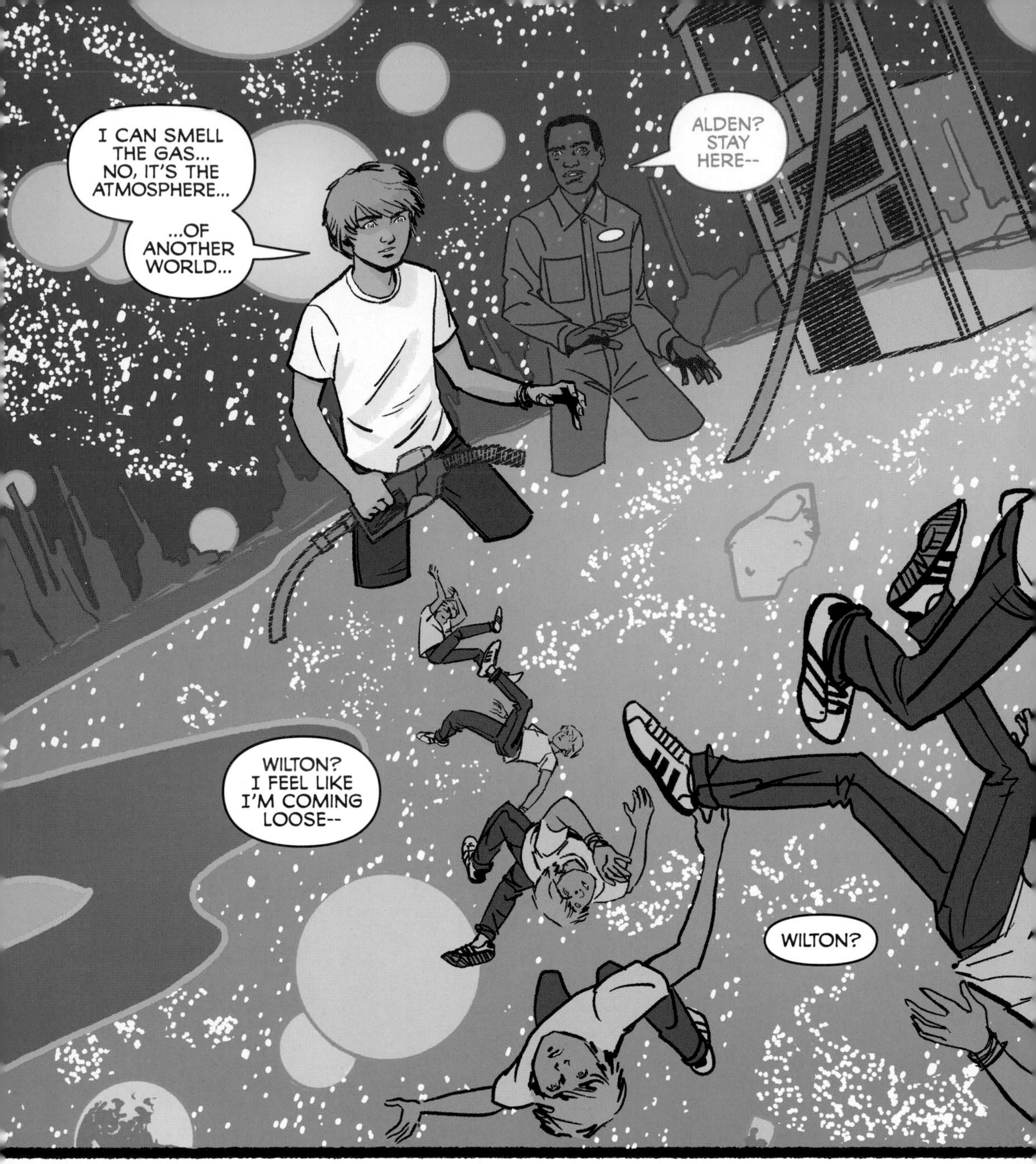
I CAN SMELL THE GAS... NO, IT'S THE ATMOSPHERE...
...OF ANOTHER WORLD...
ALDEN? STAY HERE--
WILTON? I FEEL LIKE I'M COMING LOOSE--
WILTON?

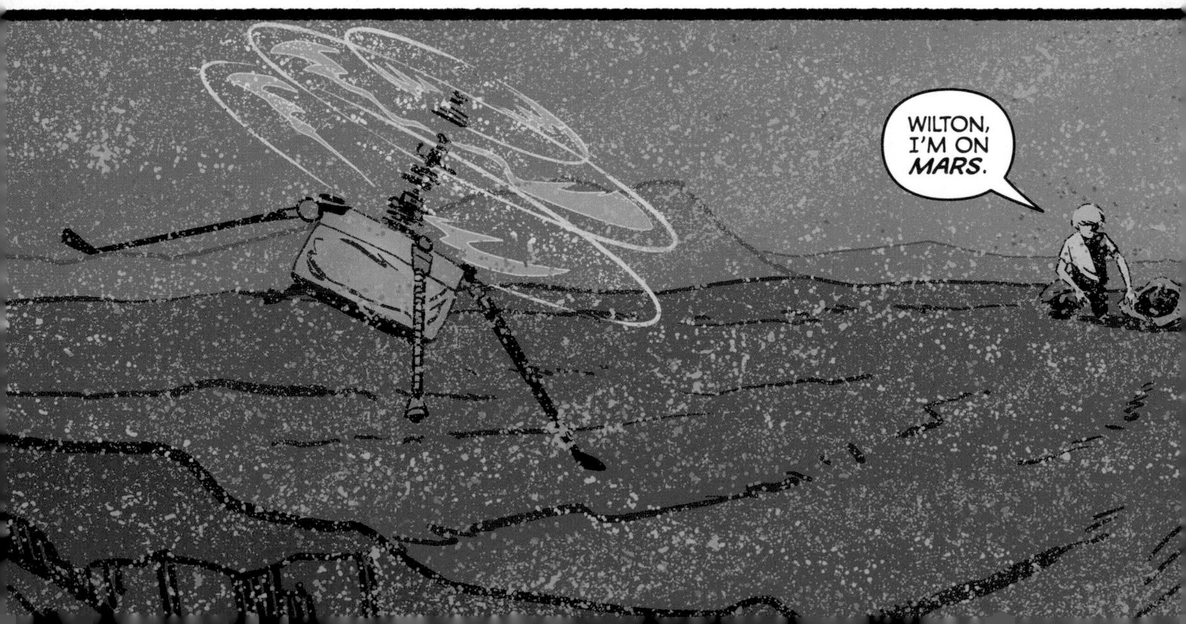
WILTON, I'M ON *MARS*.

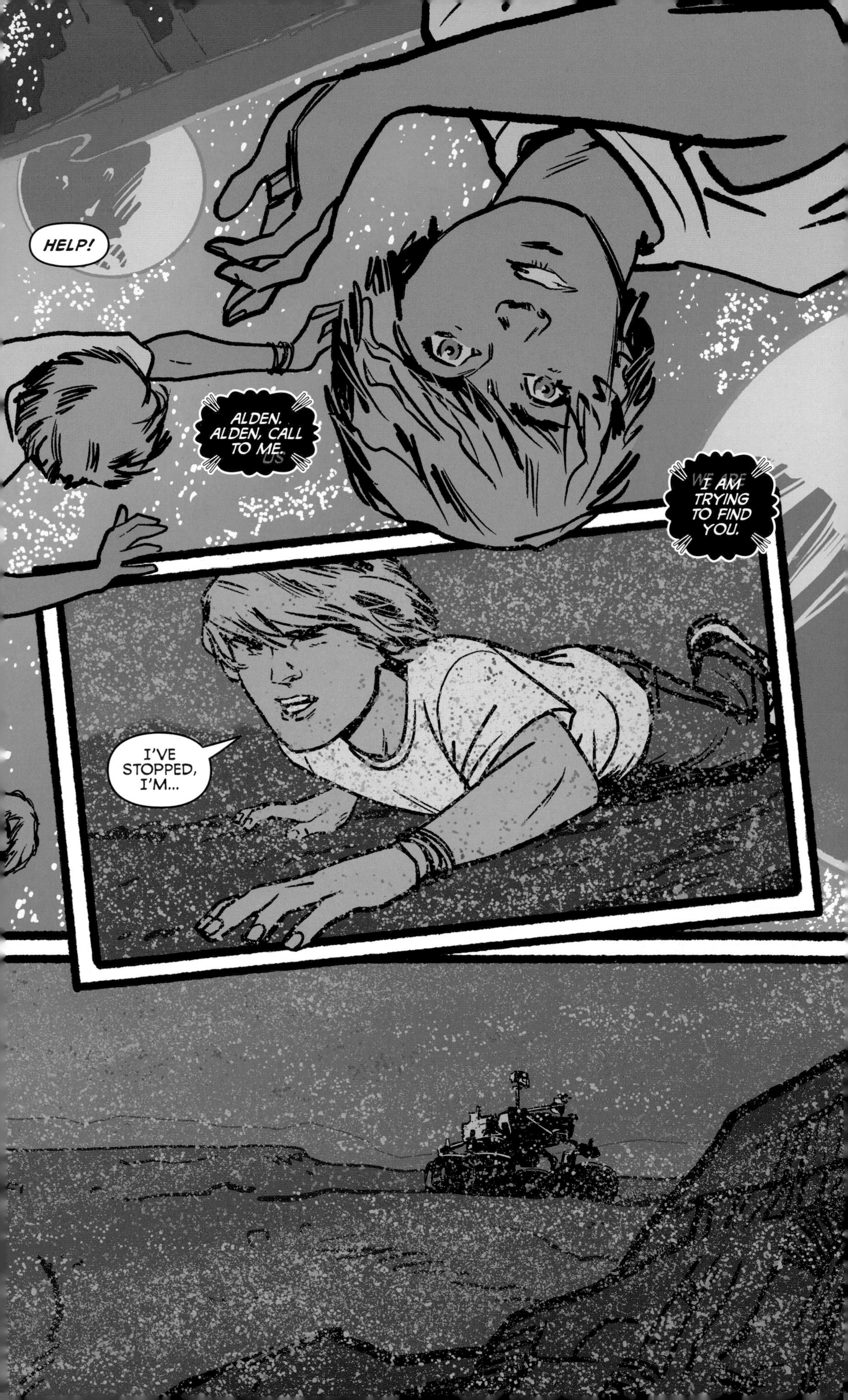
HELP!
ALDEN. ALDEN, CALL TO ME.
I AM TRYING TO FIND YOU.
I'VE STOPPED, I'M...

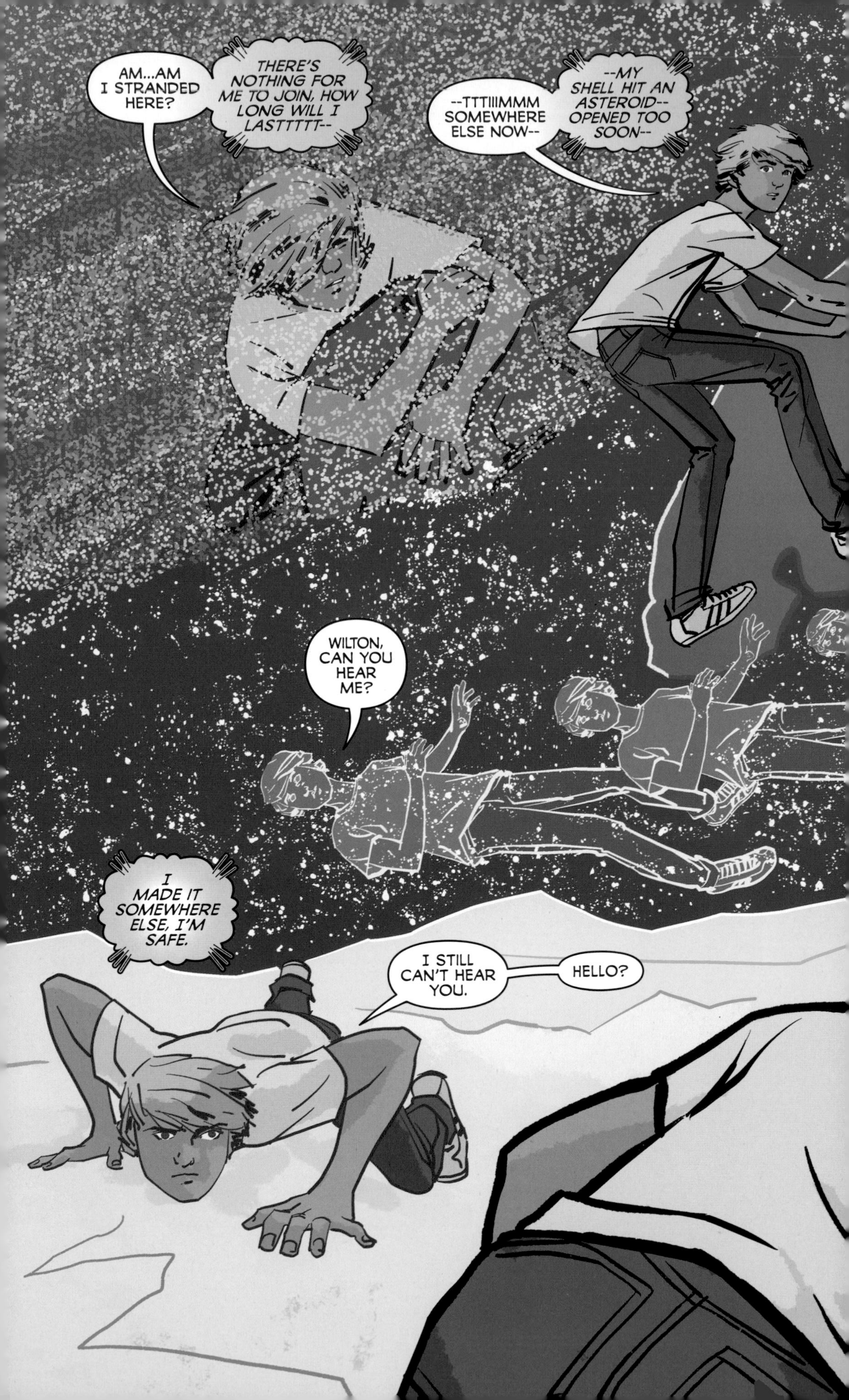
AM...AM I STRANDED HERE?
THERE'S NOTHING FOR ME TO JOIN, HOW LONG WILL I LASTTTTT--
--MY SHELL HIT AN ASTEROID-- OPENED TOO SOON--
--TTTIIIMMM SOMEWHERE ELSE NOW--
WILTON, CAN YOU HEAR ME?
I MADE IT SOMEWHERE ELSE, I'M SAFE.
I STILL CAN'T HEAR YOU.
HELLO?

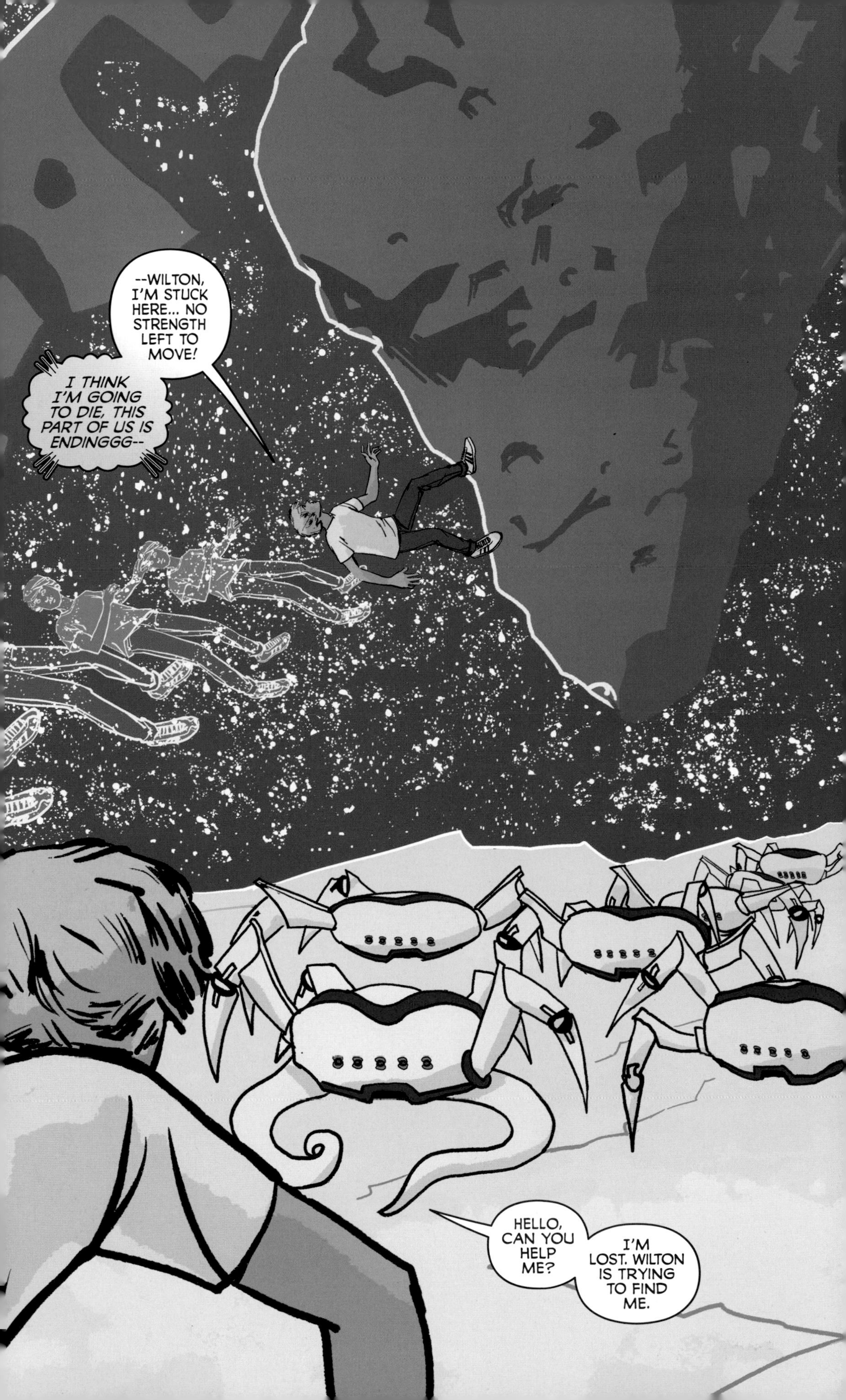
--WILTON, I'M STUCK HERE... NO STRENGTH LEFT TO MOVE!
I THINK I'M GOING TO DIE, THIS PART OF US IS ENDINGGG--
HELLO, CAN YOU HELP ME?
I'M LOST. WILTON IS TRYING TO FIND ME.

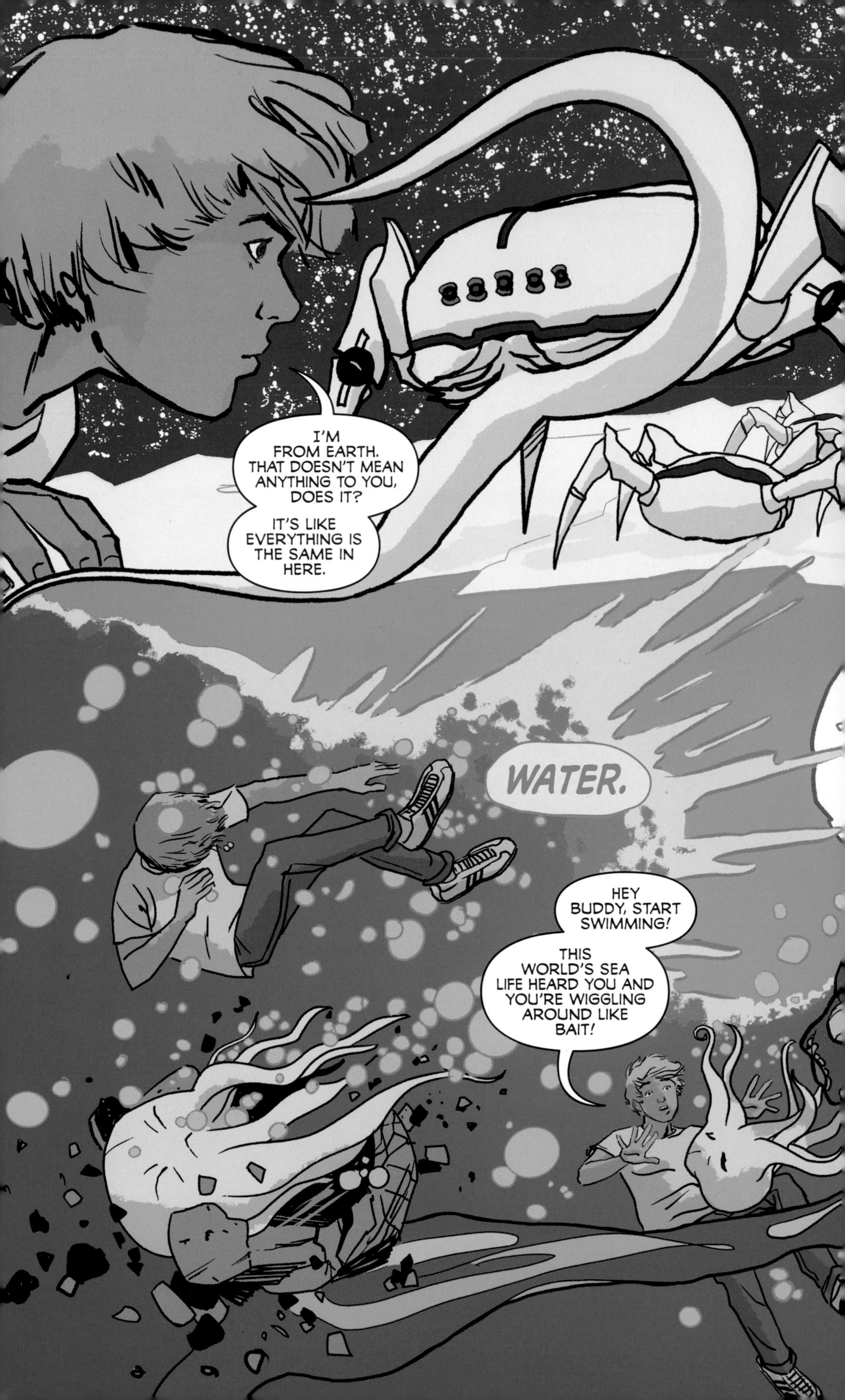
I'M FROM EARTH. THAT DOESN'T MEAN ANYTHING TO YOU, DOES IT?
IT'S LIKE EVERYTHING IS THE SAME IN HERE.
WATER.
HEY BUDDY, START SWIMMING!
THIS WORLD'S SEA LIFE HEARD YOU AND YOU'RE WIGGLING AROUND LIKE BAIT!

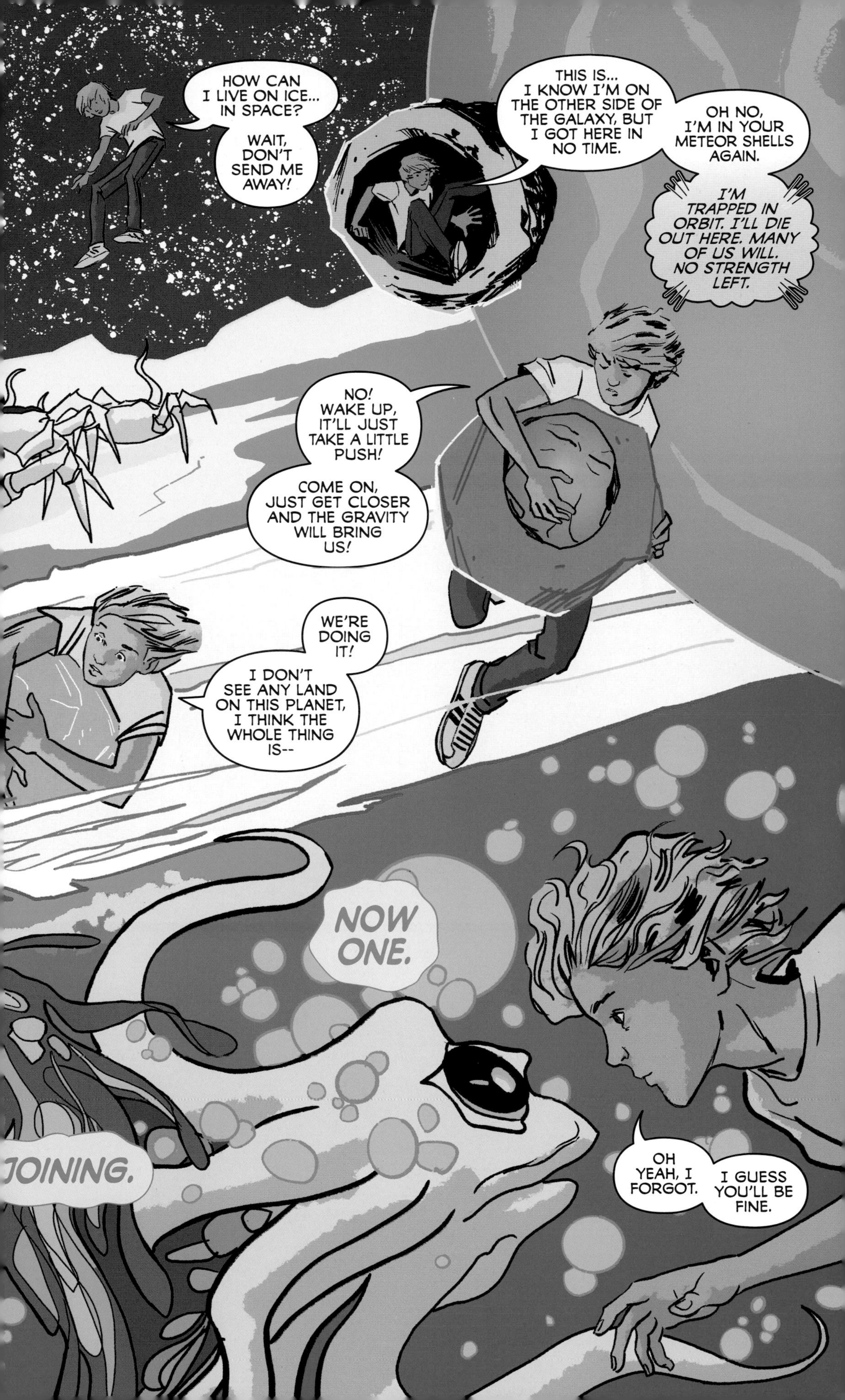
HOW CAN I LIVE ON ICE... IN SPACE?
WAIT, DON'T SEND ME AWAY!
THIS IS... I KNOW I'M ON THE OTHER SIDE OF THE GALAXY, BUT I GOT HERE IN NO TIME.
OH NO, I'M IN YOUR METEOR SHELLS AGAIN.
I'M TRAPPED IN ORBIT. I'LL DIE OUT HERE. MANY OF US WILL. NO STRENGTH LEFT.
NO! WAKE UP, IT'LL JUST TAKE A LITTLE PUSH!
COME ON, JUST GET CLOSER AND THE GRAVITY WILL BRING US!
WE'RE DOING IT!
I DON'T SEE ANY LAND ON THIS PLANET, I THINK THE WHOLE THING IS--
NOW ONE.
JOINING.
OH YEAH, I FORGOT.
I GUESS YOU'LL BE FINE.

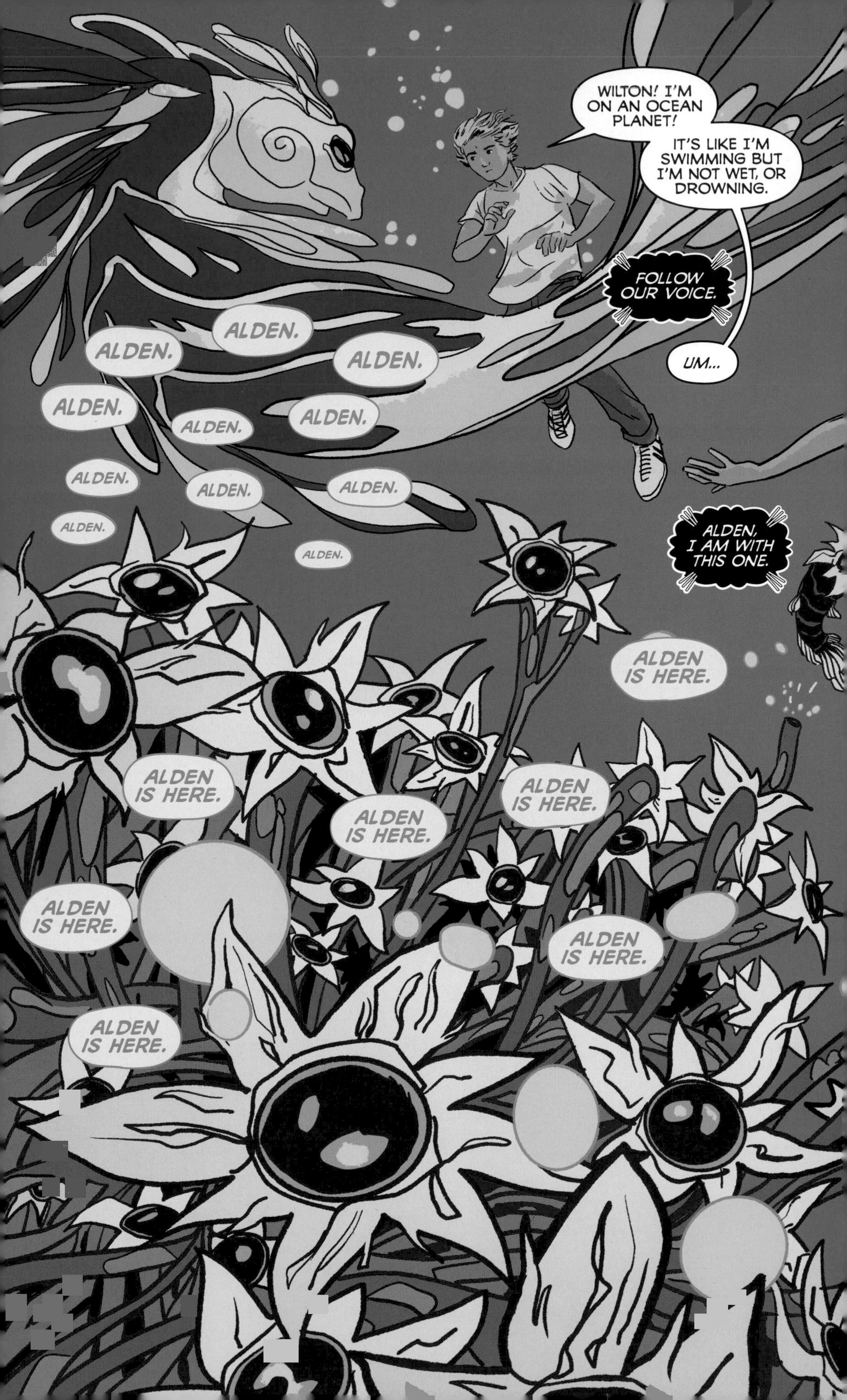
WILTON! I'M ON AN OCEAN PLANET!
IT'S LIKE I'M SWIMMING BUT I'M NOT WET, OR DROWNING.
FOLLOW OUR VOICE.
UM...
ALDEN.
ALDEN.
ALDEN.
ALDEN.
ALDEN.
ALDEN.
ALDEN.
ALDEN.
ALDEN.
ALDEN.
ALDEN.
ALDEN, I AM WITH THIS ONE.
ALDEN IS HERE.
ALDEN IS HERE.
ALDEN IS HERE.
ALDEN IS HERE.
ALDEN IS HERE.
ALDEN IS HERE.
ALDEN IS HERE.

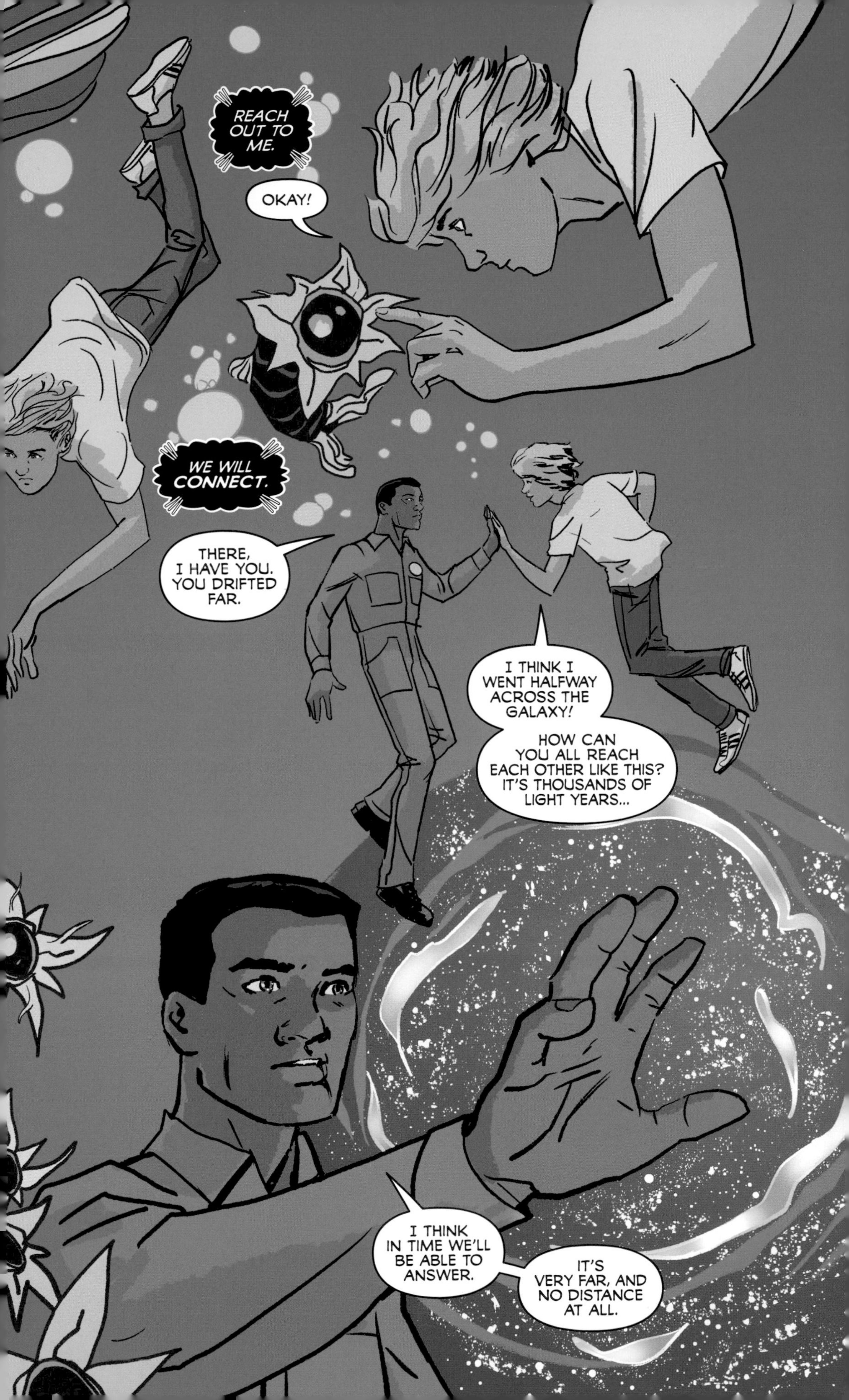
REACH OUT TO ME.
OKAY!
WE WILL CONNECT.
THERE, I HAVE YOU. YOU DRIFTED FAR.
I THINK I WENT HALFWAY ACROSS THE GALAXY!
HOW CAN YOU ALL REACH EACH OTHER LIKE THIS? IT'S THOUSANDS OF LIGHT YEARS...
I THINK IN TIME WE'LL BE ABLE TO ANSWER.
IT'S VERY FAR, AND NO DISTANCE AT ALL.

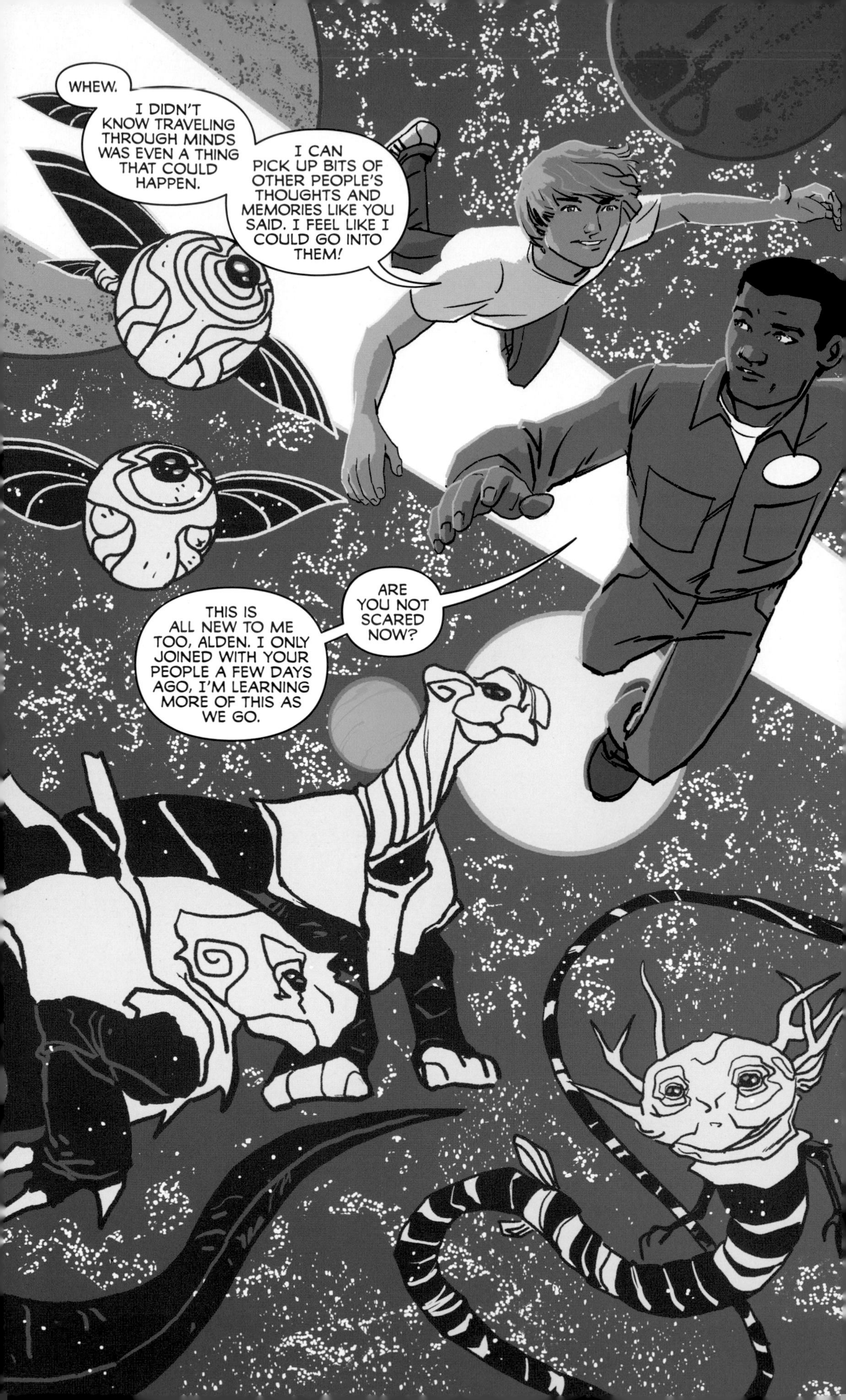
WHEW.
I DIDN'T KNOW TRAVELING THROUGH MINDS WAS EVEN A THING THAT COULD HAPPEN.
I CAN PICK UP BITS OF OTHER PEOPLE'S THOUGHTS AND MEMORIES LIKE YOU SAID. I FEEL LIKE I COULD GO INTO THEM!
ARE YOU NOT SCARED NOW?
THIS IS ALL NEW TO ME TOO, ALDEN. I ONLY JOINED WITH YOUR PEOPLE A FEW DAYS AGO, I'M LEARNING MORE OF THIS AS WE GO.

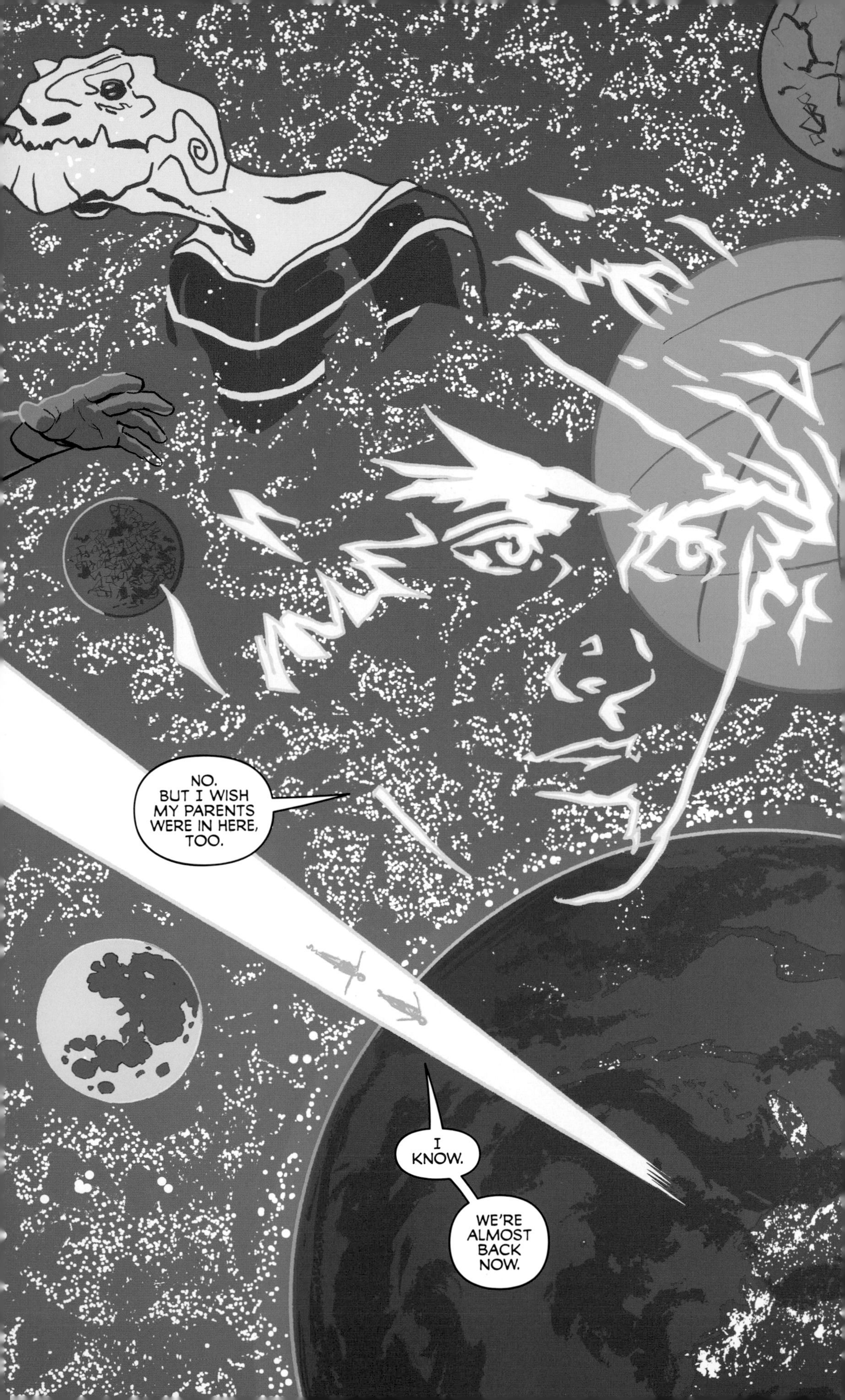

NO. BUT I WISH MY PARENTS WERE IN HERE, TOO.
I KNOW.
WE'RE ALMOST BACK NOW.

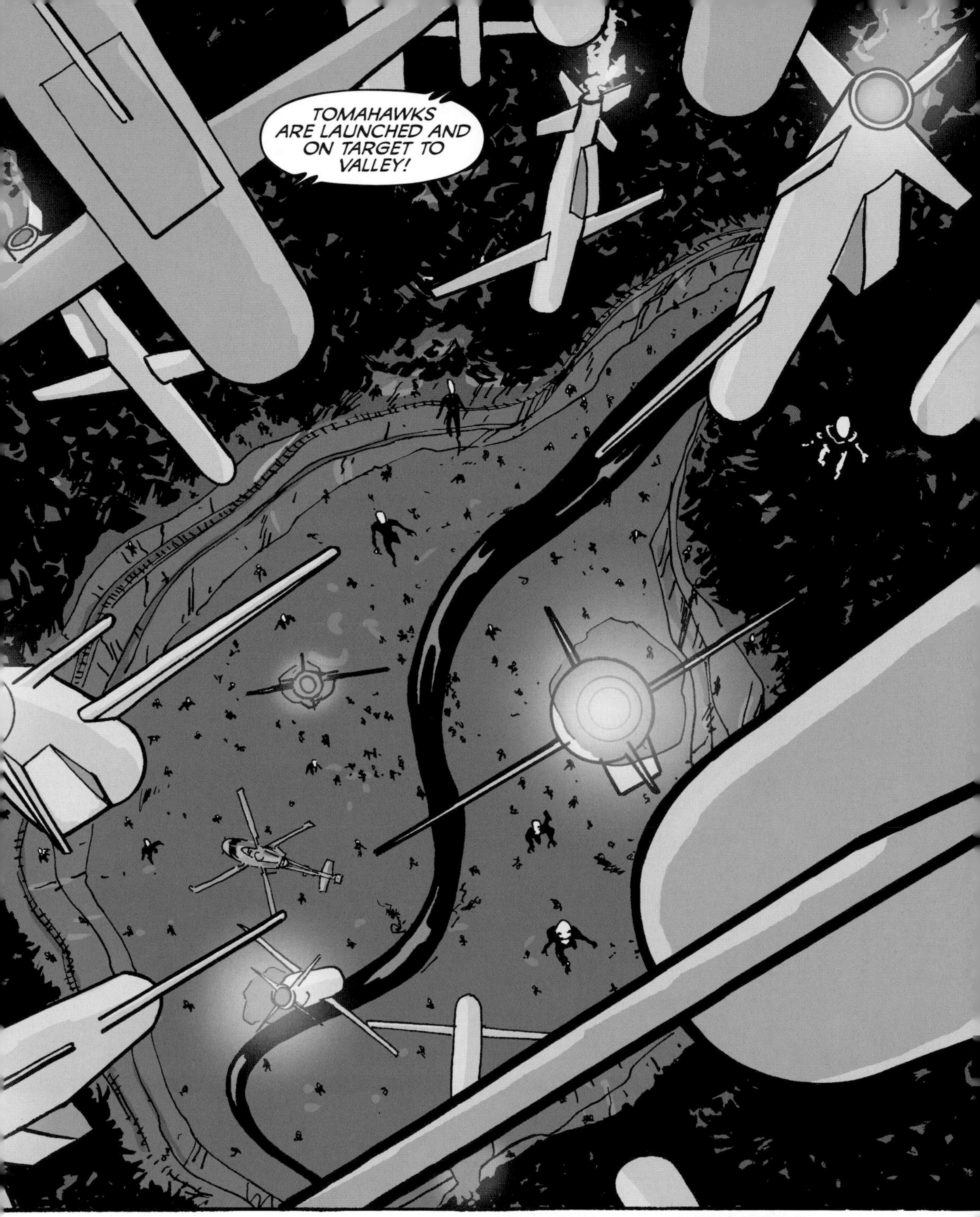
TOMAHAWKS ARE LAUNCHED AND ON TARGET TO VALLEY!

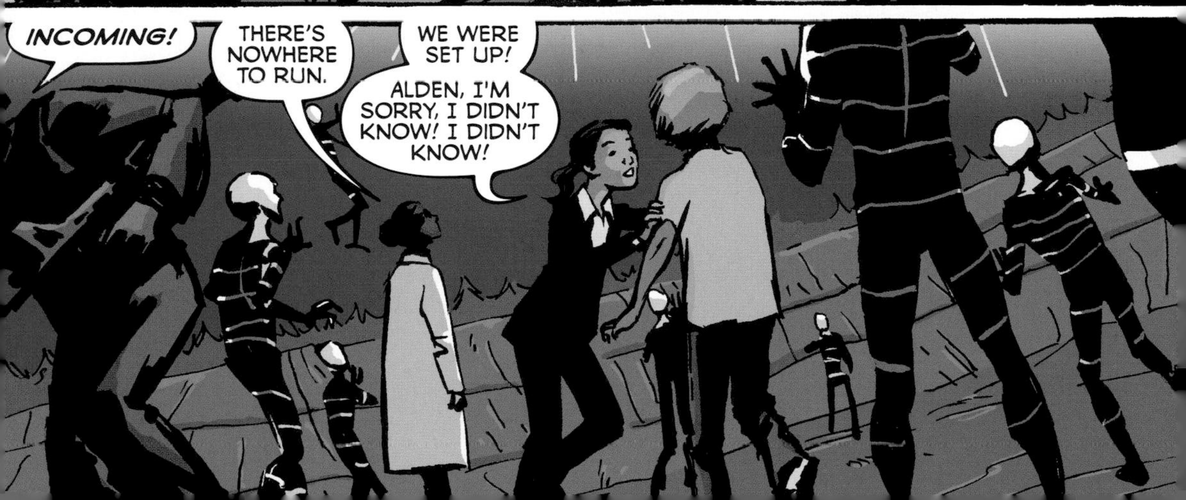
INCOMING!
THERE'S NOWHERE TO RUN.
WE WERE SET UP!
ALDEN, I'M SORRY, I DIDN'T KNOW! I DIDN'T KNOW!

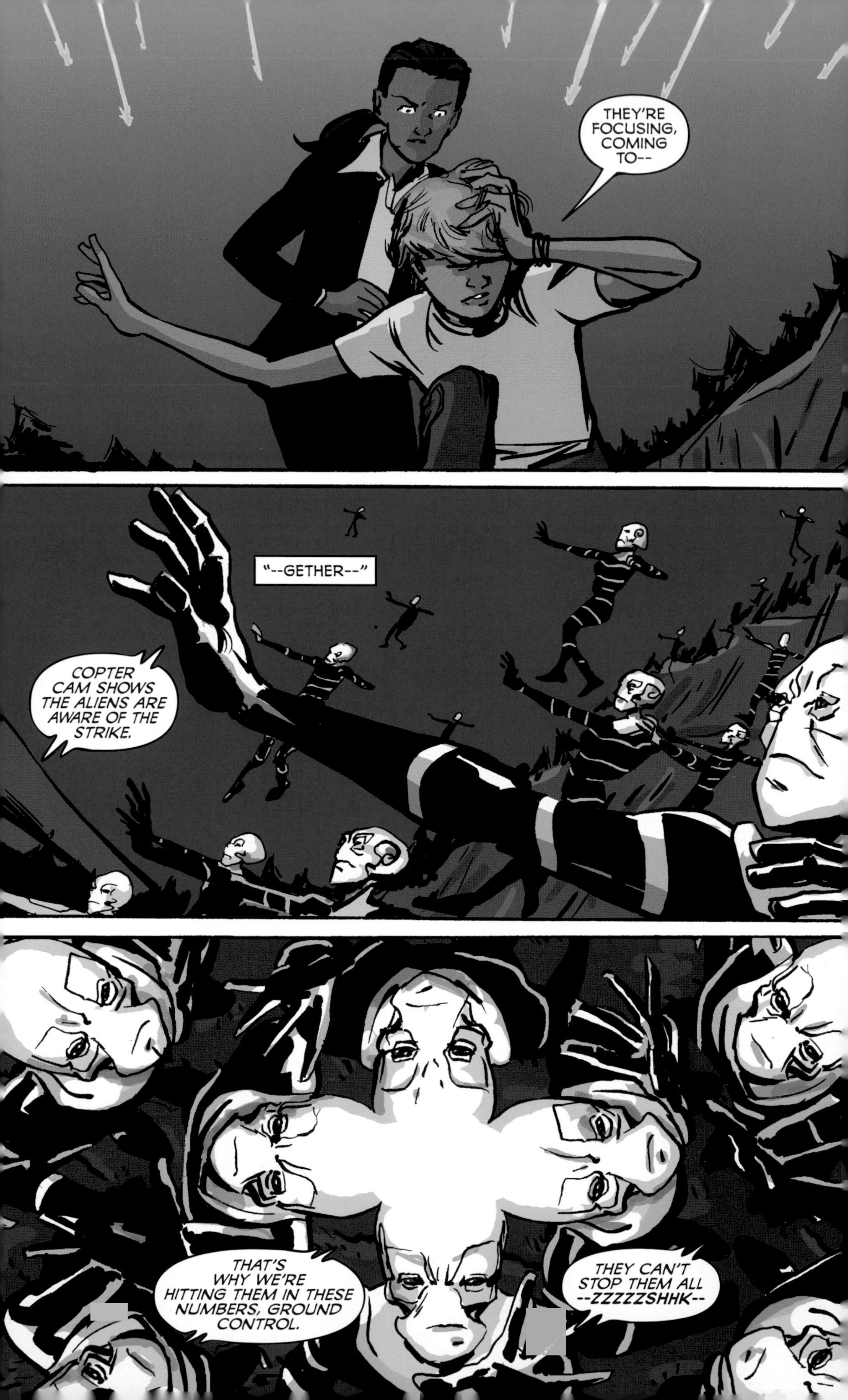
THEY'RE FOCUSING, COMING TO--
"--GETHER--"
COPTER CAM SHOWS THE ALIENS ARE AWARE OF THE STRIKE.
THAT'S WHY WE'RE HITTING THEM IN THESE NUMBERS, GROUND CONTROL.
THEY CAN'T STOP THEM ALL --ZZZZZSHHK--

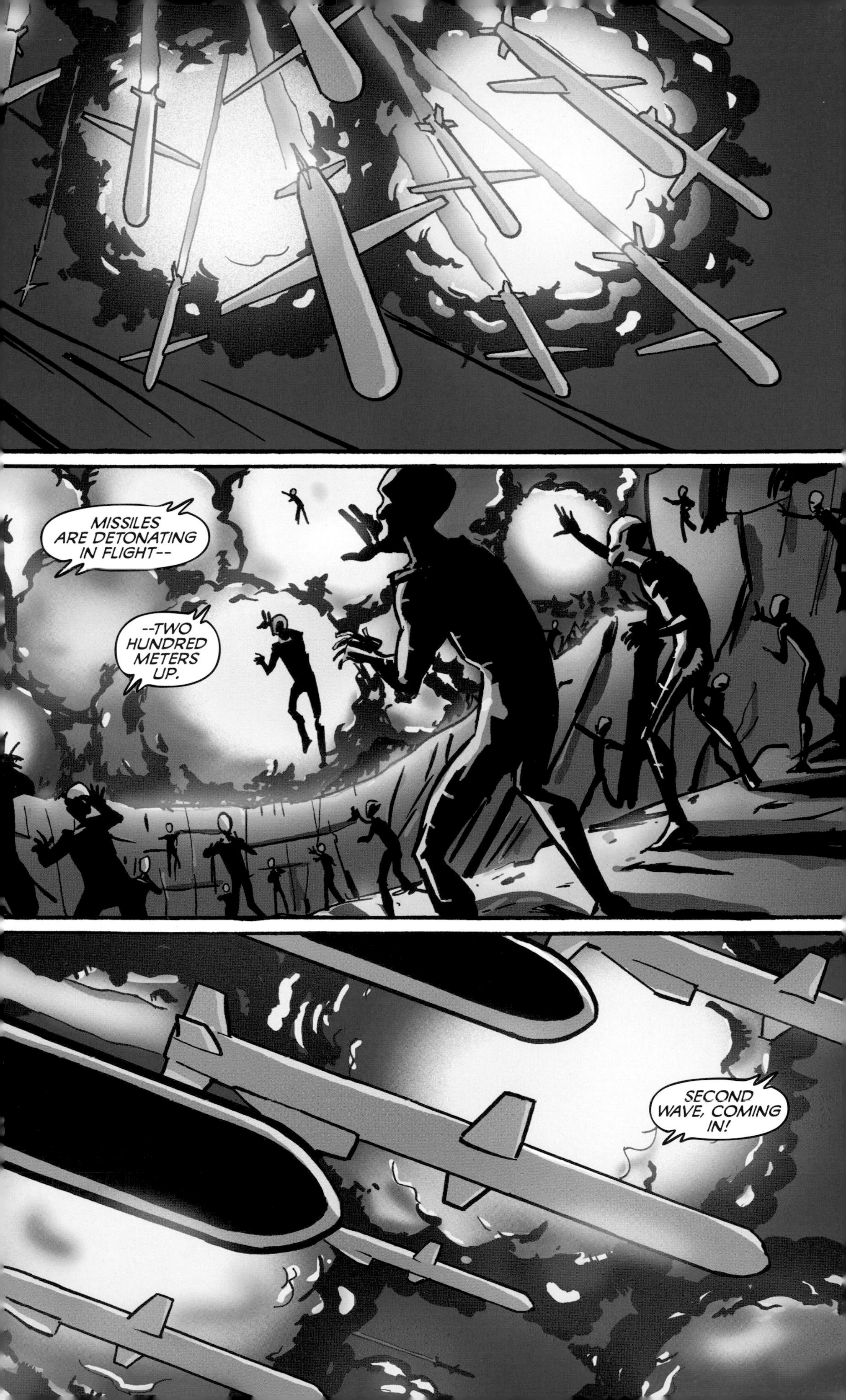
MISSILES ARE DETONATING IN FLIGHT--
--TWO HUNDRED METERS UP.
SECOND WAVE, COMING IN!

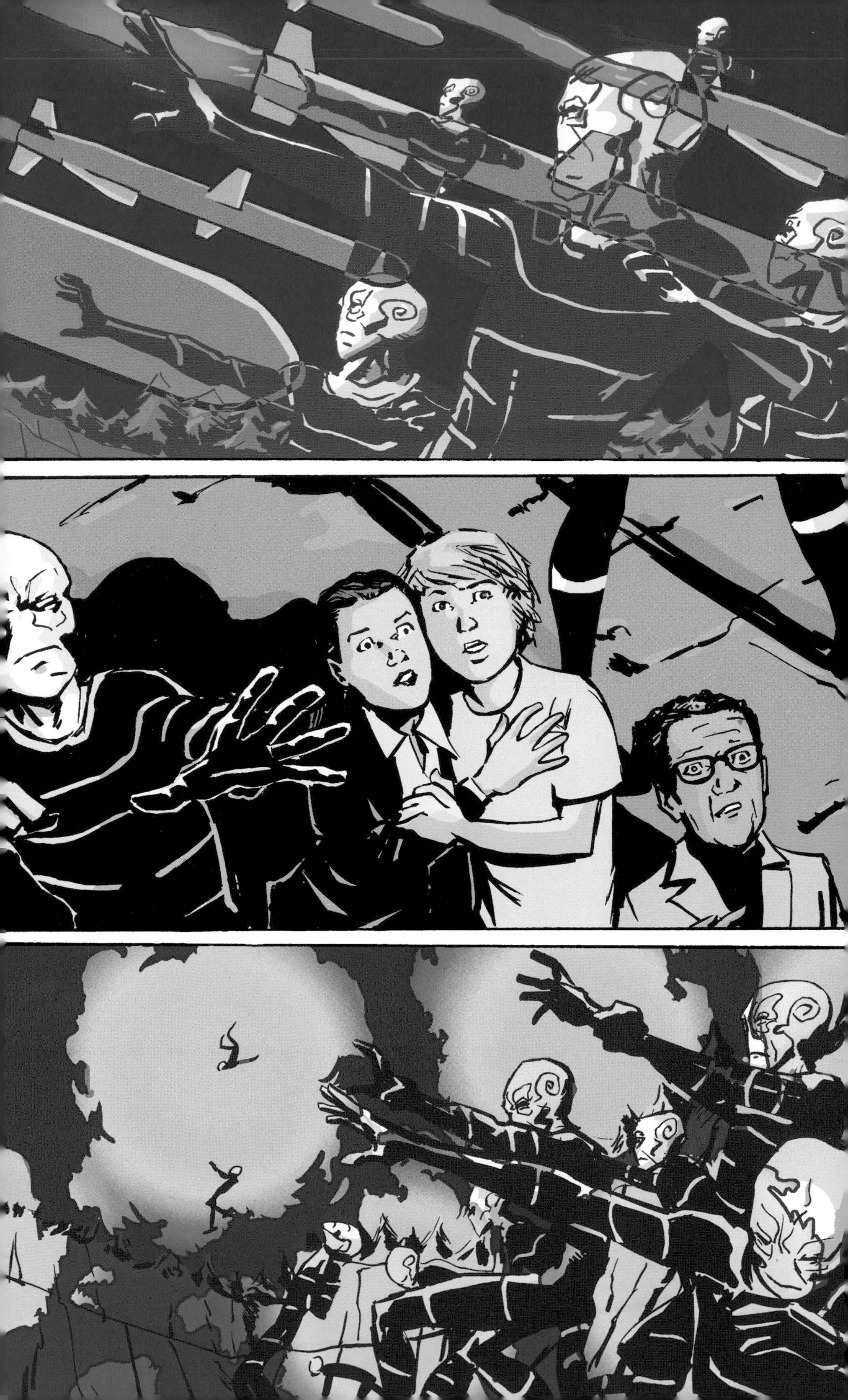

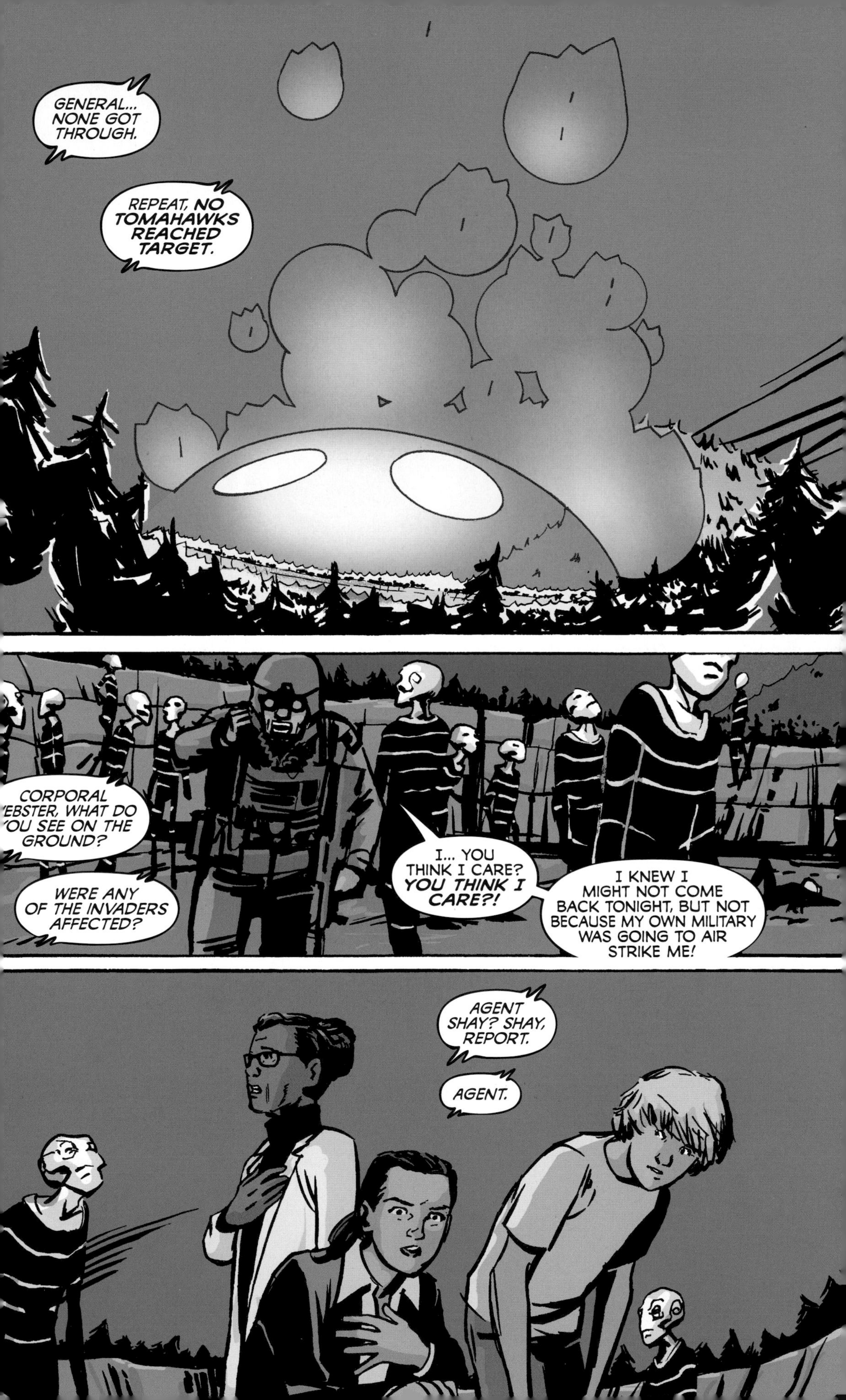
GENERAL... NONE GOT THROUGH.
REPEAT, NO TOMAHAWKS REACHED TARGET.
CORPORAL EBSTER, WHAT DO OU SEE ON THE GROUND?
WERE ANY OF THE INVADERS AFFECTED?
I... YOU THINK I CARE? YOU THINK I CARE?!
I KNEW I MIGHT NOT COME BACK TONIGHT, BUT NOT BECAUSE MY OWN MILITARY WAS GOING TO AIR STRIKE ME!
AGENT SHAY? SHAY, REPORT.
AGENT.

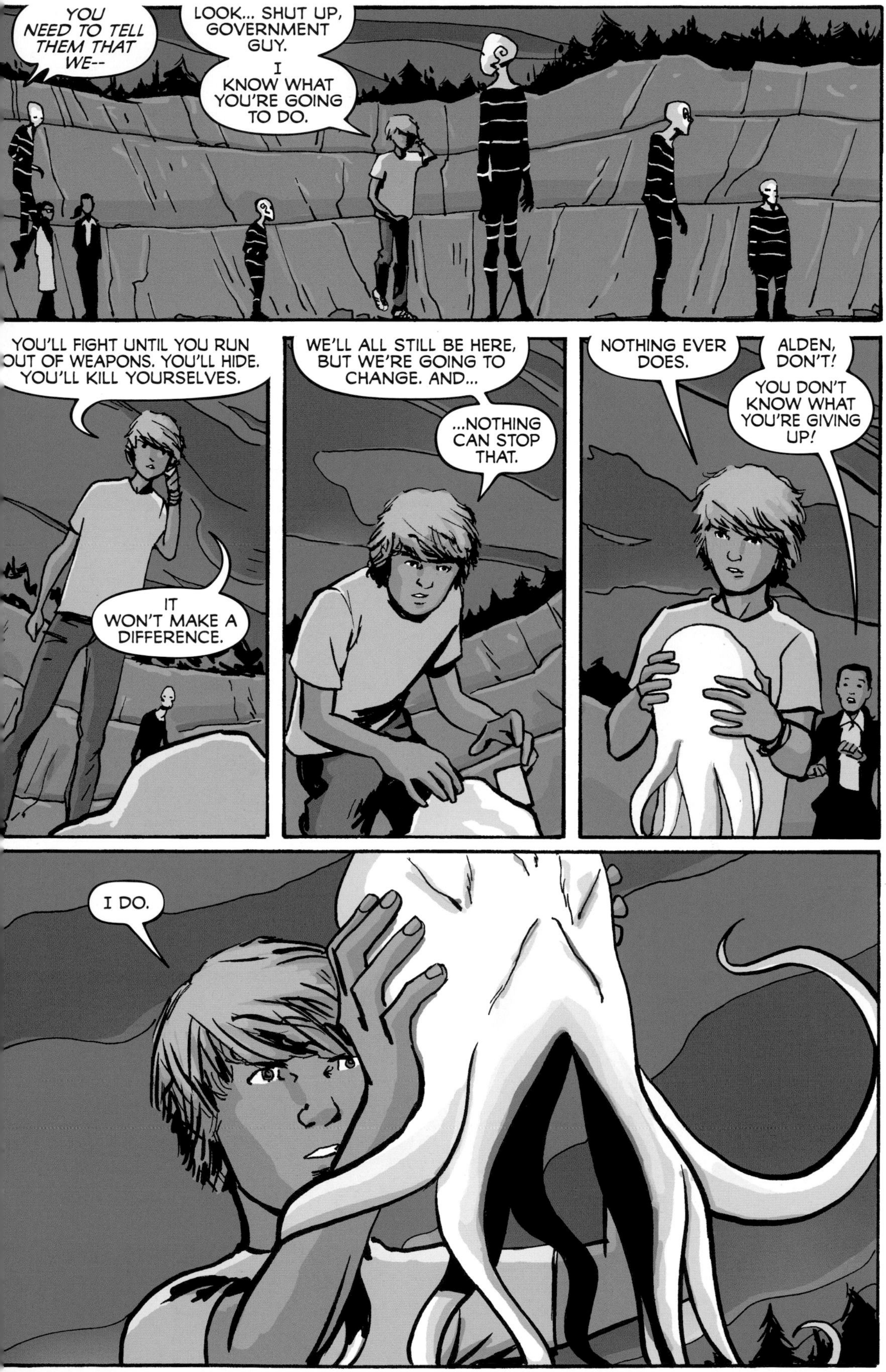
YOU NEED TO TELL THEM THAT WE--
LOOK... SHUT UP, GOVERNMENT GUY.
I KNOW WHAT YOU'RE GOING TO DO.
YOU'LL FIGHT UNTIL YOU RUN OUT OF WEAPONS. YOU'LL HIDE. YOU'LL KILL YOURSELVES.
IT WON'T MAKE A DIFFERENCE.
WE'LL ALL STILL BE HERE, BUT WE'RE GOING TO CHANGE. AND...
...NOTHING CAN STOP THAT.
NOTHING EVER DOES.
ALDEN, DON'T!
YOU DON'T KNOW WHAT YOU'RE GIVING UP!
I DO.

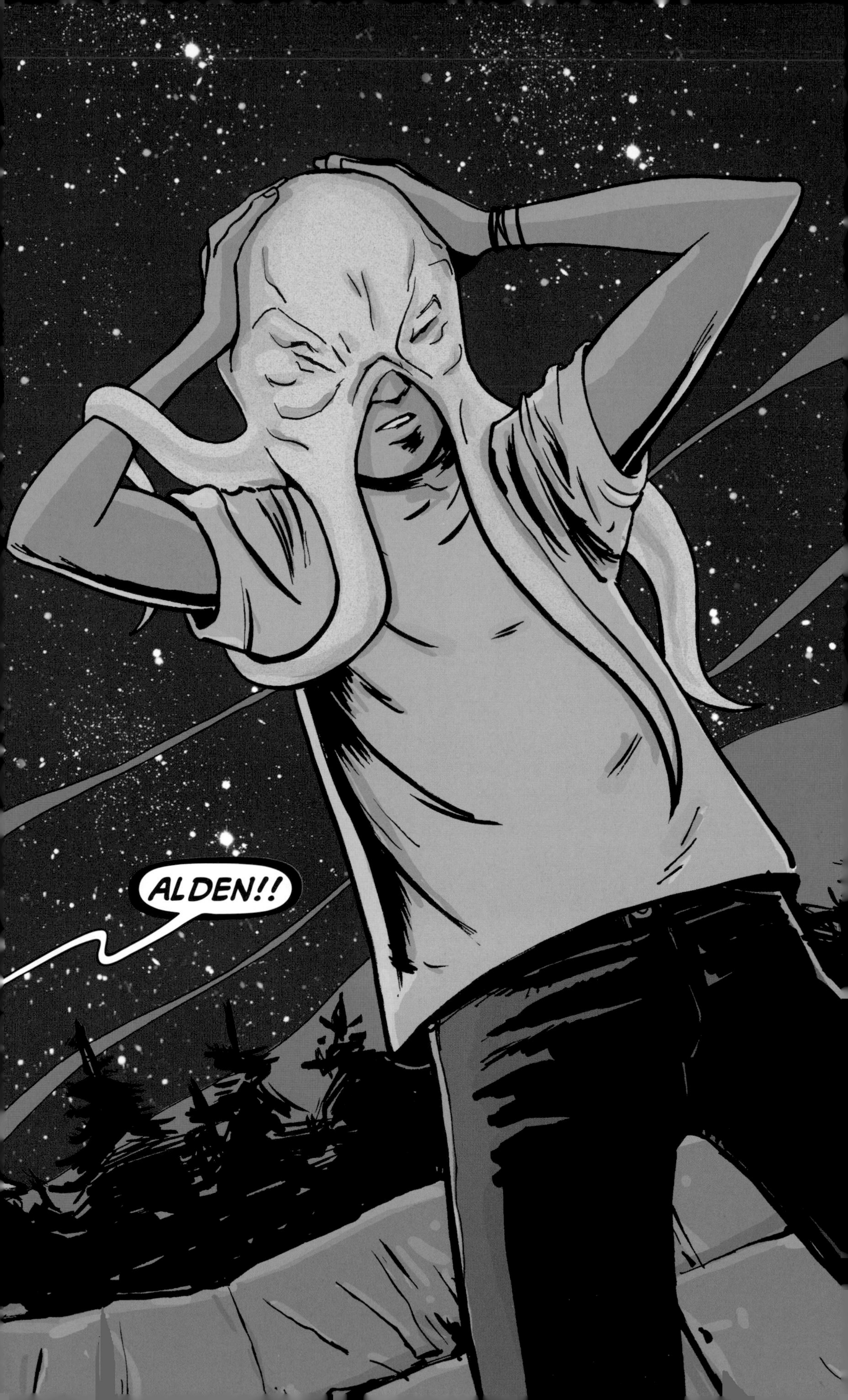
ALDEN!!

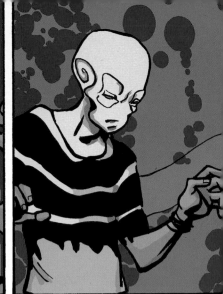

WH...
WHY?

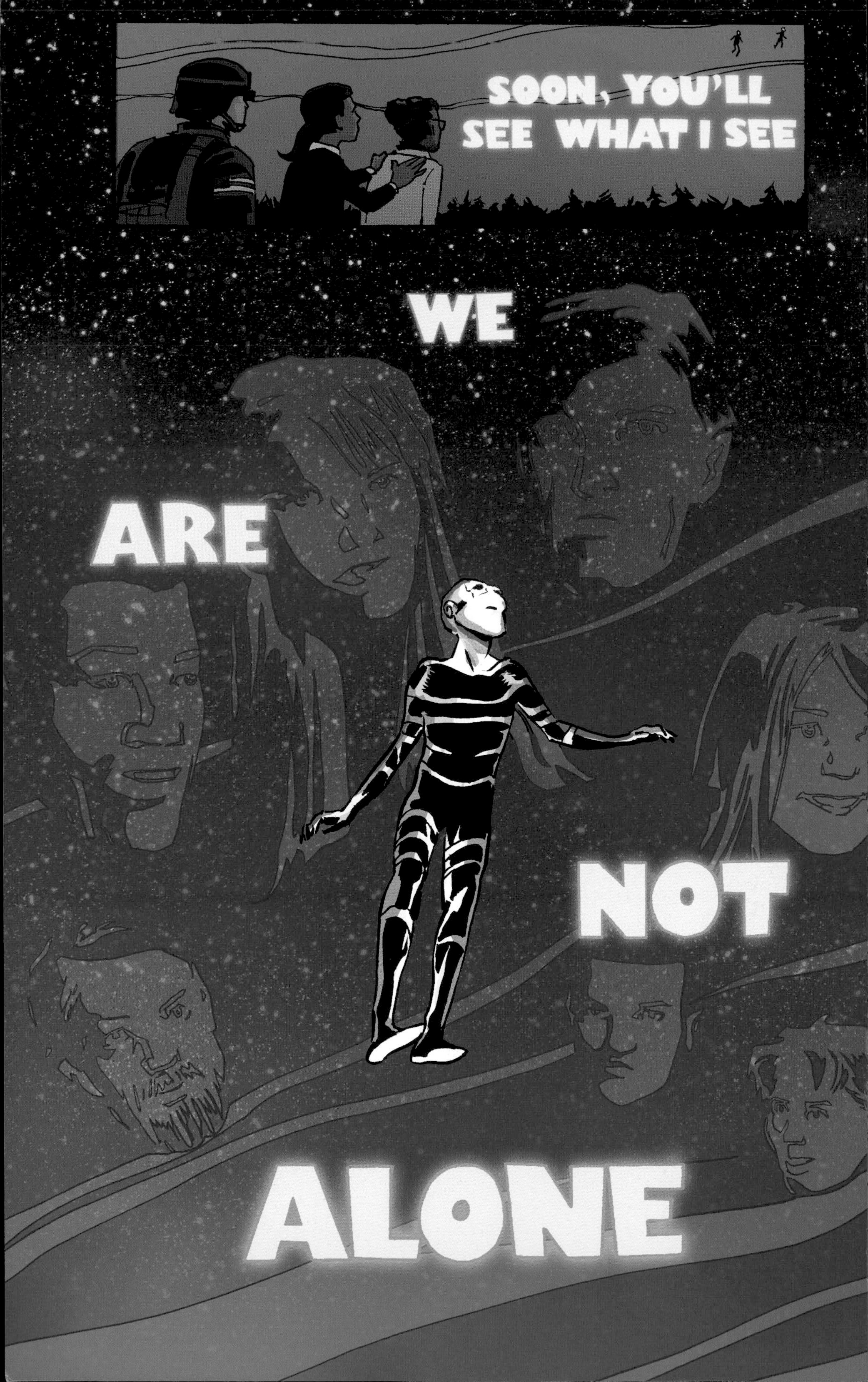
SOON, YOU'LL SEE WHAT I SEE
WE
ARE
NOT
ALONE

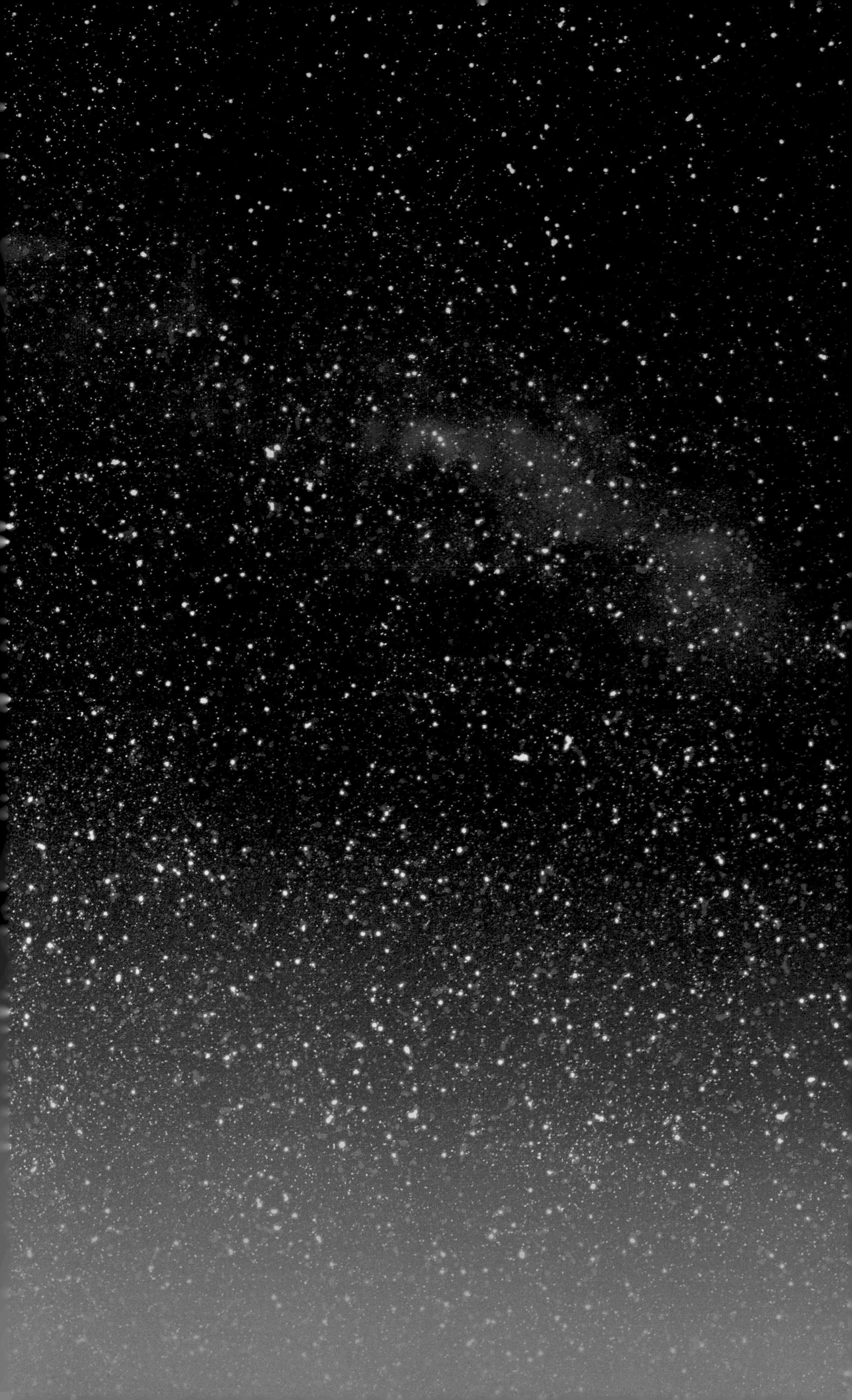

JEFF PARKER

Jeff is known in comics as the writer of *Agents of Atlas*, *X-Men First Class*, *Hulk*, *Flash Gordon*, *Batman '66*, *Aquaman*, *Future Quest*, *Thunderbolts*, *Justice League United*, and *James Bond Origin*. He's especially proud of his original graphic novel creations, such as *The Interman*, *Underground*, *Mysterius the Unfathomable*, *Bucko*, and now *Meteor Men*. On Twitter @jeffparker.

SANDY JARRELL

In addition to *Meteor Men*, Sandy has drawn *Archie*, *Batman '66*, *Black Canary*, *DC Bombshells/Bombshells United*, *Jungle Jim*, *Reggie & Me*, *Teen Titans Go!*, and Neil Gaiman's *Norse Mythology*. On Twitter @sandy_jarrell and on Instagram @sandyjarrell.

KEVIN VOLO

Kevin is an instructional technologist and teacher specializing in graphic design and video editing. He runs the popular YouTube channel 3D Printed Props, where he makes and features pop-culture props and costumes using 3D printers and EVA foam, and shows his thousands of subscribers how they can use the tools they have to create awesome, fun projects, and grow as makers and artists. In addition to his YouTube channel, you can find his work on Instagram and Twitter @3dprintedprops, as well as www.3dprintedprops.com.

CRANK!

Christopher Crank (crank!) has lettered a bunch of books put out by Image, Dark Horse, Oni Press, Dynamite, and elsewhere. He also has a podcast with comic artist Mike Norton and members of Four Star Studios in Chicago (crankcast.com), and makes music (sonomorti.bandcamp.com). Catch him on Twitter @ccrank and on Instagram @ccrank.

"My initial attempt at the alien design. I think I was going for some carved-Polynesian mask inspiration originally."

"Sandy nailed the look for Alden immediately."

"Sandy and I kept fooling with the black suit until I got further into the concept and realized they wouldn't have a 'suit.' Once I got the idea that the aliens ooze out a protective covering, we had a better look that made sense with their nature. Observers interpret it like a diving suit, assuming it's clothes!"

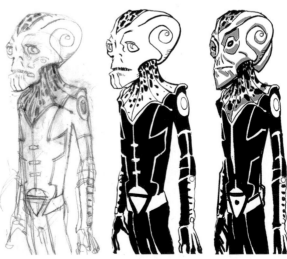

IF YOU LIKED *METEOR MEN*, CHECK OUT THESE OTHER GREAT ONI PRESS TITLES!

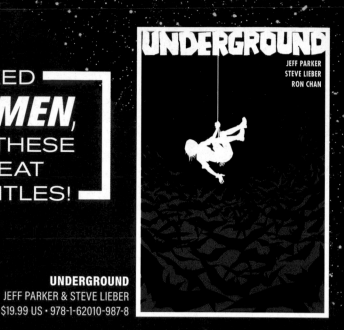

UNDERGROUND
JEFF PARKER
STEVE LIEBER
RON CHAN

UNDERGROUND
JEFF PARKER & STEVE LIEBER
$19.99 US • 978-1-62010-987-8

THE BUNKER
JOSHUA HALE FIALKOV JOE INFURNARI
VOLUME 1

THE BUNKER VOL. 1
JOSHUA HALE FIALKOV &
JOE INFURNARI
$19.99 US • 978-1-62010-164-3

LETTER 44

LETTER 44 VOL. 1
CHARLES SOULE & GUY MAJOR
$19.99 US • 978-1-62010-133-9

ONE LINE
Ray Fawkes

ONE LINE HC
RAY FAWKES
$24.99 US • 978-1-62010-934-2

CULLEN BUNN ANDY MACDONALD NICK FILARDI
ROGUE PLANET

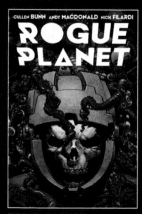

ROGUE PLANET
CULLEN BUNN,
ANDY MACDONALD &
NICK FILARDI
$19.99 US • 978-1-62010-708-9

DRYAD
VOLUME ONE

DRYAD VOL. 1
KURTIS WIEBE,
JUSTIN BARCELO &
MEG CASEY
$19.99 US • 978-1-62010-790-4

BACKTRACK 1
BRIAN JOINES / JAKE ELPHICK / DOUG GARBARK

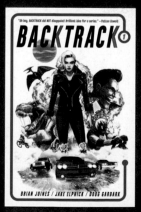

BACKTRACK VOL. 1
BRIAN JOINES,
JAKE ELPHICK &
DOUG GARBARK
$19.99 US • 978-1-62010-786-7